BUSINESS/SCIENCE/TECHNOLOGY DIVISION
CHICAGO PUBLIC LIBRARY
400 SOUTH STATE STREET
CHICAGO, IL 60605

D1802981

# PORSCHE

*By the same author*

FORD VERSUS FERRARI
FORMULA ONE
ITALIAN HIGH-PERFORMANCE CARS
(with Keith Davey)

# PORSCHE

## ANTHONY PRITCHARD

PELHAM BOOKS

*First published in Great Britain by*
PELHAM BOOKS LTD
*52 Bedford Square
London, W.C.1
1969*

© *1969 by Anthony Pritchard*

*All Rights Reserved. No part of this publication may be reproduced, stored in a retrieval system, or transmitted, in any form or by any means, electronic, mechanical, photocopying, recording or otherwise, without the prior permission of the Copyright owner*

TL
215
.P75
P7
1969 cop.1

7207 0250 x

*Set and printed in Great Britain by Tonbridge Printers Ltd, Peach Hall Works, Tonbridge, Kent, in Times ten on twelve point, and bound by James Burn at Esher, Surrey*

## CONTENTS

| | | |
|---|---|---|
| Introduction | | 11 |

*Chapter*

| | | |
|---|---|---|
| 1 | *From Inception to Power*<br>Porsche background and the evolution of the classic 356 model | 15 |
| 2 | *Purely for Racing*<br>The early competition sports cars | 27 |
| 3 | *First Porsche Single-Seaters*<br>Formula Two racing, 1957–60 | 45 |
| 4 | *Grand Prix Failure*<br>The Formula One cars, 1961–62 | 52 |
| 5 | 900 *Winning Ways*<br>The evolution of the 911 | 64 |
| 6 | 1962: *First Year of Prototype Racing* | 73 |
| 7 | 1963: *A Quiet Year for Porsche* | 80 |
| 8 | 1964: *Carrera Consistency* | 90 |
| 9 | 1965: *Another Successful Year for the* 904 | 99 |
| 10 | 1966: *Six-Cylinder Competition Cars* | 107 |
| 11 | 1967: *A Season of Unlimited Success* | 119 |
| 12 | 1968: *Porsche Versus Ford* | 138 |
| 13 | 1969: *Resumé of the Season* | 168 |
| | *Appendix* 1: *Specification of Porsche Cars* | 172 |
| | *Appendix* 2: *Porsche Competition Performances* | 180 |
| | *Index* | 195 |

## ILLUSTRATIONS

| | | | |
|---|---|---|---|
| 1 | Hairy brute – the SSKL Mercedes-Benz | *facing page* | 32 |
| 2 | Abortive effort – the 1938 aero-engined car designed by Porsche for Mercedes-Benz | | 32 |
| 3 | Mentor – Ferry Porsche, who guides the company's destinies | | 33 |
| 4 | Successor? Ferdinand Porsche Junior, grandson of the founder | | 33 |
| 5 | International Racing Debut for the Porsche team – 1951 Le Mans | | 40 |
| 6 | The works 'Spyder' which Wolfgang von Trips shared with former Ferrari driver Umberto Maglioli in the 1956 Nürburgring 1000 Km race | | 40 |
| 7 | Mechanics work on the 550 'Spyders' before the 1954 Le Mans race | | 41 |
| 8 | Le Mans 1956: Porsche RS1500 with a coupé top on the normal racing body | | 56 |
| 9 | Umberto Maglioli with his Porsche 'Spyder' in the 1957 Mille Miglia | | 56 |
| 10 | Jean Behra at the wheel of the RSK Porsche he shared with Edgar Barth in the 1958 Nürburgring 1000 Km race | | 57 |
| 11 | The 1600 Porsche of Bonnier and von Trips having a wheel changed in the 1959 Tourist Trophy | | 57 |
| 12 | Pugnacious rear end of one of the works Porsche RS60 cars | | 64 |
| 13 | Sebring, 1961: the works RS61 of Hans Herrmann and Edgar Barth | | 64 |

| | | |
|---|---|---|
| 14 | Tourist Trophy, 1961: the Abarth-bodied 2-litre Carrera of Graham Hill outdragged at the start by the Berlinetta Ferrari of Stirling Moss | 65 |
| 15 | German Grand Prix, 1960 won by Joakim Bonnier at the wheel of his works Porsche | 65 |
| 16 | French Grand Prix, 1961: the 4-cylinder Porsches of Dan Gurney and Joakim Bonnier harry the eventual winner, Baghetti's V-6 Ferrari | 72 |
| 17 & 18 | Two views of Gurney's flat-eight Porsche at the 1962 French Grand Prix at Rouen | 73 |
| 19 | Another view of Gurney in the 1962 French race | 88 |
| 20 | The Porsche flat-eight Grand Prix engine | 88 |
| 21 | Former works driver Huschke von Hanstein, until recently competitions manager of Porsche | 89 |
| 22 | Hans Herrmann, one of the mainstays of the Porsche works team | 89 |
| 23 | Vic Elford wins the 1968 Monte Carlo event with a 911S | 96 |
| 24 | Vic Elford retires his 911S at the 1968 Easter Thruxton meeting | 96 |
| 25 | The 2-litre 8-cylinder Porsche which took third place in the 1962 Targa Florio | 97 |
| 26 | The 2-litre 8-cylinder Porsche which won the 1963 Targa Florio at record speed | 97 |
| 27 | The 1963 Targa Florio-winning car overturned in the Nürburgring 1000 Km race by Phil Hill | 104 |
| 28 | Experimental 8-cylinder 2-litre car which led the first lap of the 1964 Targa Florio | 104 |
| 29 | Victory in the 1964 Targa Florio went to this 904 driven by Colin Davis and Antonio Pucci | 105 |

| | | |
|---|---|---|
| 30 | Private 904 which took 12th place at Le Mans in 1964 | 105 |
| 31 | Jo Siffert | 120 |
| 32 | Vic Elford | 120 |
| 33 | The 6-cylinder 904 which took third place in the 1965 Targa Florio | 121 |
| 34 | This 6-cylinder car of Herbert Linge and Peter Nöcker took fourth place in the 1965 Le Mans race | 121 |
| 35 | Sebring, 1966: fourth place went to the 906 2-litre 6-cylinder car of Herrmann and Buzzetta | 128 |
| 36 | Nürburgring, 1966: fourth place again, for the 906 of Bob Bondurant and Paul Hawkins | 128 |
| 37 | The 910 with 2·2-litre engine of Paul Hawkins and Rolf Stommelen which won the 1967 Targa Florio at record speed | 129 |
| 38 | Le Mans, 1967: the long-tailed Porsche 907s of Mitter/Rindt and Siffert/Hermann | 136 |
| 39 | All four wheels off the ground. The 3-litre car of Elford and Siffert which won the 1968 Nürburgring 1000 Km race | 137 |
| 40 | Tony Dean and 906 at Silverstone | 152 |
| 41 | Bill Bradley and 906 at Oulton Park | 152 |
| 42 | Neck and neck in the 1968 B.O.A.C. '500' at Brands Hatch – Spoerry and Steinemann with their 910 and the works 907 of Scarfiotti and Herrmann | 153 |
| 43 | Porsche idea of an aerofoil on the Siffert/Herrmann 3-litre car at Le Mans, 1968 | 153 |

# AUTHOR'S NOTE

Once again, the author would like to express his gratitude to Keith Davey for both his helpful advice and for his assistance in the preparation of the manuscript.

Thanks are due to the following for permission to reproduce photographs: No. 12, *Autocar;* Nos. 13, 14, 19, 30, B.P. Ltd.; Nos. 40, 41, Guy Griffiths, Esq.; No. 5, Louis Klementaski, Esq.; No. 2, Mercedes-Benz A.G.; Nos. 23, 24, *Motor;* Nos. 8, 20, 25, 26, 27, 28, 29, 33, 34, 35, 37, *Motor Sport;* Nos. 16, 17, 18, David Phipps, Esq.; Nos. 3, 4, 22, Porsche System Engineering; No. 1, Publifoto, Milan; Nos. 21, 31, 32, 36, 38, 39, 42, 43, Nigel Snowdon, Esq.; Nos. 6, 7, 9, 10, Studio Wörner.

# Introduction

Porsche have done an enormous amount of design and development work and overcome a great deal of prejudice since the first 356 model rolled out of the tiny Porsche workshops at Gmünd in Austria in May, 1948. For the first Porsche was Volkswagen-based and all the successive production variants stemmed from this until the appearance of the completely new 911 model at the 1963 Frankfurt Show. For no matter how you describe the later and very refined Super 75 and 90 and 1600C and SC models – evolved, developed, souped, modified, redesigned, hotted-up or improved – they were still of clear Volkswagen origin. Now this was all very well for the man who knew his Volkswagens – and many Porsche owners were previously VW drivers, but a driver used to a conventional sporting car such as an M.G., a Jaguar or a Triumph with its rigidly sprung rear end and pronounced understeering characteristics, found a Porsche hard to come to grips with. Typical, and not entirely unjustified, were the comments of one dissatisfied owner who put his feelings to paper in the 24th December, 1954 issue of *Autosport:*

> 'Correspondence appears to have started regarding the virtues of the Porsche, and as an owner with 25,000 miles up on one nine months old perhaps my experience may be of interest.
> 'There is no doubt that the Porsche has a very efficient and lively engine, that it is extremely comfortable and that it is a thing of beauty. At the same time, it *should* be for £2,000. If it is any satisfaction to those who pine for a Porsche there are, however, many snags.
> 'The engine performance is obtained at the expense of quite considerable noise and roughness. Maintenance by a private owner is very difficult. Changing a plug calls for a bath, and as for adjusting tappets or anything like that, it constitutes a major operation. Greasing can only be done with a pit or a lift, and if the starter goes wrong, as mine has done three times, it is impossible to get at without garage equipment, and since there is no handle one either walks home or gets a push.
> 'The service from the factory would not be tolerated from an English manufacturer. I broke a crown wheel pinion due to the

gear jumping out when the car was a fortnight out of guarantee. I had, however, complained about this gear-jumping since the car was new, despite which, however, the makers say it is out of guarantee, and I have a bill for £60, as it was also found that new reverse gears were required and new selector arms – this in a very expensive car six months old. Previously the differential broke when it was a fortnight old. One of the worst aspects of owning a Porsche is the practically complete lack of spares in the country. Every time I have wanted anything, I have had to wait for it to come from Germany, and if I wanted it airmail I have been charged for the excess and also for any cables involved.

'I may have been unlucky with mine and every time I make a complaint I get the answer that I drive quickly and do rallies in it. So I do – that's what I bought it for, and I think that if one pays £2,000 for a 1500 cc car with a claimed maximum speed of about 100 mph one should be able to drive it with the needle round the 65–70 mark without the back axle and gearbox packing in.

'To the continuous arguments about the steering and road-holding I can only add that my experience is that it is very nice at high speed if you give absolutely 100 per cent attention to your driving and never put the brakes on in a bend if it is wet or loose (yes, we all know that theoretically braking in a bend is strictly *verboten*, but all fast drivers have to do it from time to time and nothing drastic should happen unless you are going far too fast or brake far too heavily – AP). If your attention wanders for a split second, however, the engine is likely to be round the corner before the headlamps – and you don't get much warning.

'Despite my grouses, I think the Porsche is a grand car, but there are English cars as good and cheaper with much better service facilities, and, if one is prepared to go up another 500 cc, with better performance.'

The Concessionaires were hot, if not quick, to reply and the 21st January, 1955 issue of *Autosport* contained the following letter:

'May we have the courtesy of your columns in replying to the letter under the signature of ——? Obviously, as your readers will agree, it is a difficult letter to answer without becoming personal, but we would like to give the following facts:

'Mr. —— broke the star wheels in the differential when his car was nearly new. We had these wheels tested and the material was perfect but even so, although the job cost us £23 8s 9d, we only charged Mr. —— £5. This included all night work, because he wanted to be ready for another competition. Next he crashed the car; it had to be repaired in two days, and this meant another overtime job.

'The next trouble was that he broke a tooth out of the crown wheel, but on this occasion it coincided with the periodic visit of one of the Porsche Company's engineers, who stated quite definitely that it was not fair on the Company to do this work under guarantee, because there was nothing wrong with the material or workmanship. This was explained by the engineer to Mr. ——, but we suggested that we would like to have a full report from the laboratory and, therefore, the gear was sent back to the factory.

'Since then, we learned from the factory that there was nothing wrong with the material or workmanship, but in view of Mr. ——'s attitude, they suggested meeting him by halving the cost of the material and Mr. —— has been informed of this. We on our part have never said that he drove the car too fast because this is what the car is built for, but we did suggest that he drove the car badly.

'Regarding the maintenance of the car, we hold an adequate stock of spares and special tools, as suggested by the manufacturers. We also have Porsche-trained mechanics and the necessary special tools for doing every possible job on the car. Obviously, however, it is difficult to legislate for breakages which exceed the experience of the factory. However, in these circumstances, parts can be flown over within a day, but if they are not under guarantee then, of course, we expect the owner to pay for the cost of special delivery.

'We have found that all figures given by the manufacturers regarding performance are correct. Porsche claim 96 mph for the car and we believe Mr. ——himself has lapped Montlhery at 97 mph.

'The "Standard" Porsche engine is extremely smooth and flexible, but Mr. —— has attempted to improve on the factory, and in our opinion, and in the opinion of the works engineer, has spoilt the engine by his modifications.

'Regarding steering and road-holding, the reputation of the car is sufficient (? – AP) but as the car is extremely fast, then obviously it needs experienced handling to get the best out of it.

'Mr. ——'s description of difficulty of maintenance on the car is not true of a car that has not been modified; we agree that if the electric starter needs changing the engine must come out, but this can be done in 20 minutes.

'We would also add that exactly the same material is used in cars for the Mille Miglia, Pan-American, Nürburgring, etc., as Messrs. Porsche do not use different material for their own cars, and that is why they fail to understand how Mr. —— can break things which they cannot in events such as the Alpine, and others mentioned above.

'Incidentally, the basic price of the car is now £1,260 and the total price with purchase tax is £1,786 2s 6d.

'Finally we took over the Porsche concession because we considered it to be an exceptional car. We like the car immensely, and the more we use it ourselves the more we like it, and we feel that this is the opinion of most of the owners in the world.'

W. H. ALDINGTON
A.F.N., Ltd., Isleworth, Middx.

These letters have been reproduced, without expurgation, after an interval of fifteen years not to discuss the merits of the particular case, but because, despite the 'puff' contained in both, they vividly highlight the two sides of the great Porsche controversy. For fifteen years ago the Porsche *was* a highly controversial car. There were many private owners as dissatisfied with their cars as Mr. —— and many others who felt just as enthusiastic as did the Concessionaires. For the Aldingon brothers, builders of Frazer Nash cars and importers of B.M.W. products, were keen sporting motorists who would not have handled a car that they did not like.

Today, however, the Porsche is appreciated by all enthusiasts almost without exception, it is an Internationally recognised status symbol and it has a record of success in races and rallies matched by only a handful of the world's racing car entrants. The change in the Porsche image, the intensive development work that has put Porsche at the forefront of motoring technology and the make's racing record are the main themes of this book.

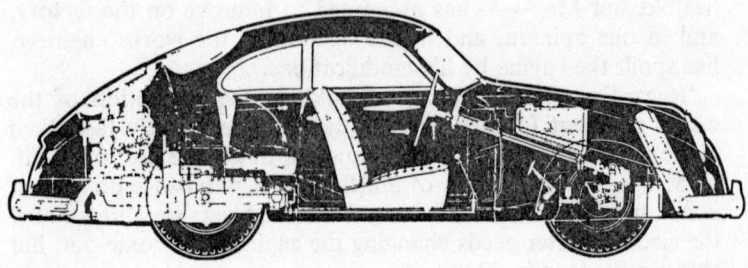

# ONE
# From Inception to Power

*Ferdinand Porsche*

No car has a longer or more intensive engineering development history than the Porsche. Ferdinand Porsche was the most prolific of automobile designers and one of the most successful – but even he had his failures and mistakes. None of his designs can be described as an unqualified success, even the Volkswagen with a production output in millions that some other manufacturers would envy in thousands, and many of his ideas have been superseded. Ferdinand Porsche was born in Maffersdorf in 1875. From an early age Porsche was interested in electricity and spent hours carrying out electrical experiments. At the age of eighteen, Porsche went to Vienna to work for the Bela Egger electrical equipment manufacturers and from there he moved to the Lohner concern where in 1897 he designed an electrical car known as the Lohner-Porsche with hub-mounted motors. In 1905 he became technical director to the Austrian Daimler Company. His most successful design was probably the 86 hp 'Prince Henry' model with so-called 'tulip'-shaped body, a primitive attempt at streamlining. These cars took first three places in general classification in the 1908 Prince Henry Trial. As well as designing cars, Porsche worked on aircraft engine designs, certain of which were made under licence by the Beardmore concern in England. During the war years, Porsche became managing director of Austro-Daimler which, just before the war, had amalgamated with the Skoda concern.

In post-war years Porsche developed a small capacity model to which he gave the name 'Sascha'. Porsche was keen on pursuing a very active racing policy and a Sascha with Neubauer at the wheel finished seventh in the 1922 Targa Florio. A 2-litre car was also raced that year. Unfortunately the rest of the Austro-Daimler directors did not feel that the expense of a racing programme was justified. Bitter arguments ensued, the result of which was that Porsche moved on to Stuttgart in the Spring of 1923 to become technical director of Daimler.

Ferdinand Porsche had the reputation of being quick-witted, but short-tempered – ingenious, but on occasion abusive to his colleagues and it is doubtful whether he would have been able to hold down his appointments had he been an average technician; but such was his brilliance that he became almost indispensable wherever he worked. At Mercedes, Porsche designed a 2-litre 4-cylinder car which became the first successful supercharged racing car ever to compete when it ran at Indianapolis in 1923, and the following year, one driven by Christian Werner won the Targa Florio. But the other side of the coin was that when Raymond Mays drove one of the later 8-cylinder cars in 1927 he found '... that with its poor acceleration and appalling road-holding the car was useless for Shelsey Walsh ... I learned that these straight-eights have never been considered good on corners.' (*Split Seconds*, G. T. Foulis, 1951).

During his five and a half years as technical director at Daimler-Benz (as it was known after the amalgamation of the two companies) Porsche produced many designs, but probably the most successful was the series of really big cars ranging from 6·8 to 7·1-litres and known in its ultimate form as the SSKL. These cars scored a large number of major victories, although they were originally designed for fast touring. They were vast, cumbrous brutes, weighing even in short chassis form close to two tons, and needed a great deal of strength to drive. Ettore Bugatti supposedly described Bentleys as being like lorries, but the description was far more appropriate to these Mercedes and, indeed, a race at the Nürburgring between an SSK and a modern Mercedes lorry proper might be informative as well as amusing!

Relations had become sufficiently strained at Mercedes for Porsche to leave and join the Steyr Company at the beginning of 1929. A merger between Steyr and Austro-Daimler, with whom Porsche had had so many disagreements, resulted in his setting up as an independent design office in Stuttgart with Karl Rabe and eight other associates on December, 1930. The first design was a 2-litre car for Wanderer which was given the design number 7 so that it would not *look* like the first design by the new office.

During the 'thirties Porsche and his collaborators designed a number of prototype small cars, all of which were in one way or another the forerunners of the Volkswagen. The Volkswagen is a car which has already been the subject of several books, including *Small Wonder* (Hutchinson, 1968) and *Beyond Expectation* by K. B. Hopfinger (G. T. Foulis & Co.), and it suffices to say here that the Porsche 356 was an evolution of the thinking that went into the Volkswagen in its final production form. The 'missing link' between the two is the streamlined coupé version of the Volkswagen, so smooth it could achieve 87 mph on 40 bhp, that was built to compete in the cancelled 1939 Berlin-Rome open road race. Three of these cars were constructed and one has survived. As late as 1951 this ran in Austrian rallies.

The other outstandingly important Porsche design was the Auto Union which was produced for the 1934 season of Grand Prix racing held to a new formula with no limit on engine size but a maximum weight of 750 kg (14·73 cwt) without water, oil or tyres. In the main, the new Formula and its successor of 1938–40 with capacity limits of 3000 cc supercharged and 4500 cc unsupercharged, was led by Mercedes-Benz in terms of both technical development and racing successes. Porsche's Auto Union design was novel in more respects than one. It was rear-engined and it was in fact the first successful rear-engined racing car. The engine was right at the back of the car and the driver right at the front. Not only did this mean that the driver became aware much later of the sliding action of the tail than he would with a conventional car, but the preponderance of weight on the rear wheels meant that the limit of adhesion was reached very early and the car displayed pronounced oversteering tendencies – but traction was excellent. Even the Auto Union directors came close to conceding that the rear-engined layout was inherently wrong but felt that a change of layout would be bad for the Company's image. Instead, as the design was developed, the engine was progressively moved further forwards, and it is accepted that a modern rear-engined racing car is in effect mid-engined, with the engine ahead of the rear axle. The other outstanding features of the Auto Union were the power unit and the front suspension design. The engine was a complex V-16 of 4360 cc with the valves operated by a single overhead camshaft, and a power output of 295 bhp. Porsche also planned an aerodynamic coupé sports car with the same engine detuned to develop 200 bhp and the same 5-speed gearbox. If this had achieved fruition, it's estimated top speed of

125 mph would, 35 years ago, easily have made it the world's fastest production car. The front suspension of the Auto Union was the much admired and much imitated Porsche trailing link system whereby each wheel was carried on two trailing arms connected to transverse torsion bars – a layout subsequently copied by E.R.A., B.R.M., Healey and Alfa Romeo, among others. A full technical analysis of the Auto Union is contained in the book *The Grand Prix Car, Vol.* 1 by the late Laurence Pomeroy (Motor Racing Publications) and the full racing history is told in both *Case History* by Norman Smith (Autosport) and *Competition Cars of Europe* by Pritchard (Robert Hale).

From Auto Union racing cars Porsche progressed to full-time work on the design of tractors, but in 1937 his design studio had entered into an advisory contract with Daimler-Benz, and for Mercedes he designed an impressive contender for the World's Land Speed record. This was rear-engined with three axles and the engine driving the rear two. The engine was a 44-litre aero-engine developing up to 3030 bhp in short bursts. The car was just under 30 ft long and weighed 56 cwt. It was completed in 1938, but development was not finished before the outbreak of war.

During the war years Porsche was engaged on war production, and his tank designs included the famous 'Tiger' so loved by German Panzer divisions. In 1944 Porsche received an order to move his works from Stuttgart to the small Corinthian town of Gmünd. The 69-year old Porsche did so with considerable reluctance. With the fall of Germany, Porsche and his son Ferry found themselves at his estate near Zell am See and because of his German nationality he was not allowed to cross the frontier into Austria to go to his works at Gmünd. In June, 1945 the Americans took Porsche to an old castle at Hessen where prominent Germans were being held for interrogation. Porsche was well treated and not too unhappy. In the meanwhile, at Gmünd, Rabe and his colleagues were trying to make some money from repairing Volkswagens, of which a large number had fallen into the hands of the allies. Professor Porsche and his son-in-law, Dr Piëch were then taken to Baden-Baden. In France the Renault concern had been taken over by the Government and production of a small rear-engined car on the lines of the Volkswagen was planned.

Discussions took place as to Porsche's willingness to co-operate in the design and then without warning he was arrested and imprisoned – and without being told why. After a few weeks, Porsche was taken to Paris and given accommodation at the porter's lodge at the late Louis Renault's villa. There he was shown early prototypes of the Renault 4CV and asked his opinion, which he readily gave. His son Ferry Porsche had already been released and had returned to Gmünd to try to put the Porsche firm back on its feet again. It was at this stage that the Porsche firm received what seemed a gift from Heaven. Piero Dusio, managing director and principal shareholder in the recently-formed Cisitalia car works, a firm with an emphasis on motor sport, decided in 1946 to build a Grand Prix car and entrusted the design the Porsche team.

Ferry Porsche had already been working on a Volkswagen-powered sports car design to which the number 356 had been allotted. Work on the Cisitalia caused the 356 to be shelved and the money from Grand Prix design was urgently needed to ransom Ferdinand Porsche. The Cisitalia, typed the 360, featured a horizontally-opposed 12-cylinder engine of 1492 cc. With twin single-stage eccentric vane-type supercharges, power output was estimated to be 296 bhp at 8500 rpm. As would now be expected of a Porsche design, the engine was at the rear and there was, optionally, two- or four-wheel drive. The Cisitalia Company ran out of money after the first car was completed and it remained unraced in Europe. Eventually it went to the Argentine where it was renamed the Autoar and heavy-handed, unknowledgeable attempts to make it race-worthy came to nothing. The car was eventually traced and is now back in the Porsche works again.

*Austrian Porsche*

Despite all the economic and political difficulties in early post-war days and a desperate need throughout Europe for low-priced family saloons – just the sort of car that was built by Volkswagen in Germany, by Renault and Citroen in France and studiously ignored in Britain because it was so much easier to put pre-war cars back in production – Ferry Porsche decided to build sports cars. This was primarily because the Porsche family had no money and sports cars based on the Volkswagen, with which they were intimately familiar, were cheap and easy to construct.

Work started at Gmünd in early 1948 – by then the Cisitalia project had been wound up – the chassis was completed by March and two months later the car was ready to be tested. The power unit was the standard 1131 cc Volkswagen with careful cylinder-head work by Ferry to increase the power output to 40 bhp on a compression ratio of 7 : 1. The chassis was built up from any old tubing that the team could lay their hands on and suspension, steering and transmission were all standard Volkswagen. Swiss electrical equipment was used. The body was an open two-seater roadster without any luggage space. After tests on the Katschberg Pass (which at the time had a gradient of one in $3\frac{1}{2}$ on the Northern side) Porsche number One was sold because the money was needed to build the next car, a fixed-head coupé, which had been planned earlier. This original Porsche was acquired back by the works in 1958 and it was with great amusement that a piece of construction iron, used as a temporary repair after a breakage, was noticed to be still in place.

Ferry and his team were well satisfied with the original car and no changes were made to the coupé, which was ready by September, 1948. The first Porsche catalogue was published shortly afterwards and in this capacity was referred to as being 1131 cc – the normal Volkswagen size – but from the first cars capacity was reduced to 1086 cc to make them eligible for the 1100 cc category in competition. Another turning point for Porsche in September, 1948 was the signing of a royalty contract with Volkswagen which brought in much needed money and Porsche still receive a royalty from this source because of the development and experimental work carried out for VW. During the Autumn of 1948 Porsche production attained a level of five cars per month, but a major snag was that there was only one bodybuilder. The first exhibition appearance of a Porsche was at the Geneva salon in March, 1949. These early coupés had alloy coachwork and were easily distinguishable by their divided windscreen. In all, fifty of them were built in Austria, where the total Porsche staff was around 100. Four of these original cars were retained at the Porsche works for competition use. Apart from the coupés, six open cars were built by the Swiss Beutler concern between January and August, 1949 and, like the coupés, they had divided windscreens.

After lengthy negotiations, arrangements were made for Porsche to return to Zuffenhausen, a suburb of Stuttgart, in 1950, and as a temporary measure they occupied part of the Reutter body works. It had been decided that the Porsche concern would no longer go on making their own bodies and relying on one worker who on a number of occasions was too inebriated to do his job. Reutter had been chosen to make the bodies, so there were good prospects of the arrangements working well. The bodies built by Reutter were in steel, had a one-piece windscreen and modified VW brakes replaced the special Duplex brakes fitted to the early cars. Originally Porsche planned to build between eight and ten cars a month in the 500 square metres allotted to them at Reutters, but eventually they were building cars there at the rate of 80 a month!

*Production Developments*

During 1950 works Porsches made no competition appearances, though private owners were already rallying the cars, and concentrated on production. That year a total of 410 cars in coupé and cabriolet form were completed. Even so, half the Company's resources were devoted to design consultancy work. A privately-entered car won the 1100 cc G.T. class in the 1950 Midnight Sun Rally in Sweden and not long afterwards another class victory was gained in that year's Austrian Alpine Rally.

No substantial changes were made to the design until 1951, when a 1300 – the extra capacity was achieved by increasing the bore from 73·5 to 80 mm – was introduced. Power output rose to 44 bhp at 4200 rpm and features of the car were perforated wheels and finned front brake drums. Later, in October of that year, Porsche development went a stage further with the introduction of a 1488 cc (80 × 74 mm) version. This was the first Porsche to have a roller bearing crankshaft and its power output was restricted to 60 bhp at 5000 rpm in the interests of gearbox reliability. Eleven months later, in September, 1952, followed a 1500 'Super' with a roller bearing crankshaft, an output of 70 bhp at 5000 rpm and a claimed maximum speed of 105 mph. To cope with the extra power the car was, for the first time, fitted with an all-synchromesh gearbox, the baulk-ring type developed for the Cisitalia Grand Prix car, and larger, 11 in brake drums. The ordinary 1500 was at the same time renamed the 'Damen' (lady), given a plain bearing crankshaft and detuned to develop 55 bhp at 4400 rpm. Another development in 1952 was the production of 15 only 'America' roadsters with detachable windscreens and cut-down doors and intended purely for the North American market. These were powered by the 1500 'Super' engine before it became available in coupé form.

In the Autumn of 1951, 76-year-old Ferdinand Porsche suffered a stroke; he had been too weakened by two years of internment to recover from this and he died on 30th January, 1952.

## Porsche Debut at Le Mans

It had been the intention to field two 1100 cc cars at Le Mans in 1951 and there was still sufficient anti-German feeling in France for the entry to be resisted. The situation was eventually smoothed over by Charles Faroux, one of the oldest and most respected of French journalists, and Porsche's appearance at the Sarthe circuit did much to ease the way for Mercedes-Benz to make their re-entry into racing in 1952. The cars for Le Mans were examples of the early alloy-bodied production run and were finished in silver-grey. The engines had been tuned to develop 44 bhp and wheel spats were fitted front and rear. Unfortunately, one of the cars, driven by Rudolph Sauerwein, crashed badly in the wet in practice, and was so severely damaged that it could not be repaired in time for the race. The other car, in the hands of French drivers Veuillet and Mouche, both of whom were more experienced with the traditional style of French sports cars such as the Delage, had a completely trouble-free race and covered 1766·33 miles at 73·59 mph. The Porsche won the 1100 cc class and was 20th overall. This success was repeated in 1952.

In August 1951, Porsche fielded two cars in the Liège-Rome-Liège Rally, probably the toughest of all the classic European rallies. One car, an 1100, was driven by Huschke von Hanstein (who joined Porsche as Press director shortly afterwards) and Petermax Müller, while the other ran in the 1500 cc class. This was entered as a 1300 cc, but in fact it had a 1500 cc unit of the type which became available to the public in August. Despite covering the last 200 miles of the rally with third gear only operative, the 1500 driven by von Guilleaume and Count von der Mühle won its class and was third overall. The 1100 finished second in its class.

Just before the Paris Salon, two Porsches, and 1100 and a 1500, went to Montlhéry to tackle long-distance records, with a team of drivers including von Hanstein. There also went to the circuit an open two-seater Porsche known as the Glöckler-Porsche, which is described in the next Chapter. The records achieved were sufficiently impressive to warrant reproduction in full:

#### 1100 cc Class, Porsche Coupé

|  | Old Record | New record |
|---|---|---|
| 500 miles | 158·00 kph | 161·8 kph |
| 6 hours | 159·4 | 162·8 |
| 1,000 kilometres | 159·7 | 162·71 |

#### 1500 cc Class, Porsche Coupé

| 3,000 kilometres | 153·33 | 158·96 |
|---|---|---|
| 2,000 miles | 153·7 | 159·04 |
| 24 hours | 152·00 | 159·00 |
| 4,000 kilometres | 152·00 | 159·13 |
| 3,000 miles | 147·67 | 159·25 |
| 5,000 kilometres | 147·23 | 159·19 |
| 4,000 miles | 147·29 | 158·00 |
| 48 hours | 147·94 | 156·66 |
| 5,000 miles | 144·36 | 156·49 |
| 10,000 kilometres | 127·8 | 154·29 |
| 72 hours | 145·5 | 152·34 |

#### 1500 cc Class, Glöckler-Porsche

| 500 kilometres | 185·3 | 188·1 |
|---|---|---|
| 1,000 kilometres | 182·4 | 186·18 |
| 6 hours | 181·8 | 184·66 |

The 72 hours record included covering the last stretch with third gear only operative and the car was then taken in its dirty, oil-grimed state for display on the Porsche stand at the Salon.

By this time Porsche had moved into a new factory alongside the Reutter works – the competitions department then consisted of two cars and four mechanics and production had just reached a total of 1,000 cars.

## Later Competition Appearances of the 356

In 1953 came the 1300 'Super' model featuring roller main bearings, alloy cylinders and hard-chrome liners. Capacity was slightly greater at 1290 cc and this was the first 1300 to use the 'standard' Porsche stroke of 74 mm. The following year the 'normal' 1300 received the same dimensions and remained unchanged until the 1300 was dropped in 1957. A substantial technical development in 1954 was the abandonment of the Volkswagen crankcase and the introduction of one to Porsche design and constructed in three parts. 1954 also saw the introduction of the 'Speedster' open model, which was an instant success in the States despite leaking like a sieve, and the fitting of an anti-roll bar at the front, the first tentative step towards eliminating the notorious oversteering tendencies of the Porsche.

The year 1955 was one of substantial modifications to the design and Porsche production and staff figures up to that time from 1950 make interesting reading:

|      | Staff | Production |
|------|-------|------------|
| 1950 | 108   | 298        |
| 1951 | 214   | 1,103      |
| 1952 | 332   | 1,303      |
| 1953 | 437   | 1,978      |
| 1954 | 493   | 1,934      |
| 1955 | 616   | 2,952      |

A lesson in efficiency that certain British manufacturers would do well to heed!

In the Autumn of 1955 there appeared the improved 356A series; the cars were a little heavier, the body was 'cleaned up' in detail and there were slight suspension modifications aimed at reducing the oversteer still further. The most important modification, however, was in the increase in capacity to 1588 cc by retaining the stroke of 74 mm and increasing the bore to 82·5 mm. There were now two basic models offered in coupé, cabriolet and 'Speedster' forms:

1600N or standard: 60 bhp at 4500 rpm
1600 'Super': 75 bhp at 4500 rpm
1300N or standard: 44 bhp at 4200 rpm
1300 'Super': 60 bhp at 5500 rpm

The 1600 standard which, in Great Britain, cost in 1956 £1,891 inclusive of Purchase Tax, would attain a maximum speed of 101 mph, would accelerate from rest to 60 mph in 15·3 seconds (prior to the 911 range, all production Porches had sluggish acceleration) and would average 30 mpg. By March, 1956, total Porsche production had amounted to 10,000 cars.

## The Carrera

Named after the Carrera Panamericana Mexico race which was not held after 1954, the Carrera was simply the 356A (it appeared at the same time) powered by the 1498 cc four overhead camshaft engine from the sports/racing 'Spyder' and developing 100 bhp at 6200 rpm. The 'Carrera' was a wonderful beast, rather intractable for road use, excruciatingly difficult to service and heavy on oil, but ideal for G.T. racing. To drive one on the road was like driving a really hot sports/racing car, but with an unexpected degree of comfort, and accompanied by all the mechanical clatter and exhaust roar of a competition car. 125 mph was the top speed attainable by most examples.

For 1957 the 'Carrera' was offered with the choice of 100 and 110 bhp engines depending on the compression ratio, and became known as the 'de luxe' or the 'G.T.', and the makers glibly quoted the same top speed of 125 mph! In 1958 capacity was increased to 1600 cc and the two power outputs rose to 105 and 115 bhp. When Porsche produced the 356B in 1959 (see below) the Carrera was temporarily dropped from the range. However, a further 60 were built in 1960. Of these, 40 had the normal steel body by Reutter, but Abarth of Turin built the rest with their own style of coachwork. In order to achieve the necessary structural rigidity, the all-aluminium Abarth bodies weighed almost as much as the standard product, but they were very much prettier and had a smaller frontal area. One of the Abarth-bodied cars won the Grand Touring section of the 1960 Targa Florio.

The Carrera came back with a bang in 1962 in vastly improved form. It retained the 356 body shell (although cars were also bodied by Abarth), but had a 2-litre four-cam engine developing 130 bhp. Maximum speed was close to 130 mph and acceleration from rest to 60 took a not dreadfully impressive 9 seconds. To stop the Carrera 2, Porsche gave it disc brakes developed from those on their Grand Prix cars. These were exceedingly expensive to make and had the brake caliper mounted inside the disc, which was bolted to the wheel carrier and not to the hub. The 2-litre car proved far more popular than its makers anticipated and remained in production until 1965.

## Final Production Versions of the 356

In 1957 Porsche stopped using the roller-bearing crankshaft on the pushrod cars, a shorter gear-lever was used and a hard top for the cabriolet became optional. The following year the 'Speedster' was dropped in favour of the Convertible D with a body by Drauz. In late 1959 this was replaced by the Roadster and the 356B appeared. Among modifications were the raising of bumpers and headlamps, a cleaner nose for better air penetration, a still shorter gear-lever and better brakes and a larger windscreen. The Carrera was dropped and three variants were offered:

|              | *Power output*      | *Claimed top speed* |
|--------------|---------------------|---------------------|
| 60 'Normal'  | 60 bhp at 4500 rpm  | 100 mph             |
| 75 'Super'   | 75 bhp at 5000 rpm  | 109 mph             |
| 90 'Super'   | 90 bhp at 5500 rpm  | 115 mph             |

The Super 90 was fitted with a single transverse leaf spring fixed to the differential, but free to ride with the half-shafts. By shifting wheel loading from the wheel on the outside of the curve to that on the inside, it improved handling and was offered as an optional extra on the 1600C and 1600SC models which appeared later.

These, the very final version of the 356, took their bow in July, 1963, just before Porsche completed their 50,000th car. This series of cars had ATE disc brakes made under licence from Dunlop and incorporating small back drums for the handbrake. The main changes to the engine were improved cylinder heads and a stronger crankshaft. The 356C could be distinguished by a larger rear window and twin air vents in the engine cover.

Two versions were offered:
1600C: 75 bhp at 5200 rpm on Zenith carburation
1600SC: 95 bhp at 5800 rpm on Solex carburation.

When the 356 was finally superseded in May, 1965, its place was taken by a line of cars that was to strengthen Porsche's place in the sports car markets of the world even further and was to represent a complete break with the 17 years' development of a single theme that had its origins in a car of purely economical conception.

TWO
# Purely For Racing
# The Early Competition Sports Car

## *A Private Prototype*

Motor racing runs in the blood of the Porsche family, who see it not only as a source of publicity and engineering experience, but as an end in itself. The early attitude of Porsche and von Hanstein was that it was primarily a sport, and indeed, as the years have passed the Competitions Manager has increasingly grown to dislike the rat race and business pressure of modern motor racing. In the early 'fifties the Porsche factory was too busily engaged with expanding production to build a sports/racing car proper and the first Porsche in this category was the work of a private owner. This car was the Glöckler-Porsche, the creation of Walter Glöckler, the main Volkswagen distributor in Frankfurt.

During 1950 Glöckler had entered an 1100 cc car with a power output of 58 bhp, but for the following season he produced a diminutive sports car with a Porsche 1500 cc engine and a wheelbase of only 6 ft 6 in. Despite a low power output of 90 bhp, the small frontal area permitted the Glöckler to attain speeds of up to 130 mph. The car took part in the record attempts at Montlhéry in 1951, where it greatly impressed the Porsche team, and was subsequently sold to Max Hoffmann, the New York Porsche representative.

## *The 550 'Spyder'*

Directly inspired by the Glöckler was the factory's decison to build a sports/racing car. It was decided that the existing push-rod engine would not be fast enough, and so work was put in hand on a flat-four, air-cooled engine with twin overhead camshafts per bank of cylinders. This engine, typed the 547, had a capacity of 1498 cc

(85 × 66 mm) and was in due course developed to push out 110 bhp at 6200 rpm. The engine was developed over the winter of 1952–3, but was not raceworthy until well into the 1953 season. To take the new engine, a new chassis, specially cross-braced, was constructed; suspension was similar to that of the production cars with two square laminated torsion bars at the front and, at the rear, two shorter and thicker round-section bars. Transmission was by the same 4-speed gearbox as the production cars, and this was mounted behind the rear axle and had a hydraulically-operated clutch.

A prototype of this car with a tuned 1500 'Super' engine ran in a minor race at the Nürburgring in 1953 and Helm Glöckler drove this to victory ahead of the works Borgwards. Next on the calendar was Le Mans, and Porsche fielded two of the tubular chassis cars fitted with the coupé tops. In this form they were uncomfortable and the ventilation was atrocious, but with their good aerodynamic shape these push-rod cars were timed at 123·6 and 122·4 mph on the Mulsanne straight. The leading car of von Frankenberg and von Hanstein covered 2,070·5 miles in the 24 hours at 86·78 mph and won the 1500 cc class, while Glöckler, co-driving with the young Hans Herrmann, finished 16th. The two Le Mans cars, with the aerodynamic tops removed, next ran at the sports car race accompanying the German Grand Prix and for this event the push-rod engine was tuned to develop 98 bhp. Herrmann scored an easy victory. In practice for the race ran a third car, driven by von Hanstein and Herrmann, and this was the four-cam engine making its first public appearance. The now complete competition car was typed the 550 and was exhibited at the 1953 Paris Salon. At the instigation of the American agent, who thought that an attractive name would be necessary if the cars were to sell well, the new model was called the 'Spyder', a nickname given to American sports roadsters in the late 'twenties. In November, 1953 Porsche entered two of the 550 'Spyders' for Hans Herrmann and Karl Kling in the 1,934-mile Carrera Panamericana Mexico, run in eight stages spread over five days. At the end of the first stage Herrmann was leading his class, but both 'Spyders' retired.

## The 'Spyder' in 1954

The first 1954 entry of the 'Spyder' came in the Mille Miglia, that exciting road race round Italy, where Hans Herrmann, by then a Mercedes-Benz Grand Prix team driver, was accompanied by Herbert Linge, who enjoyed at that time more of a reputation as a mechanic than as a driver. The race was exciting and there was a close duel on time between the Porsche and the Italian Oscas. Herrmann lost twenty minutes while Linge sorted out soaked electrics and the car had a dangerous moment when Herrmann found a level crossing closed against him; both men crouched low in the cockpit and the low Porsche slid under the barrier and across with an approaching train a mere 100 ft away. Herrmann won the 1500 cc class of the race, finishing sixth and averaging 78·74 mph for the 992 miles.

Next on the calendar was the Le Mans race where Porsche fielded three normal 550 'Spyders' plus an example fitted with an 1100 cc engine. The race was something of a disaster. Incorrect ignition settings on the 1500 cc cars caused overheating and burnt pistons and thus the retirement of two of the cars; the third, driven by Johnny Claes and Stasse, also burnt a piston, but staggered round on three cylinders for the last five hours of the race to win its class and finish 12th. Fourteenth and also victor in its class was the 1100 cc car driven by Chevrolet development engineer Arkus Duntov and Olivier. But gearbox trouble caused this to 'stagger' in the closing stages. A fortnight later the 'Spyders' vindicated themselves by finishing first and second in their class in the Rheims 12 hours race.

During the remainder of the season a number of minor successes came the way of the 'Spyders', including first four places in the 1500 cc sports car race at the Nürburgring on 1st August. But at the 1500 cc sports car race at Silverstone on the day of the British Grand Prix, Herrmann was beaten into third place by the Lotus cars of Colin Chapman and Peter Gammon; von Hanstein, however, won the 1100 cc class. In November the team again contested the Carrera Panamericana Mexico race and 550s were driven by Herrmann and Guatemalan driver Juhan; they took the first and second places in their class after the faster Borgward of Bechem had been involved in a multi-car crash at Rio Hondito whilst leading the class.

At the end of 1954 the first 550s were sold to private owners and in all over 100 were built; all pushed out a reliable output of between 110 and 115 bhp and could safely be taken up to 7500 rpm. The majority of the production went to the United States.

## The 'Spyder' in 1955

First Porsche success in 1955 came in the Buenos Aires 1000 Km race in January where Jaroslav Juhan drove solo the same 'Spyder' as he had in the Panamericana race (and now sold to him) into fourth place and defeated such heavier machinery as the 3-litre Gordini of Bayol and Schell. Porsche were prominent in March in two events of rather different calibre. In the Lyons-Charbonnières Rally the race-bred 'Spyder' of drivers Gacon and Arcan, looking rather out of place on the snow-bound Col de la Faucille, lost first place when its intrepid drivers took a wrong fork, but finished third in the 1600 cc sports class. At Sebring, Porsche fielded a 550 driven by von Hanstein and Linge which ran well to finish eighth overall and win the 1500 cc class. In the Mille Miglia it was eighth place again and a class win for the 550 of Seidel. Victory in the 1300 cc G.T. class went to Richard von Frankenberg with a 356. A fortnight later was the Paris 1000 Km race over the 4·97-mile Montlhéry circuit and limited to cars of up to 2000 cc. Victory went to the private 'Spyder' of Veuillet and Olivier from the similar car of Jeser and Mme Bousquet at 82·21 mph. Third was a 2-litre Maserati.

The most important race for Porsche in 1955 was Le Mans on 11th-12th June and once again a strong team of four 'Spyders' was fielded. The race was marred by the horrible crash involving Levegh's Mercedes, in which over eighty spectators lost their lives. The other two cars of the Mercedes-Benz team were withdrawn and the carnage of mechanical failure which eliminated the entire Ferrari team and all but one of each of the works Jaguar and Aston Martin entries permitted the Porsches to come through to prominent positions in the results:

1st   J. M. Hawthorn/I. Bueb (Jaguar D-type), 2,594·58 miles (107·07 mph)
2nd   P. Collins/P. Frère (Aston Martin DB3S)
3rd   J. Claes/J. Swaters (Jaguar D-type, privately entered)
4th   H. Polensky/R. von Frankenberg (Porsche 550 'Spyder')
5th   W. Seidel/A. Milhoux (Porsche 550 'Spyder')
6th   H. Glöckler/J. Juhan (Porsche 550 'Spyder')

The 1100 cc car of Duntov and Veuillet finished 13th and won its class.

In July privately entered 550s also took first three places in the Civil Governor's Cup at Lisbon, Portugal, and in August the works car of von Frankenberg won the production car race accompanying the Swedish sports car Grand Prix. Porsche were, however, beginning to face stiff opposition in their class from British cars in short distance races and in the longer races from Maserati, E.M.W. and Borgward. Two 550s were entered in the Goodwood Nine Hours race on 20th August; one was driven by Stirling Moss and von Hanstein, but the Porsche team manager was close to 10 secs a lap lower than the English Grand Prix driver and in the 1500 cc class Colin Chapman's Lotus forged ahead; the Porsche was eliminated during the evening (the latter stages of the race were run in the dark) when it collided with Tony Crook's Cooper-Bristol which had spun on a patch of oil; the irony of the situation was that the oil had been dropped by the other works Porsche of Wolfgang Seidel and Dickie Steed! This 550 finished second in the class to the Connaught of Les Leston and Archie Scott-Brown. A second defeat came in the Nürburgring 500 Km race on 28th August. As well as the works 'Spyders', there were 12 privately entered cars in the race; the Porsche factory felt a moral obligation to keep an eye on these and the work proved too much for their resources; the situation was not helped by von Frankenberg crashing one of the works entries in practice and von Hanstein also had a minor shunt. In the race Herbert Linge drove instead of von Hanstein, but the Porsches were soundly trounced by the brand new Maserati 150S (virtually a scaled-down version of the Modena concern's Grand Prix car) of Jean Behra which galloped to victory at record speed. In this race occurred the first fatality to a Porsche driver in the many thousands of racing miles the Stuttgart cars had covered – amateur driver Spingler inverted his 356 coupé and received injuries from which he died.

At the last Tourist Trophy held on the superb Dundrod circuit in Northern Ireland, in September, the new breed of British sports cars, Lotus, Cooper and Connaught, revealed their fragility in long distance racing, and first three places in the 1500 cc class went to works Porsches: the leading Zuffenhausen entry, which took ninth place in this race dominated by the other Stuttgart team from Untertürkheim, was driven by the American pair Carroll Shelby and Masten Gregory. One other race was still to come for the works team in 1955; at the Avusrennen, held on the notorious Berlin track with its steep, brickfaced banking, von Frankenberg won from the East German E.M.W.s of Rosenhammer and Thiel.

*Later Developments of the 550*

The stiff opposition faced by the 550 in 1955 activated a programme of intensive development work on the basic design. The chassis was stiffened and a 5-speed gearbox was introduced; first gear was for starting only, was unsynchronised and was engaged by means of a locking catch. During the winter months a further development, the 'Spyder' RS was produced – RS stood for *Rennsport*. The chassis was based on an entirely new space-frame, inspired by Lotus practice, and weighing 90 lb less than the original; it is, perhaps, a sad fact that Porsche have shown far more initiative in engine and body design than chassis and suspension developments for which they have tended to lean rather heavily on the inspiration of British designs, notably Lotus. Fuel capacity on the RS was increased from the 20 gallons of the 550 to 28.

Porsche's first race in 1956 was the Sebring 12 Hours where two 'Spyders' were entered, for Herrmann and the young and very talented Graf Wolfgang von Trips, and for Americans McAfee and Peter Lovely and with Huschke von Hanstein supervising operations in the pits. The Porsches motored with tremendous speed, leading Ferraris and D-type Jaguars, and the German drivers took sixth place overall, and won both their class and the Index of Performance; the Americans were seventh and second in the class.

Two 550s ran in the Mille Miglia, but it proved to be one of Porsche's less successful outings. Herrmann suffered valve trouble at Aquila and Gianni Bracco (winner of the 1952 race with a Ferrari) found his brakes inoperative in the wet and decided to retire before anything unpleasant happened. The new RS cars made their competition debut in the Nürburgring 1000 Km race where they were driven by Hans Herrmann/von Frankenberg and von Trips/Maglioli (the latter a former works Ferrari driver and, like Vaccarella today, a master of the open road rather than the closed circuit). Von Trips and Maglioli were the stars of the Porsche team and finished fourth overall and won their class. And Porsche also derived great satisfaction from having soundly thrashed the East German A.W.E.s (formerly E.M.W.s) which had in 1955 threatened to topple Porsche supremacy in the class. A fortnight later an RS was entered in the Targa Florio and Maglioli, co-driving with von Hanstein, hurled

*Above:* Hairy brute – the SSKL Mercedes-Benz designed by Ferdinand Porsche. This is the car in which Rudolf Caracciola and Christian Werner drove to victory in the 1931 Mille Miglia (Publifoto). *Below:* Abortive effort – the 1938 aero-engined car designed by Porsche for Mercedes-Benz. It was intended for an attack on the World Land Speed Record, but the outbreak of war prevented the attempt

Mentor – Ferry Porsche, who guides the company's destinies

Successor? Ferdinand Porsche Junior, grandson of the founder, who designed the 911 body and who is destined one day to take over from his father

the 'Spyder' through the twists and turns of the little Madonie circuit to win from Piero Taruffi, past-master of the Targa, with a 3-litre Maserati.

In 1956 there were two 12 Hours races at Rheims and in that for cars up to 1500 cc Porsche entered two cars. After the retirement of the very fast Lotus of Ivor Bueb and Herbert Mackay Fraser with the race two thirds run, the Porsches were first and second, the RS of von Frankenberg and Storez leading home the 550 of the brothers Goethals. Because of the circuit modifications that took place after the 1955 disaster, the Le Mans race was put back until the end of July. One of the race regulations – and they were sufficiently peculiar to exclude the 1956 Le Mans event from the Sports Car World Championships – was the compulsory fitting of full-width screens, and so the two works RS Porsches ran with coupé tops; these had rings mounted in the doors to operate the door locks and the tail panel and roof-top recognition lights. The RS of von Frankenberg and von Trips never missed a beat throughout the 24 hours and finished fifth overall at 98·19 mph, won its class and was second in the Index of Performance. The other works car driven by Herrmann and Maglioli dropped a valve – in practice it had jumped out of third gear causing the engine to soar up to 8900 rpm and it is probable that this started the damage. A further victory for the RS was gained when Herrmann won the 7-lap accompanying race to the German Grand Prix from the Maserati 150S of Stirling Moss.

In the autumn of 1956 Porsche put the RS into production and about thirty were built for sale to private owners.

## Porsche in 1957

Porsche skipped the first two races in the Sports Car Championship in 1957 – at Buenos Aires and Sebring – but privately entered cars waved the Stuttgart flag in Florida by finishing eighth and ninth and winning the 1500 cc class. A Stuttgart flag, incidentally, closely resembles the Ferrari emblem, with a black prancing horse on a yellow background, but the Stuttgart horse faces right and the Ferrari horse left. First serious Porsche appearance in 1957 was in the Mille Miglia where a single RS was driven by Umberto Maglioli. He finished fifth overall and won his class – but he almost threw away the race by forgetting to refuel at Bolgna and coming to a stop with a dry tank; by good fortune he was able to tank up at a small garage nearby. The Carrera of Strahle and Linge won the 1600 cc G.T. class.

At the 1000 Km event at the Nürburgring, Porsche's new RSK model appeared in practice, but for the race the team relied on the faithful RS. The race was won by an Aston Martin DBR1 from two Ferraris and fourth, winning its class and on the same lap as the winner was the Porsche of Maglioli and former E.M.W. *pilote* Barth. The second car of the team finished seventh. The RSK model, typed the 718, was known as such because the carrier tubes of the front suspension formed roughly that shape of a 'K'. The front suspension also incorporated ball-swivels instead of king-pins and the chassis was lower and lighter. The steering box was mounted centrally (with an eye to Formula Two), the spare wheel was mounted horizontally in the nose and the front brakes were of a new turbo-finned type. At the back the new car had the low-pivot swing-axle mounted on coil springs and the body was distinguished by twin tail fins – another feature derived from British sports car practice. With two twin-choke Weber carburettors power output was now 148 bhp at 8400 rpm.

One of the RSK cars was entered for Edgar Barth and Umberto Maglioli to drive at Le Mans, but the race proved a disaster for the team. The new car ran well until it hit the wreckage of Tony Brooks' overturned Aston Martin and the other two entries, both RS models, retired. Herrman/von Frankenberg were out before midnight because of a burnt piston and the Storez/Crawford car retired in the last hour of the race with a broken crankshaft.

## *RSK to the Fore, 1958*

In 1958 Porsche's efforts were much more intensive and widespread and the results were to be seen in their placing in the Sports Car Championship. For the first time Porsche entered the Buenos Aires 1000 Km race, held in January on a 5·888-mile circuit which took in the outer track of the Autodrome and part of the adjacent dual carriageway. Because their Maserati had been too badly damaged to be repaired for the race, Stirling Moss and Jean Behra accepted von Hanstein's offer of an RS Porsche with an enlarged engine of 1587 cc. These two put up a magnificent performance to finish third overall behind two 3-litre Ferraris and fifth place went to the other Porsche team car, a normal RS, in the hands of Barth and one-time Maserati Grand Prix driver Mieres. RS cars ran in this race because they could be sold afterwards whereas as RSKs would have had to be taken back to Stuttgart.

RS cars, for the same reason, were entered at Sebring and they put up an excellent performance that repeated the Argentinian results. Harry Schell and Wolfgang Seidel finished third behind two Ferraris at 83·6 mph compared with the winners' 86·6 mph and tenth were von Hanstein (having temporarily swapped team manager's for driver's hat) and Linge.

To the Targa Florio Porsche brought two sports cars, one an RSK distinguished by its oil cooler incorporated in the surface of the nose and, for this race, an additional block-type cooler alongside the driving seat, and a normal RS shared between three drivers, Behra, Barth and Scarlatti. In addition a very hot Carrera coupé with the latest Spyder engine was driven by von Hanstein and Pucci. Ferrari led throughout the race, but the RSK driven by Behra and Scarlatti took a brilliant second place. As Denis Jenkinson wrote in *Motor Sport*, 'The Anglo-Saxon-speaking element in the Ferrari team seemed to take a very childish view of the race, which was obviously more difficult and harder work than they have been used to and for once they "had to earn their money" so it was not surprising that the little Porsche made them look silly.' And indeed the 3-litre 'Testa Rossa' Ferraris of Hawthorn/von Trips and Collins/Phil Hill were beaten into third and fourth places. The RS retired with a broken half-shaft and the Carrera finished sixth.

In the Nürburgring 1000 Km race, Aston Martin scored their second victory in succession, leading home four Ferraris. Although the RSK's failed to display the speed that might be expected of them, they took first two places in the 1500 cc class in the order von Frankenberg/de Beaufort/Barth and Frère/Schell and were placed 11th and 12th overall. The third car of the team entered for Behra and Barth retired with valve trouble.

At Le Mans Porsche fielded four RSK718s, two of 1587 cc and two of 1498 cc – all now without tail fins – for Jean Behra/Hans Herrmann, von Frankenberg/Storez, Barth/Frère and de Beaufort/Linge – names that constantly recur in Porsche history. A carnage of crashes and mechanical failures amongst the 3-litre Ferraris, Aston Martins and Jaguars combined with the speed and reliability of the Porsches resulted in exceptionally high placings for the RSKs in the final results:

1st O. Gendebien/P. Hill (Ferrari 3-litre TR/250), 106·20 mph
2nd P. Whitehead/G. Whitehead (Aston Martin DB3S)
3rd J. Behra/H. Herrmann (Porsche RSK), 1st in the 2000 cc class and a new class record
4th E. Barth/P. Frère (Porsche RSK), 1st in the 1500 cc class and a new class record
5th C. G. de Beaufort/H. Linge (Porsche RSK), 2nd in the 1500 cc class and also beating the old class record
6th A. de Changy/'Beurlys' (Ferrari 3-litre TR/250)

In addition the privately entered RS of Colas and Kerguen finished tenth. The sole works car to fall by the wayside was that of von Frankenberg and Storez which crashed, like many other competing cars, during a heavy rainstorm.

On the day of the German Grand Prix, two works RSKs faced three works Borgwards in the Rheinland Cup at the Nürburgring. Behra and Barth were first and third for Porsche, while Bonnier, Herrmann and Jüttner were second, fourth and sixth for the Bremen concern. Zeltweg airfield on 17th August was the scene of yet another Porsche triumph when von Trips, Behra and Barth took the first three places.

In September Porsche came to Britain for the Tourist Trophy held at Goodwood and the last round in the Sports Car Championship. Two cars were entered for Behra/Barth and de Beaufort/Heins. Ferrari scratched his works entries and so the race turned into an Aston Martin procession which Behra did his best to break up. The Feltham DBR1 cars took first three places, while Behra/Barth came home fourth and won their class. Porsche was joint runner-up in the Sports Car Championship with Aston Martin, each having scored 18 points compared with the maximum 32 of Ferrari (only the best four performances counted). Porsche rounded off the season with a win by Behra in the 1500 cc Avusrennen later in September.

## 1959: Another Consistent Year

There was no Buenos Aires race in 1959 and so the first round in the Sports Car World Championship was at Sebring on 24th March. Porsche took two of the 1600 cc cars and one 1500 to the race and the team included one-time Mercedes-Benz works driver, American John Fitch. The 1600 RSKs had a new form of independent rear suspension by triangular links, radius rods and coil springs – as on the Formula Two cars. After the sole British Aston Martin and the Listers had fallen by the wayside, Ferraris took the first two places, but the Porsches were not far behind and occupied the next three places in the order von Trips/Bonnier (despite clutch trouble and a suspected cracked piston!), Sessler/Holbert (a private entry), and Fitch/Barth. Von Hanstein, co-driving with de Beaufort, finished eleventh.

At the beginning of May a sole RSK was entered in the 1500 cc Spa Grand Prix for de Beaufort and he scored an easy win from Isabel de Tomaso's Osca. The next Championship race was the Targa Florio, also in May, to which Zuffenhausen sent four cars. Two were modified versions of the RSK as raced at Sebring and Spa and these were driven by Maglioli/Herrmann and Bonnier/von Trips, while a 1500 RSK was given to Barth/Seidel; to complete the team a Carrera was driven by Pucci/von Hanstein. The car driven by Bonnier and von Trips had slightly modified front suspension with the trailing arms not so far apart vertically in order to eliminate the slight wandering tendencies at high speed. Apart from the works team, Paul Strahle had two private entries, a 1957 RS and a Carrera and it was the intention that the driving should be shared between himself and two fellow-Germans, Linge and Mahle. The organisers were unhappy about this and insisted that there should be a fourth driver, so Strahle roped in local driver Scagliarini. In fact the Sicilian never even sat in either car and the Germans did all the driving – but when the cars finished high up in the results, Scagliarini made the headlines in Sicilian and Italian newspapers! Opposition to the Porsches came from a strong team of Ferraris. Of these, two of the 'Testa Rossas' retired with crown wheel-and-pinnion failure, one was crashed (by both Jean Behra *and* Tony Brooks) and the 2-litre Dino broke its gearbox. The Porsches were not exactly the epitome of reliability – although they faired much better than their rivals – and von Trips had the rear suspension collapse, while Hans Herrmann had gearchange trouble and the engine eventually broke. To prevent pillaging by the local 'bandits', Herrmann stayed with his car for thirteen hours until the team came out from the pits to collect it. Thirty-five years previously the race had been won by the Porsche-designed 2-litre Mercedes of Christian Werner and now cars bearing the same famous name had scored their second victory in the race.

*Results*

1st E. Barth/W. Seidel (Porsche RSK), 56·74 mph
2nd E. Mahle/P. Strahle/H. Linge (Porsche RS)
3rd A. Pucci/H. von Hanstein (Porsche Carrera)
4th P. Strahle/E. Mahle/H. Linge (Porsche Carrera)
5th A. Boffa/P. Drago (Maserati A6GCS)
6th 'Sepe'/C. Davis (Alfa Romeo Giulietta Sprint Veloce)

The Carreras, which had special gear ratios allowing three very close lower ratios to be used in the mountains and a very high top gear on the 6-kilometre straight, were attaining over 120 mph and 7500 rpm in top gear. After the race they were driven back to Zuffenhausen by way of Italy and the Brenner Pass.

Aston Martin gained yet another victory in the Nürburgring 1000 Km race and Ferraris were second and third – but the Porsches were very much to the fore on home territory and this is how they fared:

4th U. Maglioli/H. Herrmann (1st in class) – latest works 1600 cc RSK with wishbone rear suspension

6th H. Walter/A. Heuberger – new, privately entered 1500 cc RSK

7th W. von Trips/J. Bonnier – latest works 1600 cc RSK with wishbone rear suspension

10th H. J. Walter/P. Strahle – experimental works Carrera with disc front brakes and modified rear suspension with wide single-leaf transverse spring pivoted in the middle below the rear axle casing – the extra spring in conjunction with the torsion bars gave a double-rate suspension

13th R. Rodriguez/L. Levine – experimental 1600 'Super' with new brakes, Solex racing carburettors and revving up to 6500 rpm. The rear suspension was as on the Carrera and this was a prototype of the Super 90

Retired, E. Barth/C. G. de Beaufort – a works 1958-type 1500 RSK which was eliminated by engine trouble

Le Mans, a fortnight later, was next on Porsche's programme and the race provided Aston Martin with well deserved first and second places after ten years of misfortune at the Sarthe circuit. The race was a complete disaster for Porsche, for all six cars entered, three works, three private, retired – mostly with engine trouble; the downfall of the works cars was an outright bid for victory rather than relying on consistent running to collect a class win. First to go was the Herrmann/Maglioli 1600 which was lying eighth when it blew up its engine on the Saturday evening; by Sunday morning Porsches were fourth, fifth, sixth and seventh, but the Bonnier/von Trips 1600, the Barth/Seidel 1500 and the private car of de Beaufort/ Heinz blew up their engines in quick succession. And it was not long before the remaining two cars broke down with engine trouble out at Mulsanne.

On 1st August at the banked Avus track the works RSKs galloped home to first three places in the Berlin Grand Prix. Next and final appearance of the works sports cars in 1959 was in the Tourist Trophy at Goodwood where Porsche fielded three of the 1600 cc cars. Despite losing one of their cars in a pits fire, Aston Martins were first and fourth. The Porsche of Bonnier and von Trips was driven magnificently, leading the race at one stage, finishing second and running rings round the 3-litre Ferraris. The Maglioli/Barth car broke its engine and was pushed across the line to finish twelfth. The third car of the team, driven by Hans Herrmann and young Chris Bristow was eliminated in a collision with Alan Stacey's Lotus – both these young men were destined to be killed in the same race, the 1960 Belgian Grand Prix. In the Sports Car Championship Porsche took third place with 21 points to the 22 of Ferrari and the 24 of Aston Martin.

## *1960: Second Place in the World Championship*

A grand total of eight RSK Porsches were fielded in the 1000 Km race at Buenos Aires, restored to the calendar after a year's absence. Porsche fielded three works 1600 cc RSKs plus a Carrera and there were five privately entered. After Dan Gurney's new 'Bird-cage' Maserati had retired, works Ferrari 'Testa Rossas' were first and second, but the Porsches gave another fine display of reliability and speed. Third and winner in the 1600 cc class was the works RSK of Graham Hill and Joakim Bonnier, a Maserati was fourth and RSKs occupied fifth, sixth, seventh and eighth places. The Carrera driven by von Hanstein and Bohnen took tenth place.

Sebring became a farce because the organisers insisted on the entrants using a particular brand of fuel and one result of this was that the works Ferraris were not entered. After the retirement of the private 'Testa Rossas' and the Camoradi Team's three 'Bird-cage' Maseratis, the RSK Porsches droned into an easy lead and the works car of Gendebien and Herrmann won from a private entry shared by Holbert, Schlecter and Fowler.

To the Targa Florio came two transporters from Maranello, each carrying three cars (one for training), while Porsche sent a collection of vans and trailers with the latest RS60 models together with an RSK for practice and a Carrera which was driven from Stuttgart by Engineer Hild. Two of the new stubby, pugnacious looking RS60s had engines bored out to 1630 cc and these were shared between Bonnier, Herrmann and young Belgian driver Olivier Gendebien, while the 1586 cc model was in the hands of von Hanstein and Pucci. Paul Strahle had entered two Carreras, the 1959 fourth-place car which he and 'Keinz' were to drive and a new Abarth-bodied Carrera which he had also put himself down to handle with Herbert Linge. The Targa Florio maintained its car-destroying reputation: the Rodriguez brothers both crashed their 2-litre Ferrari – but finished! Ginther crashed his works 'Testa Rossa'; and Pucci hit a wall with the works Carrera. The Porsches were superbly driven, were handling much better than the Ferraris and had the race in their pockets once the 'Bird-cage' Maserati of Vaccarella and Maglioli had run out of petrol and clouted a bank. Once again the Stuttgart cars completely dominated the results:

1st J. Bonnier/H. Herrmann (Porsche RS60), 59·24 mph
2nd W. von Trips/P. Hill (Ferrari Dino 246)
3rd O. Gendebien/H. Herrmann (Porsche RS60)
4th W. Mairesse/L. Scarfiotti/G. Cabianca (Ferrari Dino 246)
5th E. Barth/G. Hill (Porsche RS60)
6th H. Linge/P. Strahle (Porsche Carrera-Abarth)
7th R. Rodriguez/P. Rodriguez (Ferrari Dino 196)
8th P. Strahle/'Keinz' (Porsche Carrera)

Also in May privately entered Porsches were first and second in the Spa Grand Prix. The next appearance of the works cars came later the same month in the 1000 Km race at the Nürburgring. The race proved a Maserati benefit and the Camoradi Team 'Bird-cage' cars finished first and fifth, but, numerically, Porsches completely dominated the results and won the 1600 and 2000 cc sports classes and the 2000 cc G.T. class. Works 1630 cc RS60s finished second and fourth (Bonnier/Gendebien and Herrmann/Trintignant), while the private RSK of Walter and Losinger was sixth. The G.T. victory went to the Carrera-Abarth of Strahle and Walter placed tenth overall. The 1600 cc RS60 of Hill and Barth led its class until the German driver collided with a slower car he was lapping and left the road.

Porsche also ran two experimental cars in this race. One was an Abarth-bodied Carrera fitted with Porsche's own disc brakes and was driven into seventh place by Linge and Greger and the other was a production Carrera, but with extensive modifications. The power unit was a push-rod Super 90 running on fuel injection and with an exhaust system consisting of four separate equal-length pipes with reverse-cone megaphones; Porsche disc brakes were also fitted to this car which was driven into 19th place.

Once again Le Mans proved not to be a Porsche race and all three works RS60s ran into trouble. The main factory car of Bonnier and Graham Hill developed a clonking noise early in the race – a symptom of something wrong with either the chassis or the suspension – and after a fruitless pit stop to locate the trouble, the car rejoined the race in 54th position and worked its way up to 14th only to retire with a blown cylinder head joint. A similar car in the hands of Trintignant and Herrmann went out early in the race with piston trouble. The third car of the team was an RS60 with a 1500 cc engine and although it motored for much of the race in the manner expected of a Porsche, it came into the pits with gearbox trouble in the closing stages of the race and limped around for a final lap to finish 12th. There were only five events in 1960 counting towards the Sports Car Championship with constructors' placings calculated on their three best performances. Porsche took second place in the Championship with 22 points.

At the end of July Bonnier won the six-hour Circuit of Auvergne at Clermont-Ferrand from the 250 GT Ferraris of Guichet and Bianchi. Next came the 25th R.A.C. Tourist Trophy, held at Goodwood and for G.T. cars only. It was contested primarily between six V-12 3-litre Ferraris, two Aston Martin DB4GTs, five Porsche Carreras and eleven Lotus Elites. Two of the Porsches were works cars driven by Graham Hill and Joakim Bonnier. Moss scored a brilliant victory with a Ferrari from the Astons of Roy Salvadori and Innes Ireland, while Graham Hill was fourth and won his class with an Abarth-bodied car – despite a traffic jam prang at the start.

## 1961: A Year of Further Development

The Sports Car Championship kicked off with the Sebring 12 Hours race and now Porsche was facing opposition from *rear-engined* Ferraris. The Porsche works entries were RS61s which differed only in detail from the previous season's cars and had smoother lines. Although the car entrusted to American drivers Bob Holbert and Roger Penske came through to finish fifth and win the Index of Performance, both of the other works cars, in the care of Bonnier/Gurney and Herrmann/Barth, retired with engine failure.

At the Le Mans practice Week-end in April Porsche ran a special RS61 with a coupé top; this featured an angled rear window that looked rather like a squashed-down version of that of the Ford Anglia and ran on disc brakes. A variant of this was amongst the very assorted range of cars taken by Porsche to the Targa Florio. This open car, powered by a 1987 cc version of the 4-cylinder engine, had a longer wheelbase (so as to accommodate the flat-eight engine when it became ready), a much smoother nose, a very sharply raked windscreen and a hollow hump over the tail which covered the carburettor intakes. It was the team's main hope for victory and was driven by Bonnier and Gurney. A normal RS61 car with 1678 cc engine was entered for Herrmann/Barth and there was a similar car for Moss and Graham Hill. The latter was nominally entered by the Camoradi team, but none of their personnel was present – 'Lucky' Casner merely had the privilege of paying. Two Abarth-bodied Carreras were running, one a works car, the other a new car belonging to Strahle and the driving was shared between Strahle, Linge, von Hanstein and Pucci. For training the team used a normal RS61 2-litre, a Super 90 and two RS61 2-litre-powered, disc-braked Carreras, these being prototypes of the Carrera 2 and used to collect data.

The race developed into an exciting and hard-fought duel between the Camoradi Porsche of Moss and Hill and the 246/SP rear-engined Ferrari of von Trips and Gendebien and only ended on the last lap when the German car stripped its crown-wheel-and-pinion. Even so the Porsches were second and third and largely dominated the results:

1st W. von Trips/O. Gendebien (Ferrari 246/SP), 64·28 mph
2nd J. Bonnier/D. Gurney (Porsche RS61)

3rd H. Herrmann/E. Barth (Porsche RS61)
4th N. Vaccarella/M. Trintignant (Maserati Tipo 63)
5th U. Maglioli/G. Scarlatti (Maserati Tipo 63)
6th P. Strahle/A. Pucci/H. Linge (Porsche Carrera-Abarth)
7th H. Linge/P. Strahle/H. von Hanstein (Porsche Carrera-Abarth)
8th J. Rosinsky/B. Consten (Alfa Romeo Giulietta Sprint Veloce)

Porsche entered four cars in the 1000 Ks race at the Nürburgring and for the second year in succession the race was won by a Maserati 'Bird-cage' of the Camoradi team. Second was the North American Racing Team's 'Testa Rossa' and third the works rear-engined Ferrari shared between Ginther, Gendebien and von Trips. The highest placed Porsche was a private Carrera in sixth spot and this makes its pretty clear that the race did not go according to Porsche expectations. Early in the race Barth retired the 1700 cc RS61 he was sharing with Herrmann because a cylinder head joint was leaking and Gurney at the wheel of a similar car shared with Bonnier made a very long pit stop while the mechanics reset the engine timing; this car eventually restarted to finish 10th. The third car with 'Camoradi' painted on the side as in the Targa Florio was shared by Stirling Moss and Graham Hill and although it eventually worked its way up to second place in atrociously wet conditions which seemed to suit its drivers, it blew up its engine. These two drivers then took turns at the wheel of the works experimental disc-braked Carrera with 1608 cc engine which finished eighth and won the 2000 cc sports class!

Le Mans saw Porsche field another very varied assortment of cars and although it was Ferrari – Ferrari – Ferrari – Maserati at the finish, a Porsche was fifth and the make won two classes. This is how the Porsches fared:

5th Masten Gregory/Bob Holbert with a normal open RS61 with 1966 cc engine. This won the 2000 cc class.
7th H. Herrmann/E. Barth with what amounted to a prototype G.T. Prototype for racing in 1962. This was a beautifully finished coupé with the roof cut short to provide a rearward entry for cooling and carburettor air. It had a 1608 cc engine.

10th B. Pon/H. Linge with a works entered Carrera-Abarth; this won the 1600 cc class.

Retired, J. Bonnier/D. Gurney with a car like that in seventh place; clutch failure caused its elimination.

One more race, the Pescara Four Hours, remained to complete the Sports Car Championship; because of its distance it counted for only half-points so Porsche did not bother to enter. Barth, however, was released to co-drive with private owner Orthuber and their RS61 finished second overall behind the 'Testa Rossa' Ferrari of Bandini and Scarlatti and won its class. Again Porsche sent two cars to the Grand Touring Tourist Trophy and Graham Hill drove a steady race to finish sixth and win his class. Herbert Linge retired with transmission trouble after only 15 laps. Final event of the season was the Paris 1000 Km race for G.T. cars at Montlhéry on 22nd October. Von Hanstein and Barth shared a Carrera-Abarth and won the 2000 cc class in which Porsches took the first four places. With this race over Porsche could concentrate on their ambitious 8-cylinder-based 1962 Formula One and Prototype G.T. programme.

# THREE
# First Porsche Single-Seaters

*Formula Two Racing, 1957-60*

There can be no greater decision for a manufacturer to make than that of competing in Grand Prix racing. The enormous expense can damage the Company's financial stability as it did with Lancia in 1955 and failure can also do the company's image more harm than not competing at all. To enter Grand Prix racing was Porsche's biggest mistake and it was the result of gaining success too easily in Formula Two racing and underestimating the potential strength of the opposition.

It all started when the organisers of the German Grand Prix included a class for Formula Two cars (racing cars of up to 1500 cc unsupercharged), a Formula only inaugurated that year, in the 1957 race. Having so often raced at the Nürburgring and with drivers who had an intimate knowledge of its twists and turns, ascents and descents, it was almost inevitable that Porsche should enter the race and they fielded three of the 1500RS 'Spyders' for Edgar Barth, driver of the East German A.W.E. (née E.M.W.) cars until that concern ceased racing at the end of 1956, Umberto Maglioli, one time up-and-coming man of the Ferrari team whose star, alas, waned before it had fully waxed, and Dutchman Carol Godin de Beaufort. Facing the Stuttgart cars were six of the purpose-built, small, light, but rather underpowered Cooper-Climax Formula Two cars. In the early stages of the race, Salvadori's works Cooper led the Formula Two class, but Barth worked his way up to come to grips with Salvadori, and the Porsche and Cooper passed and repassed each other until lap 11 when the right-hand rear wishbone broke on the Cooper. Barth was now in complete command of the class and finished 12th overall, having covered 21 laps out of the full 22. A lap behind came Brian Naylor's Cooper and third in the class was de Beaufort. A broken stub axle was the cause of Maglioli's retirement on lap 14.

Porsche were sufficiently encouraged by this success to have a go at a couple of the more important Formula Two races in 1958. The first of these was the Coupe de Vitesse which preceded the French Grand Prix at Rheims on 17th July. Here Porsche entrusted one of the Le Mans RSK sports cars, but with central driving position, to B.R.M. team-member Jean Behra. Behra found that the Porsche with its superior aerodynamics was fastest along the straights, but because of the greater weight and gear ratios that were not quite right lacked acceleration out of the corners. His best lap time of 2 min 37·4 sec was slower than Peter Collins' Dino Ferrari (2 min 36·7 sec) and Moss' Cooper-Climax (2 min 35·8 sec). Even so Behra led from the fall of the tricolour to the chequered flag – except when Moss got past for a short while on lap three – and his victory was an embarrassing shock for both Scuderia Ferrari and the British Cooper boys. Behra's average speed was slightly higher than that of Fangio's winning Mercedes-Benz on this circuit in the 1954 French Grand Prix.

Once again there was a Formula Two class at the German Grand Prix and, naturally enough, Porsche entered – a single central-seater appeared in the hands of Edgar Barth; de Beaufort ran his private 1500RS. Fastest of the Formula Two cars in practice was, however, Phil Hill with the V-6 Dino Ferrari that had been overshadowed at Rheims; Hill's fastest time was 9 min 48·9 sec compared with the 9 min 57·2 sec of Barth. Hill built up an enormous lead in the Ferrari until he went off the road as the result of hitting a patch of oil dropped by *Graham* Hill's Lotus; during his excursion through the undergrowth he tore away an engine breather pipe and oil blown on to the back tyres slowed him so that he was passed by McLaren's Cooper, Barth and Burgess' Cooper. De Beaufort retired early in the race. By no means a successful outing for either the Maranello or Stuttgart car!

For reasons best known to themselves, Porsche did not contest the Berlin Grand Prix held in September on the fast and dangerous 5·2-mile Avus circuit with a steeply banked loop at the northern end. Instead they loaned the central-seater to wealthy American Masten Gregory. This was one circuit where aerodynamics were at a premium and Gregory romped to victory at 126·08 mph ahead of the Coopers of Jim Russell and Jack Brabham.

## The First True Monoposto Porsches

Strongly encouraged by the performance of what had only been modified sports cars in 1958, Porsche took the plunge for the following season and built a pure single-seater exposed-wheel car. In essence the chassis was a development of the familiar RSK sports model, but nearly every component was new in some respect or other. The front suspension was still by two trailing arms on each side and transverse torsion bars with long, thin telescopic dampers, but at the rear there was a new layout of triangulated links and radius rods that gave the general effects of double wishbones. Drum brakes were retained. In this chassis was installed the standard 'Spyder' engine, but with two larger twin-choke Weber carburettors, and complete with sports car exhaust system. Transmission was by a new 6-speed gearbox contained in the normal RSK-type tubular gearbox housing. With this gearbox, first was purely for starting and this meant that the driver then had a fully synchromesh 5-speed gearbox for keeping the engine buzzing between 8500 and 9000 rpm. The fuel was carried in a large tank to the left of the driver, a smaller tank to the right and a saddle tank in front of the scuttle. With its high tail and low bonnet, the car looked ungainly, but it also looked very, very compact.

This car appeared at the Monaco Grand Prix where there was another single-seater Porsche. This was one Jean Behra had built for himself round an RSK engine. Normal RSK suspension was retained and there was a neat and narrower chassis (but with the usual track) and simple aluminium body, both built by Valeiro Colotti at Modena. The 'Behra-Porsche' as it was known was driven at Monaco by the young Italian girl Maria de Filippis. Unfortunately she was not fast enough to qualify as a starter, but Graf Wolfgang von Trips went great guns with the works car. He was out-accelerating some of the Formula One cars away from corners and his best lap of 1 min 43·8 sec was faster than the Formula One Cooper of McLaren and the Lotus of Graham Hill. Early in the race, however, he slid on a patch of oil, went sideways and was hit by Cliff Allison's Ferrari and Bruce Halford's Lotus.

Pau, on the 18th May, saw the next appearance of the Behra-Porsche, but the car proved no match for the Coopers and finished a poor fifth. The Coupe de Vitesse at Rheims attracted the works car, completely rebuilt since its Monaco prang, and this was driven by

Joakim Bonnier, while a works central-seater RSK was in the hands of von Trips. Hans Herrmann drove the Behra-Porsche. This year the Formula Two race was run after the Grand Prix to prevent vast quantities of rubber being distributed over the track before the main race. It provided a close dice between Stirling Moss (Cooper-Borgward) and Herrmann and this was the order in which they finished. Third was Bonnier with the works car – but only after Schell's Cooper boiled and Allison's Ferrari blew up. Herrman also drove Behra's Porsche in the Formula Two Rouen Grand Prix, but retired when the transmission seized up. Tragedy struck at the Germany Grand Prix meeting at Avus when Behra, driving his RSK in the sports car race, spun over the edge of the banking and was killed instantly. This brought to an end the career of his promising single-seater, for although it was acquired by the Camoradi team, it was not persevered with.

## *1960: First Full Year of Formula Two*

So great had been the promise shown by the prototype Formula Two car in 1959 that not only did the works team run cars for Joakim Bonnier and Graham Hill (both works B.R.M. drivers), but Rob Walker was loaned one for Stirling Moss to drive. Only minor changes had been made – the bodywork was slightly sleeker and the wheelbase was 10 cm longer. Walker's car first appeared at Syracuse and although already finished in his distinctive colours of dark blue with a white stripe across the nose, it was only officially handed over to its owner after the race. Moss was fastest in practice, set a new class lap record in the race, but retired because of a broken valve.

On April 10th Moss drove the Walker car in the Brussels Grand Prix, a race decided on the aggregate of two heats, and this race also marked the first appearance of a works car proper in 1960, in the hands of Jo Bonnier. Bonnier led in the opening laps, but Moss had soon squeezed his way past and then led all the way to the chequered flag. Towards the end of the heat the works car developed a horrible flat engine note and Bonnier continued at reduced speed until the engine seized up altogether. Before the second heat, the Porsche team made great play of getting Bonnier's car refuelled, claiming that it had only clutch trouble – which had now been cured – but the only Porsche to appear on the grid was that of Moss.

The second heat was run in the wet, Moss's car handled atrociously and was pointing in every direction except the way it ought to be going. The roads started to dry out towards the end of the heat, but the Porsche jumped out of first under acceleration from a bend and spun. Moss finished third which gave him second place on aggregate. It was interesting to note that the Walker mechanics had scrapped the horrible Porsche gear-gate and fitted one that had been made up for the Moss Maserati 250F car some years previously. This had the gear-lever spring-loaded away from the two left-hand slots, these being reverse and first on the Mazer, but first and second on the Porsche which had no reverse gear.

On 18th April, Easter Monday, a works car was loaned to Equipe Nationale Belge for Olivier Gendebien to drive in the Pau Grand Prix. The Porsche gear-change was an atrocious device and swapping cogs around the 6-speed gearbox meant that the Belgian driver lost a lot of time over the twisty 1·7-mile circuit and he finished third, two laps behind the leading Cooper-Climaxes of Maurice Trintignant and Jack Brabham. The three Porsches entered in the Aintree '200' – reduced in distance from 200 miles to 200 kilometres – dominated the race with ease. In practice Moss lapped in 2 minutes dead, an unofficial Formula Two record of 90 mph, but he was content to sit back in the race and take the lead at half-distance by when both the works Coopers had retired. The race then became a Porsche procession, with Moss at the wheel of the Walker car winning at 88·41 mph from the Stuttgart entries of Bonnier and Graham Hill.

In July there were two Formula Two races in Germany. The first was the Solitude Grand Prix on the 24th; this was held on an excellent circuit a few miles outside Stuttgart and taking its name from the Schloss Solitude, an old German castle on top of one of the hills overlooking the valley in which the circuit lies. A grand total of five cars was fielded by the Porsche team who were particularly anxious to do well on their home circuit. On this occasion their entry embraced the entire B.R.M. Grand Prix team of Hill, Bonnier and Dan Gurney plus a car for Hans Herrmann and the Walker car, with the normal Porsche gear-change refitted, entrusted to Motorcycle World Champion John Surtees. Gurney's car was brand new and instead of having the usual bulbous hump over the engine was fitted with an angular engine cover having a concave grilled opening on top of the tail. The Cooper opposition was surprisingly weak, but there was a new and very fast rear-engined Ferrari in the hands of von

Trips. It was a Porsche-Ferrari dog-fight all the way, the Maranello car taking the lead on the 16th lap of the 20-lap race to win by just over 4 sec from Herrmann's Porsche. Third, fourth and fifth were the Stuttgart cars of Bonnier, Hill and Gurney. After the race, Gurney was heard to say, 'I've never had to drive so hard in my life just for fifth place.' Surtees, not yet having got the hang of four-wheel racing and very troubled by the inadequacies of the Porsche gear-change, had an unhappy race, constantly missing 'changes, and on lap 16 took a corner in fourth instead of changing down, ran wide on to the loose stuff at the edge of the track, spun and stalled.

The second race was the German Grand Prix on 31st July. This was held on the shorter 4·81-mile South Circuit of the Nürburgring, a tight, winding course, crammed with ascents, descents and corners and usually used for the Eifelrennen. The race was run to Formula Two rules, partly as a try-out for the Formula One of the following year and partly because there were strong hopes of a German victory. Four works Porsches were fielded for Bonnier, Hill, Barth and von Trips, while Hans Herrmann, originally entered by the Camoradi on the old Behra-Porsche, was given the Walker car but had to qualify as a starter. The race was run in atrocious conditions – heavy rain and thick mist. The tubby silver cars of Bonnier and von Trips galloped away from the rest of the field, the fog became thicker and thicker and the cars lapped slower and slower. At the finish of this miserable 154-mile race, only the five Porsches and Brabham's works Cooper-Climax were on the same lap. The finishing order was: 1st, J. Bonnier, 80·28 mph; 2nd, W. von Trips (Porsche); 3rd, J. Brabham (Cooper-Climax); 4th, G. Hill (Porsche); 5th, H. Herrmann (Porsche); 6th, E. Barth (Porsche).

In September was the Italian Grand Prix. It proved quite a race, but lacked its usual top drawer entry because of a complete boycott by Cooper, Lotus and B.R.M. This was because it was held on the 6·241-mile combined road and banked track circuit and the British teams refused to enter, saying that their cars were not suitable – which meant, in effect, that they were not strong enough to withstand the stresses and strains of the banking and the chassis-pounding of its bumpy surface. It would probably have been a very different story if Brabham had not already assured himself of victory in the Drivers' Championship with points gained elsewhere. The organisers made up the entries with Formula Two cars and Porsche fielded works cars for Herrmann and Barth, while the Camoradi team ran the Behra-

Porsche for Fred Gamble. Pit-stops, an unusual happening in 1960 were a feature of this race, for all the Ferraris had to come in for tyres (they were checked, but not changed on the Formula Two car) and the Porsches for fuel. Formula One Ferraris occupied the first three places at the finish followed by the Cooper-Castellotti (a Ferrari 'Squalo'-engined Cooper) of Cabianca and von Trips with the Formula Two Ferrari which had got well ahead of its German rivals by slip-streaming its bigger capacity team-mates. Herrmann and Barth took sixth and seventh places and the Behra-Porsche was tenth and last, nine laps in arrears.

Although the 1960 Formula Two Manufacturers' Championship had long been settled as a tie between Porsche and Cooper, a number of races for the 1500 cc cars remained to be run. At Zeltweg airfield in Austria on 18th September, Stirling Moss, now fully recovered from his crash at Zandvoort with Rob Walker's Grand Prix Lotus, drove *le patron*'s Porsche to an easy victory ahead of the works cars of Herrmann and Barth. A fortnight later there was another tremendous duel between the works rear-engined Ferrari and Porsches in a 100-lap race at Modena Autodrome. The race was a close-fought battle between von Trips with the red of Maranello and Bonnier with the silver of Stuttgart until lap 90 when Bonnier had a small lead and von Trips was forced to ease off by failing brakes. The bearded Swede then scored an easy victory, avenging the Solitude defeat back in July, and his team-mates Herrmann and Barth were fourth and fifth behind. Ginther finished second with a front-engined Ferrari and von Trips took third place.

## FOUR
# Grand Prix Failure

*The Formula One Cars, 1961-62*

So successful had been the Formula Two category of racing from 1957 to 1960 that the same capacity limit was adopted for Grand Prix racing for the years, 1961-65 – despite the vociferous protests of the British constructors who wanted the existing 2½-litre Formula One to continue unchanged. Porsche's very considerable success in Formula Two encouraged them to support the new Grand Prix Formula which had the added inducement that the capacity limit was similar to that of their production cars. A completely new flat-eight car was designed and both Dan Gurney and Joakim Bonnier were induced to leave B.R.M. to drive the new Porsche. According to Porsche, Gurney was not paid and so would have to rely on prize money. It was announced that the new Porsche engine would develop 200 bhp, but when it was first tested the true output was found to be a derisory 120 bhp – 40 bhp less than the old 4-cylinder engine was pushing out. Porsche had no alternative but to continue racing the old 4-cylinder cars and if British constructors had not found themselves in a similar position, the season would have been truly disastrous for Zuffenhausen. As it was, the only constructor who was ready for the new Formula was Ferrari and even the Maranello team was forced to use their 1960 engine in the early part of the season.

For the first race of the year, the Brussels Grand Prix on 9th April, Porsche fielded two of the 1960 cars, completely unchanged apart from starters and batteries, made compulsory by the new regulations, and crash bars welded on to the chassis behind the driver's head. The race was decided on the aggregate of three heats and Bonnier won the first; but after only three laps Gurney was out because of a broken lever in the gear-change transfer-mechanism. And poor Bonnier was eliminated in the second heat when his car was struck up the rear by Surtees' Cooper, the cars spinning against each other and damaging each other's rear suspension.

Next on the calendar was the Syracuse Grand Prix, a race which provided a fine display of dominance by Ferrari, of the sound merit of the 1960 Porsche and the unhappy state of British motor racing in 1961 prior to the appearance of the first of the new V-8 engines. Fractionally fastest in practice was Gurney's Porsche, but young Giancarlo Baghetti, a novice driver taking part in his first Grand Prix, assumed the lead on lap six of the race and held it throughout the remaining 56 except when he and Gurney were lapping the tail-enders and the Porsche driver slipped ahead for a short while. At the finish the Ferrari was 5 sec ahead of the Porsche, but Dan Gurney derived some consolation from setting fastest lap, only 0·6 sec slower than the absolute lap record which stood to the credit of Stirling Moss with a Vanwall. Joakim Bonnier's Porsche finished third, a lap in arrears.

To the Monaco Grand Prix Porsche brought four new cars. Two of these were the chassis intended to take the flat-eight engine when it was ready; although the general layout was similar to that of the old design, one car had a slightly longer wheelbase and both were wider at the back. Front suspension was by double wishbones and coil springs and these cars were easily distinguishable by slightly sleeker nose cowlings and more bulbous tails. All four cars had fuel injection incorporating a Kugel-Fischer injection pump instead of carburettors and sports car 5-speed gearboxes of which only the upper four ratios were being used. Dan Gurney drove one of the cars of older pattern, as his lanky frame would not fit into the newer type, and these were driven by Bonnier and Hans Herrmann. The race was dominated by Stirling Moss with Rob Walker's old Lotus-Climax 4-cylinder car, but Bonnier mixed it with the Ferraris until lap 60 when a vapour-lock in the fuel pumps caused the engine to die; he abandoned the car out on the circuit, not realising that the system would return to normal once it had cooled off. Dan Gurney finished a poor fifth, behind Moss and three Ferraris.

The next round in the World Championship was the Dutch Grand Prix at Zandvoort. The race provided a near-walk-over for the lithe red Ferraris, rear-engined like every other Grand Prix car of the time and distinguished by their twin-nostril air intakes; they finished first, second and fifth, split by Clark and Moss with Lotus-Climax cars. The Porsche entries trailed home at the tail of the field and von Hanstein blamed the team's inexperience with fuel injection for the poor performance of their cars. What was remarkable about this race was that there were 15 starters and 15 finishers. It was much the same story at the Belgian Grand Prix where Gurney and Bonnier were back on the fourth row of the grid and could manage no better than sixth and seventh places in the race.

## A Change in Porsche Fortunes

The failure of the 8-cylinder cars to prove a raceworthy proposition and dissatisfaction with the handling of the new chassis resulted in the team fielding three 1960 cars – all on Weber carburettors – at the French Grand Prix held on the very fast Rheims circuit. These were driven by Bonnier, Gurney and Count Carol Godin de Beaufort, a Dutch driver whose car was prepared and looked after by the works, although, nominally, it was a private entry. When the cars lined up on the grid for the start, sunshine of almost tropical intensity was blazing and already the tarred surface of the track was treacherously sticky. Right from the fall of the flag the works Ferraris of Phil Hill, von Trips and Ginther and the outdated Lotus of Stirling Moss commanded the leading places in the race, but all these cars fell by the wayside. Von Trips came into the pits with water running out of the right-hand exhaust of his Ferrari's new 120-degree V-6 engine – an unexpected failure as this engine had previously been completely troublefree; Moss spent a long time in the pits because of brake trouble; further back Bonnier and Gurney, unable to catch the leading Ferraris, were dicing with the fourth car of the Maranello team, the older 65-degree V-6 car of Baghetti; de Beaufort went into the pits to retire on lap 23 with oil all over the rear of the car and oil smoke gushing out of the exhausts – a state of affairs attributable to his driving methods. Phil Hill spun on the wet tar on lap 38, his car was thumped by Moss' Lotus and was unable to restart. Now Ginther was all on his own at the head of the field, but the intense heat was causing a fall-off in oil pressure; he came into the pits briefly, but as the FIA regulations no longer permitted oil to be taken on during a race, he was sent out again and three laps later he was forced to stop out on the circuit to prevent the engine blowing up.

Thus the whole face of the race changed and the sole remaining Ferrari driver, the almost totally inexperienced Baghetti who had only driven in Formula Junior races prior to Syracuse, was left battling for the lead with the vastly experienced Gurney and Bonnier. Lap after lap the three cars fought for the lead, with now a silver car leading, now the red, and sometimes the three were abreast, but always with only inches separating them. On lap 50 Baghetti snatched a slight lead and Bonnier staggered into the pits with smoke and oil pouring from the rear of the car only to be sent out again with orders to finish if he could. Into the Thillois hairpin on the last lap but one Gurney snatched the lead, held it along the straight to the finishing line and then the Ferrari went ahead; out of Thillois on the last lap Gurney led, the Ferrari in his slipstream. Some 300 yards from the finishing line, Baghetti shot out of the Porsche's slip-stream, forged ahead and won by less than a car's length. As Denis Jenkinson so prophetically wrote in *Motor Sport*, 'This was motor racing, and Giancarlo Baghetti had arrived, even if he never wins another race, for he had ensured that the 1961 French Grand Prix will go down in history just as Mike Hawthorn did in 1953'—Baghetti never did win another major race!

Although Gurney had never been able to keep up with the fastest Ferraris, it is results that count and the Porsche team left the circuit in a very much happier frame of mind than they had after any Grand Prix so far in 1961.

## *Return to Mediocrity*

In complete contrast with Rheims, the British Grand Prix on the bleak, characterless Aintree circuit was held in pouring rain and was probably the wettest in the series. Although Bonnier succeeded in getting his Porsche on to the front row of the grid with a time of 1 min 58·8 sec – exactly the same as recorded by the three works Ferraris – it was the Maranello cars that completely dominated the race once again and took the first three places. The Porsches had the legs of most of the British cars and Bonnier and Gurney finished fifth and seventh.

Two German races followed. The first was on the delightful 11·417-kilometre Solitude circuit and a total of five cars was entered from the local Porsche works. Gurney and Bonnier were backed up by entries for Herrmann and Barth and de Beaufort had his works-supported car. Barth had an experimental low-chassis car of the type intended to take the flat-eight engine when it was ready. Cooling was by a horizontally mounted fan driven by a short shaft and bevel gears, an arrangement intended for use with the 8-cylinder engine and similar to that fitted to the production Chevrolet Corvair. Another unusual feature was the use of disc brakes made under licence from Dunlop. There were no Ferraris entered in this race.

Bonnier and Gurney were fastest in practice, but Bruce McLaren with a Cooper-Climax was only fractionally slower; when the flag fell, Innes Ireland shot through from the second row of the grid with his works Lotus and at the end of the first lap he and McLaren led the Porsches. While McLaren gradually fell back, a four-sided fight developed for the lead between Ireland, the two Porsche drivers who were furiously scrapping with each other and Jack Brabham. On this circuit full of swerves and curves the British 4-cylinder Climax-powered cars were a match for the Porsches and Ireland managed to hold a narrow lead until lap 23 – the last lap but one – when Bonnier squeezed by. It now looked as if Porsche were going to score the victory on home territory that was expected of them, but Innes was in a fighting mood. Pushing to the back of his mind what Colin Chapman would have to say if he crashed the Lotus, he slip-streamed Bonnier down the straight and then, after pulling out in an unsuccessful attempt to get past, he outbraked Bonnier who was using all the road, took to the grass and scrambled by into the lead. Through the winding section of the circuit and the short stretch of straight before the finishing line Ireland maintained his narrow lead and took the chequered flag a mere three feet ahead of Bonnier, with Gurney the same distance behind. If the finishing line had been another couple of hundred feet further on, Bonnier would have won! Barth, troubled by heavy steering and loss of oil, took eighth place behind McLaren, Brabham (who had fallen back in the closing stages of the race), Herrmann and Clark.

Porsche fortunes reached their lowest ebb in the German Grand Prix a fortnight later – at Solitude they suffered an honourable defeat, but at the Nürburgring they received a severe thrashing. The race was completely dominated by the maestro, Stirling Moss, who led with his almost antique Lotus from the first lap to the finish, trailed by the works Ferraris which finished second and third. Bonnier suffered a puncture on the first lap and later in the race retired with valve trouble; Gurney's first lap misfortune was a minor

*Above:* To comply with the rather odd Le Mans regulations in 1956, Porsche ran their familiar RS1500 cars with a coupé top on the normal racing body (*Motor Sport*). *Below:* One-time works Ferrari driver Umberto Maglioli with his Porsche 'Spyder' in the 1957 Mille Miglia. He won the 1500 c.c. class

*Above:* Frenchman Jean Behra at the wheel of the RSK Porsche he shared with Edgar Barth in the 1958 Nürburgring 1000 Km race. They held third place overall before retiring with valve trouble. *Below:* The 1600 Porsche of Bonnier and von Trips having a wheel changed in the 1959 Tourist Trophy. They took second place after one of the Aston Martin team cars caught fire

collision, he was never able to challenge the leaders and finished a poor seventh.

Fastest Porsche driver in the Italian race, held on the full Monza road and track circuit, was Bonnier who was on the fourth row of the grid. A first lap crash eliminated Clark (Lotus) and von Trips (Ferrari), costing the life of the Ferrari driver who was leading the World Championship, the elimination of these cars together with the retirements of much of the faster opposition, including the Ferraris of Ricardo Rodriguez and Richie Ginther, the new Climax V-8-powered Cooper of Brabham and Moss's Lotus resulted in Gurney coming through to finish second to Phill Hill's Ferrari. On the third lap Surtees collided with Bonnier, the Yeoman Credit Cooper riding up over the Porsche's tail. The British driver came into the pits, but the pig-headed Bonnier plodded on with a vibration that became worse and worse until even he dared to press on no further. Later in September Bonnier was third in the Circuit of Zeltweg.

The Porsche team then took the long trek to the 2·3-mile Watkins Glen circuit for the United States Grand Prix. With the Driver's and Constructors' Championships in the bag, Ferrari did not bother to enter and so, once again, Porsche found themselves racing against the British teams only. Early in the race the two Porsches ran together in the middle of the field, but retirements and pit stops by the opposition and Gurney's steady and consistent driving brought the American through to take second place and third place in the Drivers' Championship with Stirling Moss, both drivers having scored 21 points. Bonnier finished sixth. Porsche took third place in the Constructors' Championship.

So the 1961 season ended on a far from unsatisfactory note. Many things had gone wrong for the Stuttgart team during the year. Development work on the 8-cylinder engine had taken far longer than was anticipated; the new chassis intended for the 8-cylinder engine was a complete failure; and the old cars were outclassed on many circuits. Porsche had, however, two strong factors in their favour – the almost legendary reliability of their cars and the intelligent, skilful and restrained driving of Dan Gurney. During 1963-65 when he was driving works Brabhams, the tall American with the cheerful grin gained a reputation as an exceedingly fast driver, but one who was far from kind to the mechanics of his car. His driving of Grand Prix Porsches was the complete opposite – certainly he was fast, within the limitations imposed by his cars, but he nursed them carefully and drove with restraint. During the winter Bonnier drove in South Africa and took third place in the Transvaal Grand Prix.

## The New Flat-Eight Car

At the 1962 Dutch Grand Prix the new flat-eight Porsche Grand Prix car designed by Helmuth Boll, still head of the Racing Department, made its long-awaited appearance. Even then the claimed output of 200 bhp – a figure that would have topped the output of both the B.R.M. and Coventry-Climax V-8 engines in their original forms – was not being achieved and the Porsche engineers had been forced to settle for 180 bhp at 9300 rpm, a good 10 bhp *less* than the British engines were developing. It was this engine that made the Porsche the least conventional of the 1962 Grand Prix cars. It was an air-cooled, horizontally opposed unit (whereas everyone else used a conventional water-cooled unit with the cylinders in vee formation) with a cast Elektron crankcase and aluminium alloy cylinder heads. Bore and stroke were 66 × 54·6 mm which gave a capacity of 1494 cc. The crankshaft ran in nine main bearings and drove the overhead camshafts by a series of shafts and bevel gears and a similar arrangement was used to drive the resin-bonded glass-fibre cooling fan. There were two plugs per cylinder, the sparks were provided by four coils and two distributors and there were four twin-choke, downdraught Weber carburettors.

Transmission was by a mechanically operated 6-speed gearbox in unit with the final drive and with selection of the gears by a very complicated, but, nevertheless, very effective linkage. The engine characteristics were such that full use of all six gears was necessary to keep the engine in the most useful part of the power curve.

The first new chassis, which had appeared in 1961, had been a failure primarily because the double wishbone front suspension, inspired by the practice of British racing constructors, was vastly inferior to the Volkswagen-type trailing links of the 1959-60 cars. For 1962 a new suspension layout with a wide-based bottom wishbone and a narrow-based cantilever top wishbone was adopted. The top pivoted wishbone on the chassis and acted as an adjustable longitudinal torsion bar. After the 1962 Monaco Grand Prix a long top radius arm was added to stabilise the suspension and to react braking loads. The coil spring units were mounted inboard front and rear, a feature designed to reduce unsprung weight and copied from

1961 Lotus practice. The degree of body roll was restrained by a short torsion bar connected to the top wishbones – another Lotus feature. Basically, the rear suspension was similar, but both wishbones were quite narrow-based. The mild-steel multi-tubular chassis had a great deal of bracing added after its first race, especially to the side-frames and scuttle. The steering was by rack-and-pinion, a departure from normal Porsche practice.

A much lower body than that of the 1960-61 cars was fitted. The cockpit was very stark, with only three instruments – the tachometer and oil pressure and temperature gauges – and the steering wheel had to be removed for the driver to get in or out.

## Early In The 1962 Season

Two of the old works cars were sold to the Italian Scuderia Serenissima Republica di Venezia team run by former Ferrari and Maserati team manager Nello Ugolini for Count Volpi. Volpi was closely associated with the A.T.S. Grand Prix car which raced with such little success in 1963. Other ex-works cars were acquired by Wolfgang Seidel who raced one entered by his Auto-Sports team and Dutchman de Beaufort continued to race a car entered by his Ecurie Maarsbergen. With one of the Venezia cars Bonnier finished second in the Brussels Grand Prix in April and third in the Lombank Trophy at Snetterton later in the month. At Pau, Nino Vaccarella was sixth with a Venezia car and Bonnier retired with gearbox trouble.

The new works cars did not appear until the Dutch Grand Prix where neither Gurney nor Bonnier was happy with the handling. This was hardly surprising for the Porsches were completely unsorted. Although the first car had been completed by the end of February, its testing was delayed by bad weather and argument within the Porsche organisation as to whether they should continue racing; when the Grand Prix car did eventually reach the test track, it was almost completely destroyed in a crash caused by brake failure. At Zandvoort Gurney managed the respectable time of 1 min 34·7 sec by dint of an untidy "blood and guts" lap and this put him on the third row of the grid. When the flag fell for the start of the race Gurney shot through to hold third place behind Clark (Lotus) and Hill (B.R.M.) and there he stayed until lap ten when the gear-lever came out of its mounting and he crawled round and into the pits. He rejoined the race six laps in arrears, but went out of the race altogether on lap 48 when a bracket in the gear-change linkage broke. Bonnier had an unhappy slow race to finish seventh and was unable to get past de Beaufort's old 4-cylinder car.

There were very mixed feelings at the Porsche works about fielding cars at Monaco, for the team was bitterly disappointed by its Zandvoort showing, yet, at the same time, were encouraged by the way the 8-cylinder G.T. Prototype had performed in the Nürburgring 1000 Km race. Dan Gurney and team manager Huschke von Hanstein were all for racing the cars as they felt that this was the only way to get them fully sorted – no amount of private testing will reveal the faults than can be exposed by one race. Eventually von Hanstein and Gurney won the day and one car was fielded for Gurney, while Bonnier had to make do with one of the Venezia cars loaned back to the works. In practice at Monaco Gurney recorded the very satisfactory time of 1 min 36·4 sec which put him on the second row of the grid, but his race was short-lived. On the first lap Mairesse (Ferrari) arrived at the Gasworks hairpin much too fast and his frantic braking and full-lock slide caused a chain-reaction down the line of cars. Ginther (B.R.M.) hit Trintignant (Lotus) who spun and hit Ireland (Lotus). Ginther bounced off the Lotus and hit the rear of Gurney's Porsche, tearing off the back of the gearbox. Bonnier was fifth, seven laps in arrears with the 4-cylinder car.

## Championship Victory

Although the flat-eight had no chance to show its paces at Monaco before it crashed, the Porsche team skipped the Belgian race so as to carry out further development testing. It was Ferrari who missed the French Grand Prix at Rouen and Porsche fielded flat-eights for Gurney and Bonnier. Rouen is a far slower circuit than Rheims, but far more interesting and varied and, perhaps, rather more dangerous. Gurney was sixth fastest in practice and held fourth place after ten laps. Retirements were rife amongst the fastest of the British cars – Surtees, in second place, brought his Lola into the pits with fuel feed trouble, Clark had a ball-joint come adrift in the suspension of his Lotus, and on lap 42 Graham Hill came into the pits with the throttle linkage of his B.R.M. having come adrift. So the three leading cars were eliminated and delighted Porsche pit found their American driver in the lead. While Bonnier, who had already made a fruitless pit stop to discover why his car was running on only six of its eight cylinders, stopped out on the circuit, the Porsche pit hung out a red signal (meaning 'slow') to Dan Gurney. After a rough and uncomfortable ride over 54 laps of the Rouen circuit Gurney took the chequered flag to his – and Porsche's – first World Championship race victory. It may have been a victory by default, but it was a victory that made all Stuttgart's Grand Prix efforts seem worthwhile.

A week later the Grand Prix Porsche team was out in the Solitude Grand Prix and the sole serious opposition came from the Lotus works entries driven by Jim Clark and Trevor Taylor. Dan Gurney went straight into the lead at the start of this 25-lap race on a circuit which he knew intimately through extensive Porsche testing. Mainly because Clark's car was down on power he drew further and further away into the lead and when Clark spun and retired, Bonnier moved up into second place.

When Porsche travelled to Aintree for the British Grand Prix, they had all the confidence gained from two victories and two fine drivers at the peak of their form. Gurney was both skilful and courageous and he had improved immensely during the season, while Bonnier was courageous and a great fighter even though his skill tended to be clouded by his obstinacy and occasional 'bloody-mindedness'. Only one Ferrari ran at Aintree and, in any case, the Maranello V-6 cars were no longer truly competitive, but the British teams were on absolutely top form. Porsche hopes of another victory went unfulfilled, for Joakim Bonnier retired after 26 laps with gearbox trouble, while Dan Gurney, having fought his way up to third place, fell back to finish ninth because of a slipping clutch. The race was won by Jim Clark's Lotus with Surtees' Lola in second place.

Next on the calendar was the German Grand Prix where Porsche brought along three cars for the use of their usual two drivers. Gurney was always at his best at the Nürburgring and as late as 1967 set a new lap record there with his Eagle. In practice he managed fastest lap in 8 min 47·2 sec, while Bonnier was fast enough to get on to the second row of the grid. The race started on a soaking wet track and with gentle rain falling. Gurney's slim Porsche (looking far more of a 'silver arrow' than the so often described Mercedes W.196 ever did) went straight into the lead and came round at the end of the first long, tortuous lap ahead of Graham Hill (B.R.M.) Phil Hill (Ferrari) and Surtees (Lola). The B.R.M. was pressing hard, but Hill dare not risk pushing his luck on the treacherously slippery surface and had to wait for Gurney to make a mistake. By the time the cars had reached the pits on the second lap, Hill had found his chance and pushed the B.R.M. through into the lead. Gurney did not give up the struggle easily, but on lap five his battery came loose in its holder and while he was reaching down to re-fix it, Surtees nipped past to take second place. At the end of two and a half hours hard and miserably wet racing, Graham Hill took the chequered flag – but there was only 4·4 sec separating the first three cars. Bonnier was seventh. Maybe the race was not a Porsche triumph, but Gurney had driven a very fine race and it was a remarkable fact that six different makes occupied the first six places for Clark's Lotus, McLaren's Cooper and Rodriguez' Ferrari were fourth, fifth and sixth.

The same two drivers with three cars turned up for the Italian Grand Prix at Monza, but held on the road circuit only. The race proved another B.R.M. triumph with Hill and Ginther romping home in first and second place, while the Porsches battled in mid-field with the Coopers. Bonnier's Porsche finished sixth, but Gurney's race ended with a crawl into the pits to retire with crown wheel-and-pinion failure.

Final round in the 1962 World Championship was the United States Grand Prix at Watkins Glen. Gurney and Bonnier drove their usual cars and at the start Gurney was on the second row of the grid with a time of 1 min 16·9 sec – compared with pole position man Jim Clark who had recorded 1 min 15·8 sec. Once again the Porsches were unable to get to grips with the fastest of the British cars and although Gurney worked his way up to third place, his engine started to run rough and he fell back to finish fifth, a lap in arrears. Bonnier spun early in the race, hit a guard rail which upset his gear-selector mechanism and after a series of pit stops finished 13th and last – 21 laps in arrears!

Failure was an almost unknown word at Zuffenhausen and it makes Grand Prix racing seem even more expensive than it really is when there is no prestige and publicity and, therefore, no sales promotion gained. Prior to Porsche's entry into Grand Prix racing the company had enjoyed an almost unparalleled reputation for competition reliability and unmatched success in their class of sports car racing. The general feeling at the works was that Grand Prix racing was doing the company's reputation more harm than good. After Watkins Glen, the Grand Prix cars returned to the factory and were never again raced. Porsche felt that they had learned a bitter and expensive lesson, notwithstanding the Rouen success, and in future resolved to concentrate solely on Grand Touring and Prototype racing. Porsche's official reason for giving up Grand Prix racing was lack of support from components manufacturers.

## FIVE
# 900 Winning Ways
# The Evolution Of The 911

*The Original 911*

Excluding racing models, the 911 was the first new model to appear from the Porsche factory since the make's inception. It was also the first production model with its own direct as opposed to Volkswagen ancestry. It had been planned in the late 'fifties, but did not take its bow until the Frankfurt Motor Show in 1963. It was originally christened the 901 because that was its project number, but Peugeot decided that they had a priority on three figure numbers with a zero in the middle and so to oblige them Porsche retyped the car the 911. When it was exhibited at motor shows during that year many who saw it – including the writer – felt that it was an exceptionally pretty car, but it was certainly not a true Porsche. The 911 did not enter production until 1965 and since then it has succeeded in carrying out a complete transformation of the Porsche image. No longer is the Porsche – as the 356 was – regarded as a very specialist sports car with difficult characteristics, but it is now a status symbol indicative of a fairly substantial income and impeccable taste; the 911 has made the marque Porsche acceptable at one and the same time to the enthusiast, the family motorist with sporting inclinations, the businessman and (with 'Sportomatic' transmission) it is a very 'in' car with the Chelsea dollies. And it has proved popular with 356 addicts.

The most striking feature of the 911 is the body which was the work of Ferdinand Porsche junior, grandson of the Professor, and which was completely new. It has greater glass area, crisper lines and is both more practical and much prettier than the 356. At the front the luggage compartment lid is almost flat until it plunges sharply downwards in the interests of visibility, it has much greater

*Above:* Pugnacious rear end of one of the works Porsche RS60 cars. It is seen before the start of the 1960 Le Mans race (*Autocar*). *Below:* Sebring, 1961: the works RS61 of Hans Herrmann and Edgar Barth which retired when in ninth place

*Above:* Tourist Trophy, 1961: the Abarth-bodied 2-litre Carrera of Graham Hill is outdragged at the start by the Berlinetta Ferrari of Stirling Moss. Hill finished sixth and won the 2-litre class. *Below:* German Grand Prix, 1960: the race at the Nürburgring was held that year for Formula Two cars and was won by Joakim Bonnier at the wheel of his works Porsche

capacity than that of the 356 and the tail has the fastback lines that are expected of a high-performance coupé. In height the car is almost the same as the 356, but the original wheelbase was 4 in longer, the length 6 in and it is 2·3 in narrower – the result is that it looks, deceptively, much lower. Basically the 911 is a two-seater like its predecessor, but there are rear seats to accomodate two children or the back-rests can be folded down to make extra luggage space.

Technically, the best feature of the 911 is the superb flat-six engine of 1991 cc (80 × 66 mm) which in its less robust forms is both smooth and quiet. It features a single overhead camshaft per bank of cylinders compared with the four-cam arrangement of the 910 Prototype. A train of spur gears drives a countershaft underneath the crankshaft and this carries two chain sprockets at its rear end, each of which drives one camshaft via a twin-row timing chain equipped with an automatic tensioner. The six-throw crankshaft runs in eight main bearings, like all Porsches the engine is air-cooled and it has dry sump lubrication. The ribbed cylinder barrels (with cast iron liners) are machined, like the heads, from aluminium castings. Compression ratio in the original form was 9:1, carburation was by two triple-choke Solex carburettors and power output in this form was 148 bhp at 6100 rpm – and Porsche said firmly that the red sector on the tachometer starting at 6800 rpm must never be crossed in any circumstances.

Integral construction is used for the body/chassis and this is of exceptional rigidity. The suspension design is in keeping with the performance. At the front there are Macpherson struts and wide-based lower wishbones operate longitudinal torsion bars with longitudinal telescopic dampers providing complementary location. The old swing-axle arrangement of the 356 is replaced at the rear by triangulated trailing links with transverse torsion bars. In handling characteristics, the 911 is completely neutral and the old oversteer of the 356 is gone for ever.

Transmission is by a 5-speed gearbox almost identical to that of the 904 GTS. As would be expected of a Porsche 'box, the baulk-ring synchromesh is unbeatable, but the change, which is rather like an old Ford 3-speed layout with fourth and fifth added on the right, takes getting used to. Steering is by ZF rack-and-pinion, instead of the old worm-and-peg and the brakes are ATE discs (made under licence from Dunlops) and incorporating vestigial drums for the handbrake at the rear as on the C and SC. Providing four wheel disc braked cars with an efficient handbrake was a serious problem in the late 'fifties and early 'sixties and it was a recognised fact that a driver could never park a Jaguar on the slightest slope without leaving it in gear and that the chances of passing the M.O.T. ten year test (as it was then) were almost nil.

*The Four-Cylinder Version*

The 911 was an expensive car and as the Porsche directors were anxious not to throw away the market so hard won by the 356 over the years, they decided to play safe by offering a version with the old 356 'SC' engine developing 90 bhp at 5800 rpm and with the option of a 4-speed gearbox. This was known as the 912 and was priced in 1965 at £2,466 in the United Kingdom inclusive of purchase tax compared with the £3,438 of the 911. The 912 remains in production, but 1969 is said to be its last year.

*Performance Data*

Below are average performance figures for the two models:

|  | *911* | *912* |
|---|---|---|
| Maximum in the gears: | | |
| Top | 132 mph | 119 mph |
| Fourth | 119 mph | 96 mph |
| Third | 94 mph | 75 mph |
| Second | 64 mph | 55 mph |
| Bottom | 40 mph | 34 mph |
| Acceleration from | | |
| 0-30 mph | 3·6 sec | 4·1 sec |
| 0-50 mph | 6·9 sec | 8·6 sec |
| 0-60 mph | 9·0 sec | 11·9 sec |
| 0-100 mph | 23·7 sec | 38·0 sec |
| Standing ¼-mile | 16·5 sec | 18·2 sec |
| Speed at end of Standing ¼-mile | 86 mph | 72 mph |

*Later Development of The 911*

Since the appearance of the original production cars in 1965, the 911 range has been expanded so that there is the choice of several degrees of tune. For 1969 the wheelbase was lengthened by 2·2 in on all models to improve weight distribution, the percentage of weight on the front and rear wheels now being 42/58 instead of 40/60, and all cars now have pronounced body flares round both front and rear wheels to permit wider wheels and tyres. Other changes for 1969 include larger brake pads and a new heating and ventilating system with a 3-speed blower.

The various models available are:

*911E:* This was the original 911 which became known for 1968 as the 911L with a power output of 130 bhp (DIN) or 148 bhp (SAE). It was renamed again for 1969 and was given, for the American market, a new fuel injection system that controls emissions and pushes out 12 more bhp. The injection system is developed from that used on the Prototypes and consists of a double-row, six-element mechanical pump between the two cylinder blocks and driven by a toothed belt from the left camshaft. Self-levelling Boge hydropneumatic front spring struts became optional for 1969.

*911T:* Introduced for 1968, this model has a touring engine developing only 110 bhp (DIN) and 125 bhp (SAE) on an 8·6 : 1 compression ratio and with cast-iron cylinder barrels. From a competitions point of view it has that advantage that the absence of some fairly heavy items of trim reduce weight and it has been homologated as a Group 3 G.T. car with various magnesium-alloy castings. A 4-speed gearbox is standard and there is also a de-luxe version. The model won the 1968 Group 3 Championship.

*911S:* The high-performance version of the 911 introduced in 1966. With a compression ratio of 9·8 : 1, it developed 180 bhp (SAE) or 160 bhp (DIN). It is easily distinguishable by the forged light alloy wheels. The 1969 version develops, with the new fuel injection system, 195 bhp at 6800 rpm.

*911R:* Available only to special order, this is an out-and-out competition car with many glass-fibre parts instead of steel and the engine to full Carrera specification. It ran in the 1967–68 Mugello races.

The 1969 version of the 911R is fitted with the full four-cam engine developing 230 bhp (gross). At Hockenheim in January, 1969 Porsche revealed the GT60 model with Bosch fuel injection and light alloy panels on the steel frame and this may well enter production in late 1969.

Since 1967 all production models have been available with the striking 'Targa' open bodywork, but with left-hand drive only. This, from the point of view of wind effects, retains the comfort of the coupé, as it has a body section in the form of a streamlined roll-over bar behind the front seats. The 1969 version of the Targa has a fixed rear window and this, as on all 1969 models, is heated.

All the 911 models can be fitted with the 'Sportomatic' transmission. This is not an automatic transmission, but a device which eliminates the clutch pedal. Between the engine and the 4-speed gearbox fitted to 'Sportomatic' cars there is a hydraulic torque-converter and a normal clutch. The clutch is actuated by mechanical links from a vacuum servo system, and this system is energised by an electrical contact on the gear-selector mechanism – the gear-lever operates the 'box in the normal way. When first gear is engaged, the first part of the travel of the gear-lever sets off an electrical contact which energises a solenoid setting the vacuum system in operation; this frees the clutch and the result is that the last part of the lever's movement engages bottom gear in the normal way. The torque-converter then comes into action and, as the driver accelerates, takes up the power up to 3500 rpm, when it is replaced by direct drive through the clutch. To change gear the driver simply moves the lever, and the movement of the gear-selector actuates the electrical system so that the clutch is engaged and disengaged at exactly the right moment.

## *Porsche Production*

The Porsche works in the suburb of Stuttgart known as Zuffenhausen has a staff of 3,000 and is situated in three main blocks which include the Reutter coachbuilding works absorbed in 1963. The company is divided into three sections – main production, spare parts, and experimental and racing. The latter section carries out a great deal of development work for other companies and it is this work that subsidises Porsche's motor racing programme. This section is concentrated right in the middle of the Porsche works and entrance to outsiders is strictly forbidden. Even when entering the administrative offices, a 'chit' has to be obtained from the gatekeeper and given up on leaving.

In 1965, Porsche production amounted to 11,300 cars, but by 1968 this had been boosted to 14,800 and Porsche hope to produce

18,000 cars in 1969. About 50 per cent of Porsche cars are exported to the States and in 1968 only 3,000 were sold on the home market. There is a staggering price difference between Germany and the United Kingdom:

|  | German Price | U.K. basic price | U.K. retail price |
|---|---|---|---|
| 912 | £1,750 | £2,215 | £2,894 |
| 911T | £1,950 | £2,600 | £3,397 |
| 911S | £2,500 | £3,570 | £4,663 |

In the Number 2 assembly plant production runs at an average of 63 cars a day, and the cars are painstakingly assembled on a continuous line of welding bays which weave back and forth in a comparatively small workshop. When assembly of the bare body-chassis shell is completed, the unit is loaded on to a castor-wheeled trolley and pushed into the paint department. The first operator gives the shell a coat of spray-on, sound-deadening material. After the first coat of enamel has been applied, the doors, the window-frames, etc., are given a seal of rubber compound to keep them waterproof. Nine coats of cellulose are applied by hand-spray. For each car, a card with 169 items to be checked is filled in and in this way the factory ensures that the bodywork of every car is up to its high standards.

Like most manufacturers, Porsche uses many proprietary components and, in all, some six hundred different items are bought from outside suppliers, including the ZF rack-and-pinion steering. The finned air-cooled heads of Porsche engines are individual for each cylinder. When assembly is complete, each engine is taken away for an hour's testing on a dynamometer.

Final assembly is followed by three separate road tests, two on ordinary roads and one on the company's test track outside Stuttgart.

*The 911 in Rallies*

The first really determined Porsche effort in rallying came in 1967 when the European Rally Championships was divided into three categories and there were 16 qualifying rounds ranging from Sweden to Spain and East Germany – but without a round in Great Britain. The first of the three categories was Group 1 in which Sobieslaw

Zasada of Poland was the victor. Zasada drove a Lancia Fulvia in the Monte Carlo Rally, but he acquired a Porsche 911S which he then drove into third place in the Lyons-Charbonnières event. He wrote the Porsche off in the Tulip Rally, but the works loaned him a 911S, and with this he scored a victory in the Austrian Alpine Rally. After this the Polish driver bought a 912 and he drove this Group 1 car to victory in the local Polish event. Not only did Zasada win his class of the Championship with 64 points, but in November he drove a Porsche to victory in the Gran Premio Internacional de Turismo 2000-mile road-race in Argentina.

Works driver Vic Elford campaigned a 911S in Group 3 (minimum of 500 units produced per year) and the car proved the fastest and best-handling in its class. Unlike most factories, Porsche concentrated on success in the Championship instead of making special efforts in particular events and Elford, partnered by David Stone, achieved consistently high placings throughout the year to win his class with 57 points. In the Monte Carlo event, perhaps the most renowned of all rallies, Elford was third, and he scored outright wins in the Lyons-Carbonnières, Tulip and Geneva events.

For 1968 a change was made in the regulations of the European Rally Championship, and this was now divided into two categories. First, there were seven rallies counting towards the European Drivers' Championship and secondly, there were eight rallies counting towards the European Constructors' Championship. Apart from the Porsche drivers, Pauli Toivonen and Sobieslaw Zasada, no-one made any serious attempt at winning either of the Championships. The drivers of the Stuttgart cars drove with tremendous consistency and Toivonen succeeded in winning six events outright. His successes were limited to the less prominent events – the San Remo, East German, West German, Geneva, Danube and Spanish – but even so Toivonen ranks among the top half-dozen rally drivers in the world.

The Porsche works rallied the 911T which weighed less than the 911S and was homologated in Group 3 with a large number of magnesium-alloy castings. The new car made its first appearance in the Swedish Rally which preceded the Monte Carlo to avoid a clash with the Winter Olympic Games which, in Scandinavia, would have spelt its death as far as publicity was concerned. In this event, Björn Waldegaard scored a fine victory with a 911T, but the results of the Monte Carlo event were even more outstanding – for the

911Ts of Elford and Toivonen took first two places. 1968 was a brilliant year for Porsche, who won eight of the year's Championship events and there is every prospect that 1969 will prove as successful. By February Porsche had already made a superb start to the rallying year with victories in both the Monte Carlo and Swedish Rallies.

Because of homologation difficulties over the new fuel injection models, the four works Porsches in the 1969 Monte Carlo event were 911S models with heavier bodies and engine parts and a lower power output than the stark 911Ts used in 1968. Toivonen was eliminated by a series of minor, and one more serious, crashes; but even so the Stuttgart cars were lying first, second and fourth at Monte Carlo before they set out on the mountain circuit. After Waldegaard, leading the Rally, had been delayed, Vic Elford went ahead, but he misjudged a corner and hit a tree at 50 mph. Waldegaard regained the lead to win from the similar 911S of Larrousse. In the Swedish event the winner was again Björn Waldegaard, partnered by Lars Helmer, at the wheel of a 911L prepared by Scania Vabis, the Swedish importers.

## *The 911 in Touring Car Races*

It is, perhaps, incongruous that the possession of four seats and the fact that a certain minimum number of cars had been produced should permit the 911 Porsche to run in saloon car races. In both 1967 and 1968 privately-entered 911s (in receipt of works support) hotly contested the European Touring Car Championship. In 1967, Gaban and 'Pedro' scored a brilliant victory for the make in the Spa 24 hours race and in 1968 Helmut Kelleners took second place in the over 1600 cc category of the European Touring Car Championship held to Group 5 regulations. In 1967 when the Championship was held to Group 2 rules and the over-1600 cc class easily taken by Porsche, the 911s were faster, lighter and possessed much better handling than the rival B.M.W. 1800TIs; in 1968, however, the new fuel-injection B.M.W. 2002s were slightly lighter than the Porsches and generally much more competitive. In their unsuccessful efforts to retain the upper hand, some Porsche owners fitted Bosch fuel-injection, while others used the full 'Carrera' twin-plug engine. The Porsche factory does not enter this class of racing but, once again, supported private owners in 1969.

With its domination of the rallying scene, its victories in the 1968–69 Group 3 Championships, its Touring car successes and its undoubted merits as a road car, the 911 must rank as one of the most successful production cars of all time.

French Grand Prix, 1961: the 4-cylinder Porsches of Dan Gurney and Joakim Bonnier harry the eventual winner, Baghetti's V-6 Ferrari (David Phipps)

Two views of Gurney's flat-eight Porsche at the 1962 French Grand Prix at Rouen. Although the cars were generally rather unsuccessful, on this occasion Gurney won – but only after the retirement of faster British entries (David Phipps)

SIX
# 1962: First Year Of Prototype Racing

*A New Category of Racing*

At the end of 1961, the Federation Internationale de l'Automobile scrapped the existing Sports Car Championship and said that there would only be a Grand Touring Championship – as introduced in 1961 – with classes for cars up to 4000 cc, 2500 cc and 1000 cc (in 1961 there had been a 1300 cc class). The notion of a G.T. Championship attracted a great deal of interest among high-performance car manufacturers, including Jaguar and Mercedes-Benz, but they rapidly lost interest when they learned that there would be a Championship in each class and no overall winner. As something of an afterthought the F.I.A. added a class for Prototypes (meaning Grand Touring prototypes, although they did not say so) and the category attracted hangovers from the sports racing category of the past such as the "Bird-cage" Maseratis and the latest and hottest machinery from Maranello and Stuttgart – but for these cars there was originally no Championship. Eventually, however, the Le Mans organisers, the Automobile Club de l'Ouest, conferred with the organisers of the Sebring, Targa Florio and Nürburgring races to arrange the *Challenge Mondiale de Vitesse*, open only to Prototype marques which competed in all four races. Preoccupation with their Grand Prix programme resulted in diminished Porsche efforts in the sports car field, but these efforts were reasonably rewarded – which is more than can be said for their Grand Prix programme.

*Sebring 12 hours Race*

Racing round an airfield circuit with vast turbo-prop transport aircraft and the Goodyear airship littering the vicinity must be an odd experience. At Sebring, no works Prototypes ran, but the make performed extremely well. First and second places went to the 'Testa Rossa' Ferrari of Bonnier/Bianchi and the 250GT of Phil Hill/Gendebien, but there in third spot was the RS61 car shared by America's Jennings, Rand and Woesthoff which also won the Index of Performance. Sixth overall and victor in its class was the 1600cc Carrera of works driver Dan Gurney, partnered by Bob Holbert.

*Targa Florio*

The rugged Sicilian mountain circuit, setting for the 46th Targa Florio, saw a strong clash between three works Ferraris ranging in size from 2 to 2·5 litres and two of the new 8-cylinder Porsches making their race debut. These new Porsches were based on two chassis, always intended to take the 8-cylinder engines, but raced in 1961 with the old 4-cylinder units. These chassis were similar to the familiar RSK models, with the same trailing link front suspension and wishbone and coil spring rear suspension and Dunlop-Porsche disc brakes, but a longer wheelbase. The 8-cylinder, 2-litre engines, capacity apart, were very similar to those used in the Grand Prix cars, with four twin-choke Weber carburetters and two plugs per cylinder fired by four Bosch coils. Transmission was by the now usual arrangement of a 6-speed gearbox behind the crown wheel and pinion, but because of the extra length of the 8-cylinder engine it was further back in the frame and the drive shafts were inclined slightly forwards.

One of the 8-cylinder cars was an open model with a 'deck' behind the driving compartment on which were two bulges over the rows of intakes for the carburetters. This car was driven by the usual works drivers Joakim Bonnier and Dan Gurney. The coupé, in the hands of local man, lawyer Nino Vaccarella and World Champion-to-be Graham Hill, had a roof section over the deck with a perspex division between it and the driver and a vertical perspex rear window. Air was let into the compartment so formed by scoops and it was filled by the carburetter intakes and the plastic cooling fan. At this race Porsche had collaborated over their entries with the Scuderia Venezia who were running 4-cylinder cars in Grand Prix racing and so the coupé, driven by Venezia drivers, was painted red while the open car was finished in Porsche silver with a Venezia badge. These entries were backed by two of the very pretty Abarth-bodied Carreras entered by the works for Herrmann and Linge, and

Pucci and Barth, and a 4-cylinder RS61 model in the hands of Maglioli and Spychiger. Three private Carreras were also running.

In practice, Phil Hill lost the V-8 rear-engined Ferrari, slid over the edge of the mountain road and thumped his way down the grassy hillside until a hummock arrested the progress of the severely-shaken driver and very battered motor-car. The race provided the usual excitements of clouds of dust as the cars screamed through the tight bends and roared along the narrow mountain roads and battered bodywork when the drivers misjudged things and clouted a wall or left the road altogether. Gurney was in second place to the rear-engined 246/SP Ferrari with Willy Mairesse driving when as a result of brake trouble he left the road, battered the bodywork and buckled three of the wheels. The wheels were changed at the Porsche depot out in the mountains, but when the car reached the pits proper it was retired. When the 2-litre coupé came in to refuel after three laps it was Bonnier, and not Graham Hill, who took the wheel, quickly moving the Porsche back into second place – but not a sure second place, for the 2-litre V-6 Ferrari of Bandini (co-driving with Giancarlo Baghetti) passed on time the 250GTO of Scarlatti and Ferraro and was rapidly closing up on the Porsche. When the V-6 Ferrari and the flat-eight Porsche restarted after their final pit stops, the former was battered, but healthy and the latter unbent but rough-sounding. Bandini was thoroughly enjoying his race, cornering the little Ferrari with abandon, and at the end of the ten 44-mile laps was nearly three minutes ahead of his German rival. The final results were:

1st W. Mairesse/R. Rodriguez/O. Gendebien (Ferrari 246/SP) 7 hr 2 min 56·3 sec (63·47). Gendebien had been allowed to drive for three laps so as to get his name on the list of winners for the 3rd time, a feat never before achieved.

2nd G. Baghetti/L. Bandini (Ferrari 206/SP) 7 hr 14 min 24·0 sec

3rd N. Vaccarella/J. Bonnier (Porsche 2-litre) 7 hr 17 min 20·0 sec

4th G. Scarlatti/Ferraro (Ferrari 250GTO) 7 hr 22 min 8·1 sec

5th R. de Lageneste/Rolland (Ferrari 250GTO) 7 hr 44 min 33·0 sec

6th H. Herrmann/H. Linge (Porsche Carrera) 7 hr 45 min 26·0 sec

*Nürburgring 1000 Kilometres*

The German race had increased in strength and interest each

year since the first 1000 Km event was held at the Nürburgring in 1953 and the organising club, the A.D.A.C., took advantage of having one of the longest circuits in Europe by permitting a large and varied entry; 67 cars lined up for the Le Mans-type start of the 1962 race on 27th May, and so not only did spectators have a very varied field to watch, but the race gave many drivers their first opportunity to break into International racing.

The main contenders were, almost inevitably, Ferrari and Porsche and at the start the cars were lined up in order of practice times, an excellent system except that because of a timing error, slap in the middle of the fastest cars was an only slightly modified M.G. Midget!

This is how the cars lined up:

Ferrari 246/SP (Phil Hill and Olivier Gendebien works-entered and fastest with this rear-engined Prototype with a time of 9 min 25·5 sec)

Ferrari 330GTO (a modified works-entered 250GTO with a 4-litre engine and driven by the rather wild Belgian Willy Mairesse and Englishman Mike Parkes)

Porsche 8-cylinder coupé (the Targa Florio car, driven by Dan Gurney and Jo Bonnier)

Ferrari 268/SP (the young Mexican brothers Pedro and Ricardo Rodriguez with a 2·6-litre V-8 engined Prototype)

Porsche 8-cylinder Spyder (Graham Hill and Hans Herrmann)

Aston Martin DBR1 (Bruce McLaren and Tony Maggs, the Cooper works drivers, with the now immense-looking car that had been one of those used by the Aston works to win this race in 1957–59. It had recorded a very creditable 9 min 48·9 sec)

Lotus Mk.23 (driven by Jim Clark and Trevor Taylor, the Lotus works drivers, and entered, like the Aston, by the Essex Racing Team. In contrast with its gargantuan stablemate, it was a diminutive car based on a Formula Junior chassis with the new twin-cam Ford-Lotus power unit)

Ferrari 250GTO (the Scarlatti/Ferraro car which had finished fourth in the Targa Florio)

Porsche RS61 (privately-entered by Swiss drivers Walter and Müller)

Ferrari 206/SP (Bandini and Baghetti works-entered with the V-6 rear-engined Prototype).

## 1962: FIRST YEAR OF PROTOTYPE RACING

Just before the start of the race, fine rain started to fall and there was a frantic rush to change to wet-weather tyres. So frantic, in fact, that mechanics were working on some of the cars when the flag fell and Bandini jumped into a car that was still jacked up. Aided by the wet weather and the fact that the tyre-changing operations delayed some of the cars, the little Lotus went straight into the lead and the big Aston held the rest of the field up through the twistiest sections of the circuit. At the end of the first 14·17-mile lap, the Lotus was leading from the Porsche of Gurney followed by the 4-litre Ferrari and the open 8-cylinder Porsche, the 246/SP Ferrari and the Aston, While Clark opened up a gap between himself and the rest of the field, Pedro Rodriguez spun off into a ditch and Scarlatti crashed his 250GTO. After nine laps, the bigger cars were beginning to catch the Lotus up and Clark was troubled by both gears jumping out on the overrun and exhaust fumes (the tail pipe had broken off). On lap 12, the Lotus jumped out of gear, a dazed Clark was not quick enough to control the resultant slide and the car disappeared into the shrubbery.

The 4-litre Ferrari with Mairesse driving was now leading from Gurney and the 246/SP of Phil Hill, but the rear-engined Ferrari took the lead when these cars stopped to refuel and did *not* lose it again when it refuelled. Although both Porsches were running well, they lacked the speed to catch the Ferraris. During the closing laps of the race Bonnier, with the coupé he was sharing with Gurney, made up a lot of ground on the 4-litre car only to retire out on the circuit with a broken gearbox. Even so, they were awarded second place in their class! The organisers refused to issue a list of overall placings, but only of class placings, perhaps because it was too embarrassing to admit that the fifth-place car was, under the farcical F.I.A. Championship system, the effective winner, as it was the first car eligible to score points in the Grand Touring Championship! This is how the first six finished on the road, if not in the official results:

1st  P. Hill/O. Gendebien (Ferrari 246/SP), 82·39 mph
2nd  W. Mairesse/M. Parkes (Ferrari 330GTO)
3rd  G. Hill/H. Herrmann (Porsche 8-cylinder)
4th  B. McLaren/A. Maggs (Aston Martin DBR1), 2 laps in arrears
5th  P. Nöcker/W. Seidel (Ferrari 250GTO), 3 laps in arrears
6th  E. Barth/H. Linge (Porsche Carrera-Abarth), 3 laps in arrears

## Le Mans

Concentration on the Grand Prix programme meant that there were no 8-cylinder Porsche entries at Le Mans. One had been entered for Gurney and Bonnier, together with a Carrera for Dutchman Ben Pon and Heini Walter, but it was scratched and its place taken by a second Carrera-Abarth. This was driven by Barth and Herrmann and the leading drivers of the team appeared with a Scuderia Venezia Ferrari. The race was Ferrari-dominated once the Aston Martin and Maserati challenges had faded; the Maranello cars took the first three places followed home by a brace of E-type Jaguars. Barth and Herrmann finished seventh, winning the 1600 cc class and full points in the G.T. Championship. The second car of the team retired after only five hours racing with transmission trouble.

## Post-script to the Season

Porsche's fortunes in their class of the Grand Touring Championship were well looked after by Ben Pon who ran in the 100-lap Tourist Trophy at Goodwood on the 18th August, finishing tenth overall and fourth in his class at 81·01 mph. The next qualifying round was the 245-mile Bridgehampton race in New York State on 15th September where Bob Holbert with his normal Carrera won at 79·76 mph from the Abarth-bodied car of Bob Jennings. In the Paris 1000 Km race at Monthéry on 21st October the Carrera-Abarths of Koch/Linge and Pon/Slotemaker finished sixth and seventh, scoring maximum points in this final qualifying round in the Championship. On the strength of their five best performances Porsche scored the maximum of 45 points, with Alfa Romeo in second place with 27—a rather hollow victory that meant little to anybody and a situation that the F.I.A. was to amend in due course by the introduction of a Prototype Championship proper.

The 8-cylinder Prototype did run again in 1962, but on the western side of the Atlantic. Bonnier took a poor sixth place in the sports car Canadian Grand Prix at Mosport Park on 23rd September, slightly improved on this by coming home fourth in the North-Western Grand Prix at Pacific Raceway the following week-end and then Dan Gurney finished third with this car in the Puerto Rican Grand Prix on 11th November. Final appearance of the 8-cylinder car in 1962 was in the Governor's Trophy race at

## 1962: FIRST YEAR OF PROTOTYPE RACING

Nassau where Bob Holbert finished second to Hap Sharp's Cooper-Monaco.

Although 1962 had proved unsatisfactory for Porsche in both Grand Prix and Prototype racing, the make took second place to Ferrari in the *Challenge Mondiale de Vitesse*. The following season Porsche campaigned a small number of events with carefully prepared cars and this policy was to see fruition in the concern's present near-domination of Prototype racing.

SEVEN
# 1963: A Quiet Year For Porsche

In an effort to eliminate the mistakes of the preceding season, for 1963 the Federation Internationale de l'Automobile cleaned up the rules governing G.T. racing and defined Prototypes quite simply as 'voitures prototype G.T.', but there was a clause saying that cars must be constructed in their entirety by the manufacturer concerned – a clause that was completely ignored so as to permit such cars as the Renault-powered René Bonnet and the new and very exciting Ford-powered Lola to run. For 1963, Porsche concentrated on steady development work and raced in less events than they had in 1960-62. The only new car to appear was a modified version of the 2-litre Carrera Two, the very fast road car which had been announced in 1962 (see Chapter 1), and it was a normal Carrera which scored the make's first success of the year.

This first success came in the Daytona Three Hours race held on 17th February on a combined road and track circuit and Joakim Bonnier drove a 2-litre Carrera into fifth place overall. The race was a round in the Championship for Homologated Grand Touring cars and Bonnier scored maximum points in his class. Outright winner was Pedro Rodriguez's Ferrari 250GTO.

Out of 69 starters in the Sebring 12 Hours race on 23rd March, none was a Prototype Porsche, but there were three of the 2-litre Carreras and they achieved all that could be hoped of them. The Coleman/Kolb car went out with back axle trouble, but Bob Holbert and Don Webster took ninth place and works driver Edgar Barth and Herbert Linge were tenth, taking first two places in their class and scoring maximum points in the Grand Touring Championship. After the Daytona and Sebring races, Porsche had 36 points in the 2000 cc class of the Championship compared with the nine of Simca-Abarth and three of Volvo!

## 1963: A QUIET YEAR FOR PORSCHE

### *The Targa Florio – A Magnificent Porsche Victory*

The wild Sicilian roads – dusty when it was dry and treacherous when it was wet – were the setting of another Porsche-Ferrari battle in 1963, just as they had been in past years and were to be almost every year until the present time. The Stuttgart factory fielded two of the flat-eight cars for Bonnier and Abate, and Maglioli and Baghetti. As a result of the influence of the British racing car constructors, the front part of the tubular chassis had been redesigned since 1962 and there was now a simple and conventional double wishbone and coil spring suspension layout – as had been pioneered on the Formula One Lotus and Cooper. Steady development work on the engine had pushed output up to close to 230 bhp. An unusual feature of these cars was that reverse gear was selected by a separate lever by the side of the driving seat and operated by a Bowden cable, and the reverse gear mechanism itself was housed in an extension on the end of the gearbox. In the hands of Bonnier and Abate was a very pretty coupé, while Maglioli and Baghetti shared an ungainly open car with glass-fibre engine cover, doors and front cover over the fuel tank and spare wheel. Running in the Grand Touring class were two 2-litre Carreras – an Abarth-bodied car per normal for Strahle and Pucci and a special car with a bodied based on the 718 Le Mans coupé in the hands of Linge and Barth. This had a long, tapering nose and a flat rear window with the roof forming a lip over the back; Weber instead of Solex carburetters were fitted and there was a glass inspection panel in the top of the oil tank mounted under the rear floor.

From Ferrari came two of the latest 250/P V-12 3-litre rear-engined Prototypes, supported by a V-6 2-litre rear-engined car entered in the Sports class. Close make-weights in the race for outright victory and certainties in their Grand Touring class were five private Ferrari 250GTOs, but the entry ranged down to a twin-engined Mini entered in the Prototype class by Downton Engineering and an ancient Ermini Italian-built sports car powered by an Alfa Romeo Giulietta engine.

To avoid damaging the race cars, the Porsche team drivers used a Super 90 and a 2-litre Carerra for practice during the week before the race. Indeed, the race cars are used very little in practice for this event, normally turning out only on the Friday when the roads are officially closed and most then only manage two laps – one for each driver.

## The 'Little Madonie' Circuit

Since 1951, the first post-war race as such – from 1948 to 1950 the Targa Florio was awarded to the winner of the Tour of Sicily – the 44·7-mile little Madonie circuit has been used for what is now the sole important long-distance road race. The roads used for the Targa Florio are the normal twisty, winding, bumpy, rough Sicilian roads with all the dangers of unfenced drops at the edge of the road, stone walls and narrow village streets – just as motor racing used to be in its early days and in complete contrast to the smooth, wide, tarmac-surfaced circuits of Le Mans and Rheims.

All the pre-race activity is centred on the seaside village of Cefalu, situated about 15 minutes from the start area. The start and finish line is just off the main road on the northern coast and at a distance of about 30 miles from Palermo, the Island's capital. From the start the road takes a steady ascent through cultivated countryside until, after nine kilometres, the narrow main street of the village of Cerda is reached. The road still goes on climbing after Cerda for another two kilometres. From this point it goes south along the west side of an enormous valley and the driver is faced with atrocious surfaces, patches of loose gravel and a succession of slow and fast corners. The road then turns towards the east, dropping in fast, sweeping curves across the olive groves of the valley and zig-zags its way up the lower slopes of Monte Caltavuturo, by-passing the village of that name which stands on an outcrop of the mountain. The steepest part of the circuit comes next and a few kilometres later an altitude of 600 metres has been reached. Here the cars pass through rugged outcrops of rock and rough countryside dotted with wild flowers and cacti.

Having skirted its way round Monte Caltavuturo, the road then plunges in a series of fast corners to a long bridge crossing the gorge at the bottom and then up through olive groves to a point at the base of Monte Caltavuturo known as Bivio Polizzi. The cars then wend their way along a fast section of ascending open curves through the foothills of Monte Cervi and descend into the village of Collesano. There is a slight curve out of Collesano and the road points north-wards along the west side of another valley which runs right to the coast. The corners are no longer so tight and twisting, but this is countered by the treacherously slippery surface, the result of constant heavy traffic. The road then drops gently into Campofelice and joins the main Messina-Palermo road; there follows the only real straight on the circuit with a length of just under five kilometres; then after nearly three kilometres of fast curves, the road climbs over low seaward hills, descends again into the plain and turns inland to the finishing line. No amount of practice can make a driver intimate with the circuit and although he may recognise many parts, he is reliant on his judgment, skill and experience for almost the entire race and can never afford to relax. The only exception is the locally born driver and there is but one of outstanding ability, Palermo lawyer and Ferrari driver, Nino Vaccarella.

# THE LITTLE MADONIE CIRCUIT

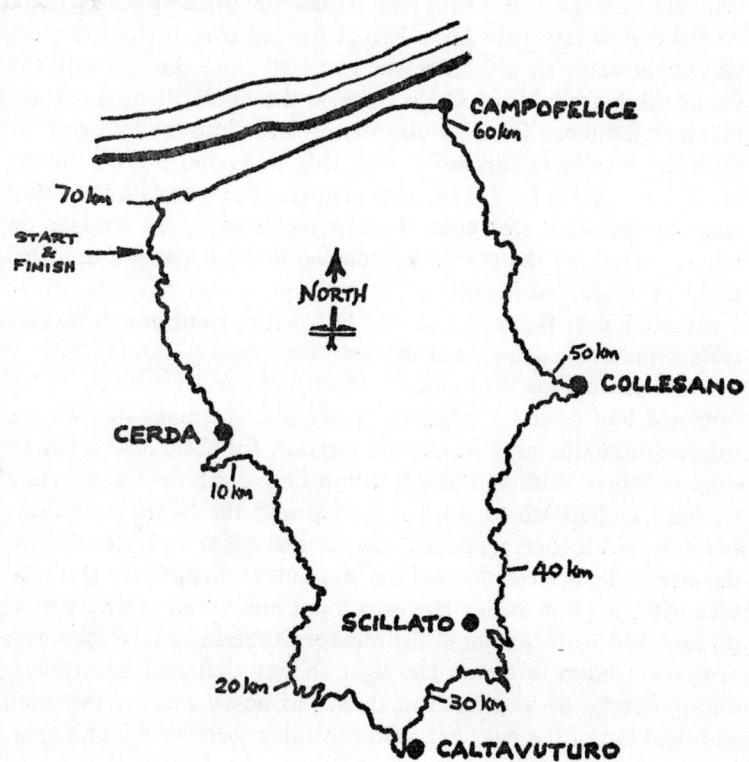

## The 1963 Race

The 55 runners left the start near the village of Cerda at 30-second intervals from 8 am onwards; the first car to break the peace and still of the morning air was an Alfa Romeo Giulietta and the last to leave the start at 8.34 was Bandini's Ferrari. At the end of the first lap the order on time was Ferrari-Ferrari-Porsche-Ferrari with the 250/Ps of Scarfiotti and Parkes leading Bonnier, who was travelling very quickly with the 2-litre Porsche, and Bandini with his 2-litre sports Ferrari. At the end of lap two Scarfiotti had fallen back and he came slowly into the pits; Belgian Willy Mairesse took over, but before he rejoined the race the engine was blipped and it sounded very, very ragged. With only another lap covered Mairesse was back in the pits; he restarted on what was to be his last lap, for somewhere on the circuit the Ferrari had bottomed, squashing the 'bump' in the bottom of the fuel tank which housed the inlet for the fuel line and the supply was restricted. At the end of lap three Mike Parkes handed over to John Surtees and at the same time the Porsche restarted from the pits with the young driver from Turin, Carlo Abate at the wheel. Because of these pit stops Bandini with the 2-litre Ferrari went into the lead and the Stuttgart 8-cylinder cars were now lying third and fourth. But on lap five the whole face of the race changed. Surtees, with the 250/P back in the lead, lost control on a bend, ploughed straight on instead of taking the corner and damaged the bodywork and fuel tank; he succeeded in getting the car back on the road, but there was fuel all over the road and very little left to run through the fuel system and so he abandoned the car.

As Abate had made up time on the 2-litre Ferrari throughout lap four and had passed it when the Maranello car made its pit stop, the situation was now serious for Ferrari, for the Porsche entries were now first, third and fourth (Barth/Linge with the Carrera) and to make matters worse, on his first lap with the 2-litre Dino Scarfiotti clouted a concrete course marker and made a pit stop for the damage to be inspected. Scarfiotti soon made amends for this mistake with two fast, steady laps which put him ahead of the Porsche on time and then came into the pits for Mairesse to take over with nearly a minute in hand. The light shower that had been falling during Scarfiotti's last lap had turned to heavy rain by the tenth and final lap of the race and – although they were six minutes apart on the road – Bonnier and Mairesse were having a real go, the former to make up time, the latter to stay ahead. By the time Bonnier had reached Bivio Polizzi, gearbox trouble had left him with only third, fourth and fifth ratios, but this was not such a disadvantage on the now near-flooded roads as it would have been in perfect conditions. When Bonnier crossed the finishing line, it was a matter of waiting and seeing how long it would be before the Ferrari took the flag. Headlamps ablaze, bonnet loose, body swaying, the tail trailing in the wind, the Maranello car crossed the line 12 sec too late for victory, a spin into a stone bollard in the fast curves at the end of the straight having cost Mairesse first place. The open Prototype 8-cylinder Porsche dropped right back in the closing stages of the race because Baghetti was forced to cover the last one-and-a-half laps with first gear only working and so he coasted in neutral wherever possible. This was Porsche's fourth outright win in the Targa Florio and the Stuttgart cars dominated the results:

1st J. Bonnier/C. M. Abate (Porsche 8-cyl), 6 hr 55 min 45·2 sec (64·57 mph)
2nd L. Bandini/L. Scarfiotti/W. Mairesse (Ferrari 206/SP), 6 hr 55 min 57·0 sec
3rd H. Linge/E. Barth (Porsche Carrera), 7 hr 26 min 19·8 sec
4th G. Bulgari/M. Grana (Ferrari 250GTO), 7 hr 26 min 31·8 sec
5th P. Strahle/A. Pucci (Porsche Abarth-Carrera), 7 hr 33 min 37·4 sec
6th G. Scarlatti/J. M. Bordeu (Ferrari 250GTO), 7 hr 40 min 16·4 sec
7th U. Maglioli/G. Baghetti (Porsche 8-cyl), 7 hr 49 min 12·8 sec
8th Z. Tchokotoua/J. Hitchcock (Ferrari 250GTO), 7 hr 59 min 33·6 sec

And once again full points for Porsche in the 2000 cc class of the Grand Touring Championship.

Next major race was the 1000 Km event at the Nürburgring, but a week after the Sicilian race was the 500 Km Spa Grand Prix, fourth race in the Grand Touring Championship and held on one of the fastest circuits in Europe. The event proved to be a complete Ferrari benefit with 250GTOs taking the first four places and the Fantuzzi-bodied 250GT of Chris Kerrison in fifth spot. Although not so conspicuous in the general classification the Porsches did all that was required of them, taking first three places in the 1600 cc and 2000 cc classes (only the latter counting for Championship points), Gerhard Koch was seventh overall with his 2-litre Carrera (but was beaten by Pat Fergusson's 1300 cc Lotus Elite) and the 1600 cc winner was English driver Dickie Stoop who has been racing Frazer Nashes and, later, Porsches since early post-war days.

*Nürburgring 1000 Km Race*

At the German race on 19th May, Porsche fielded the same two Prototypes as in the Targa Florio, but they were now fitted with oil temperature gauges on the gearbox/final drive unit. The coupé was entrusted to Bonnier and Phil Hill – the latter the 1961 Formula One World Champion who had signed up with A.T.S. for 1963, but had not so far had a drive! Hill was a skilful, vastly experienced driver, a dedicated bachelor who loved cars including early Alfa Romeos more than anything else, but not in my opinion a driver of true Championship calibre and whose laurels in 1961 were gained through the overwhelming superiority of the Ferrari and the tragic death of team-mate von Trips at Monza as much as by his own skill The open 8-cylinder Porsche was in the hands of Barth and Linge. Facing the Porsches was a strong team of three 250/P 3-litre Ferraris – but Nino Vaccarella, out of the Targa Florio because a driving offence had caused him to lose his licence, put himself out of the Nürburgring race by crashing in practice one of the 250/Ps. The two remaining cars were driven by Willy Mairesse/John Surtees and Mike Parkes/Lodovico Scarfiotti. There were no other serious challengers for outright victory, but the Ferrari 250GTOs were fast enough to pull off the unexpected if the Prototypes should fail. An especially interesting entry was the Lola G.T., low, sleek and pugnaciously potent-looking, in the hands of Tony Maggs and Bob Olthoff, but too new for much to be expected of it. There were also two brand-new lightweight racing Jaguar E-types in the hands of Peter Lindner and Peter Nöcker and British Peters, Lumsden and Sargent.

And it was Lindner's intimate knowledge of the circuit and a very swift sprint to his car at the Le Mans start that resulted in the Jaguar leading the field all the way round on the first of the 44 laps of the 14·17-mile circuit. In contrast the two 8-cylinder Porsches made poor starts and were lying in seventh and eighth positions after one circuit. Then the Ferraris forged ahead of the Jaguar and the Porsches were left desperately striving to make up lost ground. After only four laps the open Porsche of Barth and Linge retired with rear axle failure when in third place. The weather at the start of the race had been fine, but it gradually became worse and worse with rain that turned into sleet and then hail and accompanied by a fierce wind; sunshine broke through for a short while, but conditions deteriorated again, parts of the circuit were wet and slippery, parts dry or almost dry – and the result was numerous crashes. On lap 14 Surtees handed over to Mairesse and a lap later Scarfiotti handed over to Parkes. As he went through Aremberg, Parkes lost the 250/P, clouting a bridge and tearing off the rear suspension; Mairesse's 250/P was close behind and punctured the nearside front tyre on a piece of the debris. The Belgian driver lost a lot of time changing a wheel out on the circuit and stopped at the pits for the Ferrari to be checked. Phil Hill, having taken over the coupé Porsche from Bonnier, now had half a lap's lead – but not for long! Lap 16 saw inexperienced private owner Hitchcock overturn his 250GTO in the Karussel banked hairpin and there it remained for the rest of the race while the field was compelled to keep off the banking and follow the flat part of the track at reduced speed.

With 19 laps completed, Mairesse had snatched second place back from the E-type of Lindner and the 250GTO of Noblet and then there was another dramatic change of fortunes and a second crash at Aremberg – Phil Hill went straight on with the leading Porsche, damaging it too badly to continue. In all there were around a dozen crashes in this race, but no driver was seriously injured, a fine testimony to the inherent safety of the Nürburgring. Of the two brand-new Jaguars, Lindner's car was eliminated by engine trouble and Lumsden had a lurid crash; when in fourth place he lost control at the Flugplatz, the car rolled end over end and demolished 150 yards of fencing and itself. Lumsden escaped with a severe shaking.

The Mairesse/Surtees Ferrari was now completely unopposed and both drivers motored magnificently and without making a single mistake. Despite the atrocious conditions and the complete uselessness of the Ferrari's double-arm wiper (see photo. opposite Page 72 in *Ford Versus Ferrari*), Surtees, relying on his intimate knowledge of the circuit, pressed on in limited visibility without substantially reducing his speed, and Mairesse took over to complete the last four laps in much improved conditions. Porsche's interest in the race had been maintained by at half-distance switching Barth and Linge to the works Carrera and making all-out effort to catch the second-place Ferrari and be the first G.T. car home. The effort failed and it finished fourth – but first in its class. The finishing order was:

1st  J. Surtees/W. Mairesse (Ferrari 250/P), 7 hr 32 min 18·0 sec (82·72 mph)
2nd  P. Noblet/J. Guichet (Ferrari 250GTO), 7 hr 40 min 03·0 sec
3rd  C. M. Abate/U. Maglioli (Ferrari TR61), 1 lap in arrears
4th  H. J. Walter/B. Pon/H. Linge/ E. Barth (Porsche Carrera 2-litre) 1 lap in arrears
5th  "Elde"/G. Langlois (Ferrari 250GT), 3 laps in arrears
6th  D. Piper/ E. Cantrell (Ferrari 250GTO), 3 laps in arears

## Le Mans

With a repetition that was almost monotonous, Porsche fielded the two 8-cylinder cars at the Sarthe circuit, the coupé for Jo Bonnier and Cooper works Formula One driver Tony Maggs, and the open car for Barth and Linge. In an attempt to relieve gearbox stresses – and consequent failures – both cars had rubber torsional shock-absorbers in the drive-shafts. The entry was completely dominated by Ferraris from start to finish – apart from a short while when the British Aston Martin 215 led – and the Porsches never rose high in the field although they led in their class. In the ninth hour of the race the North American Racing team Ferrari with Roger Penske at the wheel burst an oil pipe and set up such a smoke screen that Jo Bonnier was blinded and ran off the road. Both the 2-litre Carreras entered retired, unexpectedly, with engine trouble and so the sole finisher was the open car of Barth and Linge. On the Sunday morning it was in fourth place when the right-hand rear axle stub sheared and Barth crept back to the pits on three wheels. The mechanics fitted a new stub axle, brake assembly, disc and wheel and the car rejoined the race in eighth place. This was where it finished, behind six Ferraris, the works Cobra and the Rover-B.R.M. gas-turbine car which did not qualify for a place in the results, but was running for a special prize.

The month of June and Le Mans brought an early end to Porsche's main racing season and there were no more important races that year. Private owners continued to keep their cars to the fore and Dickie

Concentration – another view of Gurney in the 1962 French race

A view of the Porsche flat-eight engine showing the horizontal cooling fan and covers over the carburettors (*Motor Sport*)

Former works driver Huchke von Hanstein, until recently competitions manager of Porsche (Nigel Snowdon)

One of the mainstays of the Porsche works team for many years has been Hans Herrmann who during 1954–55 was a Mercedes-Benz works driver

## 1963: A QUIET YEAR FOR PORSCHE

Stoop took 12th place overall and second place in the 1600 cc class of the Grand Touring Tourist Trophy, held over a distance of 312 miles at Goodwood. With consummate ease, the make had again won its class in the Grand Touring Championship, while Ferrari won the over 2-litre class of the G.T. Championship, together with the *Challenge Mondiale de Vitesse*. Porsche took second place in this with 30 points compared with Ferrari's 38. The Stuttgart factory had cars under development that would result in a substantial improvement in their fortunes in 1964.

## EIGHT
# 1964: Carrera Consistency

*A New Grand Touring Porsche*

Parallel lines of thought characterised the new Grand Touring cars built by Porsche and Ferrari for the 1964 season – both were low-slung coupés purely for competition work and bearing a much stronger likeness to their Prototype counterparts than to the production cars of the range. One hundred cars was the minimum necessary to qualify for homologation as a Grand Touring car and Porsche duly built one hundred of their new 904 and it was this sincerity of action that exposed the idiocy of the F.I.A.'s homologation policy. For only a dozen of the special lightweight racing Jaguar E-types of 1963 onwards were built and there were even less of the 1964 Cobra Daytona coupés which had little in common with their everyday road-going counterparts other than the chassis frame. The new Ferrari 250LM (or 275LM as it later became known) was nothing but the 1963 250/P Prototype with a roof on and initial production amounted to little more than a dozen. Accordingly its homologation was refused and it was not homologated until 1966 when the minimum necessary to qualify was reduced to 50.

Announced early in December, 1963, the 904 GTS Porsche departed from normal Stuttgart practice in a number of ways; it was the first car offered to Porsche customers with a separate chassis frame and a glass-reinforced plastic body and it was the first closed Porsche to be offered with the engine between the occupants and the final drive.

The 1966 cc flat-four engine was available in two states of tune – the standard version developing 155 bhp at 6400 rpm and the competition version developing 180 bhp at 7000 rpm. To increase the power output of the 587/3 engine of the Carrera 2-litre to these figures had meant a great deal of development work. One of the more serious problems was cooling and apart from the fitting of a large oil cooler, the depth of the cylinder finning was substantially increased from 7 mm to 20 mm. As was now normal Carrera practice, two twin-choke Weber carburetters were used and there was rather extreme valve timing on the racing version.

Basis of the chassis frame was formed by two deep box-form members fabricated from sheet steel, joined together by hollow, box-form bulkheads at either end and a pair of transverse boxed cross-members amidships. The side-members were bowed outwards so that the occupants of the car could sit low down between them and to provide leg clearance the forward transverse member was underslung. Further stiffening for the already stiff chassis was provided by the body which was both bolted and permanently bonded with adhesive to the side-members.

Front suspension was by a conventional unequal-length wishbone layout with tubular links and the wheelpost swivelling on ball joints. The rear wheels were mounted on equal-length triangulated links with the apex inboard. Parallel trailing arms provided fore and aft location of the wheels, but with the upper arms shorter so as to provide a limited degree of rear wheel steering. Co-axial coil spring and damper units were fitted and there were anti-roll bars front and rear. Large, by 1964 standards, 15-in wheels were used so that the car would be quite at home racing over rough terrain.

Transmission was by a dry-plate clutch and a two-shaft, all-independent, all-synchromesh gearbox. The body was constructed by aircraft company Heinkel Flugzeugbau and was in three units – the cab and undertray which were bolted and bonded to the chassis, and the nose and tail sections (the latter hinged for quick access to the engine, but not easily detached). The back window was a vertical panel in the fixed part of the cab and a 'hole' in the engine cover lined up with it. The headlamps were set well back in the long, sloping nose, necessitating clear-plastic fairings over the headlamps.

To coincide with the announcement of the new model, a demonstration was arranged on the Solitude circuit – with the roads still open to the public – and the favoured were taken for a few brisk laps by Edgar Barth and Herbert Linge with speeds in the region of 125 mph attained on parts of the circuit. The 904 was priced at 29,700 Dm (£2,670) at the factory, a dozen cars had been produced for the American market by Christmas, 1963 and production of the 100, intended to be completed by the end of April, was well under way by the New Year.

## Before the Start of the European Season

The Daytona race on 16th February had been extended from three hours to 2000 Km and was open only to homologated G.T. cars. It proved a complete Ferrari benefit with 250GTOs in the first three places and fifth. Fourth was the Shelby Cobra of Gurney and Johnson and the new Daytona coupé version of the Cobra had led the entire field until eliminated by rear axle failure. Though overshadowed by these giants, the 904, making its race debut in the hands of familiar Porsche exponents Barth and Linge, did all that was required of it by finishing sixth and winning the class. A month later was the Sebring 12 hours race, also held in Florida, and it proved a repetition of Daytona in many ways. Prototype Ferraris took the first three places, but in the GT category the gaudy Cobras defeated their Italian rivals and were fourth, fifth, sixth and eighth. Seventh was the 250GTO of Rodriguez and Piper. Again, out of the general classification picture and again performing in the manner that was expected of a Porsche, the 904 of Underwood and Briggs Cunningham was ninth overall, winning its class and covering 191 laps compared with the 214 of the winner. Tenth was the Carrera of Pon and Buzzetta on the same lap.

April 18th-19th was the Le Mans Test Week-end and lapping with the numerous privately owned 904s was a works car, externally similar, but fitted with the flat-eight engine.

## Targa Florio

Probably the most striking features of the 1964 race were the complete absence of the Ferrari team – Enzo, well satisfied with the results at Daytona and Sebring, had decided to concentrate his efforts on the Nürburgring and Le Mans – and a powerful entry of Shelby-Cobras from Carroll Shelby. Porsche divided their efforts two ways. The 1963 8-cylinder open prototype was entrusted to Joakim Bonnier and B.R.M. team-leader Graham Hill, driving a Porsche for the first time since the 1962 Nürburgring race, and a perfectly normal 904 apart from the 8-cylinder engine driven by Barth and Maglioli and just as had appeared at Le Mans earlier in the month. The only differences from the standard 904 chassis were a change in gear ratios and the use of rubber 'doughnut' universals in the drive-shafts instead of the Renault flexible Hooke joints. In the G.T. category Porsche fielded 904s for Pucci/Davis (Colin Davis, son of famous

Bentley driver S. C. H. Davis) and Linge/Balzarini. Backing up the works cars were four private entries, including one from the Scuderia Filipinetti. As to the opposition? – there was none, apart from two works-assisted 250GTO Ferraris, the Cobras and a pair of V-8 $2\frac{1}{2}$-litre rear-engined A.T.S. coupés making their race debut and it was certain that they would not last the race. As for the Cobras, it was doubtful whether they could beat the 250GTOs and despite a very fine team of drivers they were far too much of a handful to achieve outright victory on this circuit.

The race was held in blazing hot sunshine and right from the start, the two 8-cylinder Porsches set the pace followed by Gurney (Cobra), Guichet (250GTO) and Phil Hill (Cobra). Half-way round the second lap Bonnier's car broke a drive-shaft coupling and the Swedish driver was stranded out in the mountains at the Bivio Polizzi refuelling depot. When the Cobras came into refuel Gurney and Phil Hill were third and fourth, but such a circus act was made of pit stops that the 904s of Bulgari and the works-entered Pucci went ahead. Once again, as so often happens in this race, a series of retirements changed the whole pattern of leadership. Maglioli, at the wheel of the leading Porsche, had a spring unit break on lap five and spun into a wall; although the car was severely damaged, he managed to limp back to the pits, but so much time was lost that he dropped back to sixth place. The young Roman driver Bulgari was now in the lead with the 904, but as he sped along the final straight on lap five, he found that the car was not handling properly and when he came into the pits to hand over to co-driver Grana, it was discovered that the rear of the chassis frame had broken and the near-side rear wheel was leaning inwards.

The leader was now the 250GTO of Guichet and Facetti, but the latter, slower driver was at the wheel; Pucci handed over to Davis who began to gain rapidly with the works 904 and on lap six the Ferrari was eliminated by the back axle breaking. Second to the 904 was the Cobra of Gurney, the lanky Brabham Formula One driver putting up a really determined blood and guts drive with the unwieldy Ford-powered monster. Phil Hill's Cobra had retired with a wishbone pulled away from the chassis and Gurney's car was showing signs of breaking up; he was forced to ease up and was passed on time by the 1963 Carrera 2-litre of young German drivers Klass and Neerpasch, and not long afterwards by the Alfa Romeo TZ of Bussinello and Todaro.

Gurney finally had the rear suspension collapse and he covered the last lap with the rear wheels pointing in different directions. The Porsche pit staff were feeling complacent about the placings of their cars when Neerpasch with the 2-litre Carrera staggered into the pits with a buckled left-hand rear wheel and nearly non-existent brakes. The wheel was removed and it was found that the brake caliper had broken away from its mounting and allowed all the fluid to run out. A new pipe and wheel were fitted and Neerpasch was sent out to complete the last lap on three brakes and with the caliper of the fourth flapping in the air-stream. Only 27 out of the 64 starters completed the 48th Targa Florio and the Stuttgart team was delighted at both having won the race for the second year in succession and having four cars in the first eight finishers. Only one car out of the five Cobras entered finished, both A.T.S. entries went out with engine trouble and the rather badly driven 250GTO of Ferlaino and Taramazzo picked up for Ferrari the points he needed in his class of the Grand Touring Championship. This is how the first eight finished:

1st A. Pucci/C. Davis (Porsche 904 GTS), 7 hr 10 min 53·6 sec (62·28 mph)
2nd H. Linge/G. Balzarini (Porsche 904 GTS), 7 hr 23 min 15·6sec
3rd R. Bussinello/N. Todaro (Alfa Romeo Giulia TZ), 7 hr 27 min 7·0 sec
4th "Kim"/A. Thiele (Alfa Romeo Guilia TZ), 7 hr 27 min 38·4 sec
5th C. Ferlaino/L. Taramazzo (Ferrari 250GTO), 7 hr 28 min 25·0 sec
6th E. Barth/U. Maglioli (Porsche 904 8-cyl), 7hr 28 min 25·0 sec
7th G. Klass/H. Neerpasch (Porsche Carrera), 7hr 30 min 45·4 sec
8th D. Gurney/J. Grant (Shelby Cobra), 7 hr 38 min 5·0 sec
Fastest lap: C. Davis in 41 min 10·8 sec

*Spa 500 Kilometres Race*

On May 17th, 44 cars turned out in very hot weather for this round in the Grand Touring Championship. Overall positions were fought out between a horde of GTO Ferraris – despite promises of a challenge from Phil Hill's Daytona Cobra which suffered fuel starvation on the first lap and Dick Protheroe's E-type Jaguar which had trouble with its ZF gearbox. On this occasion Porsche were not content to let their chances rest in the hands of private owners and sent along a works 904 for Edgar Barth. He scored full points in the 2000 cc class by taking fifth place, a lap in arrears.

*Nürburgring 1000 Km Race*

Once again the Porsches were overshadowed by the Ford Versus Ferrari battle, and it was no longer the Cobras versus the GTOs, but the new Ford GT40 against the works Prototypes. Practice slashed the entry list: Brian Hetreed crashed with fatal results in his ex-works Aston Martin 215 and a similar tragedy befell Randolph Moser at the wheel of his 904; other crashes eliminated two more 904s, two Cobras, and Protheroe's E-type; Mike Spence left the road with Ian Walker's new Lotus Elan coupé and Barth pranged one of the works-entered 8-cylinder 904s because of brake trouble. As a result only a single 8-cylinder 904 ran, driven by Joakim Bonnier and short, freckled, tousle-haired B.R.M. driver Richie Ginther. A standard 904 was works-entered for Davis and Pucci and there was a host of these cars entered by private owners including one from Stirling Moss' SMART team driven by "Lucky" Casner and David Hobbs.

The race, held in remarkably warm and sunny conditions, soon became a Ferrari walk-over, for Bonnier stopped out on the circuit with sticking throttle trouble on the Porsche Prototype and the GT40, which was suffering from gear selection troubles, fell further and further back until the rear suspension mountings broke up. A long pit-stop had put the works Prototype out of the running, but it slowly worked its way through the field to finish fifth and it was the sole finisher in its class. Out of 12 904s to start, there were five in the first ten finishers, but the works car was spun off into a ditch by the Englishman. This is how the first six finished:

1st L. Scarfiotti/N. Vaccarella (Ferrari 275/P), 87·30 mph
2nd M. Parkes/J. Guichet (Ferrari 250GTO)
3rd B. Pon/G. Koch (Porsche 904 GTS)
4th L. Bianchi/G. van Ophem (Ferrari 250GTO)
5th J. Bonnier/R. Ginther (Porsche 8-cyl 904)
6th H. Müller/A. Knorr (Porsche 904 GTS)

## Le Mans

The Sarthe circuit saw another demonstration of Ferrari's stranglehold on Prototype racing and a display of tremendous speed coupled with unreliability by the new Ford GT40s. Although the Porsches were not in the running for outright victory, their star was very much in the ascendant and the Stuttgart cars put up a display of reliability of the kind that soon came to be taken for granted. But the reliability was that of the new production 904 GTS – of which all five starters finished – and not of the 8-cylinder Prototypes, which let the team down once again with mechanical disasters; the Barth/Linge car blew up its engine and the Davis/Mitter car came into the pits with clutch trouble; the clutch disc was changed in the pits – this involved removing the gearbox and rear suspension – and the car rejoined the race, only to break its engine. This is how the five 904s finished (Ferraris took the first three places):

   7th  R. Buchet/G. Ligier 322 laps (compared with the winner's 343)
   8th  B. Pon/V. Zalinger 318 laps
 10th  G. Koch/H. Schiller 314 laps
 11th  H. Müller/C. Sage 308 laps
 12th  "Franc"/J. Kerguen 307 laps
There were 25 finishers.

## Rheims 12 Hours

Re-instated after an interval of six years, the Rheims race was held as usual on the beautifully smooth circuit taking in a stretch of the main Soissons-Rheims road, the very tight Thillois hairpin, a fast stretch past the pits and an artificial stretch with three bends linking up with the hairpin Virage de Muizon at the main road once again. This artificial stretch avoids the narrow streets lined with shuttered houses and crossroads in the village of Gueux, which formed part of the circuit until 1952. Like so many Continental circuits, Rheims forms parts of roads open to traffic all the year round, and any private motorist, within the limits imposed by the traffic conditions (very heavy on the main road during the rush hour!) can try his hand. The writer has had a go round Rheims on several occasions late on a Summer evening – but the real problem is the turn back on to the Rheims-Soissons road because of oncoming traffic.

The 1964 race attracted only nine prototypes – three Fords,

A brilliant rally success was the win by Vic Elford in the 1968 Monte Carlo event with this 911S (*Motor*)

One race that Vic Elford did not win; he retired his 911S at the 1968 Easter Thruxton meeting with suspension trouble (*Motor*)

*Above:* Experimental – the 2-litre 8-cylinder Porsche which took third place in the 1962 Targa Florio. It was driven by Nino Vaccarella and Joakim Bonnier and was entered in Italian colours by the Scuderia Serenissima Republica di Venezia (*Motor Sport*). *Below:* Winner – the 2-litre 8-cylinder Porsche which in the hands of Carlo Maria Abate and Joakim Bonnier won the 1963 Targa Florio at record speed (*Motor Sport*)

three Ferraris, an Iso Rivolta, the Maserati-France 5-litre coupé and a single Porsche. The Porsche was once again a 904 with an 8-cylinder engine entrusted to Edgar Barth and Colin Davis. A grand total of eight production 904s were running, including a works-entered car for Koch and Gerhard Mitter. The race started at midnight with a Le Mans start and the early laps were all Fords and Ferraris passing and re-passing with the shafts of light from their headlamps shifting and swinging about the track and occasionally merging. Even when the Fords had fallen by the wayside, the NART and Maranello Concessionaires Ferraris were still fighting it out and these 275LMs took first and second places. The 8-cylinder Porsche had attained tenth place by the end of the first hour, but went out because a locking nut in the gearbox came undone and allowed the layshaft to move back and grind a hole in the casing, and all the oil was lost. Once again the day was saved by the standard 904s which finished fifth (Nasif/Viannini), 6th (the works car of Koch and Mitter), 7th (Pon/Slotemaker), 10th (Buchet/Ligier), 12th (Müller/Knorr), 13th (Mlle. Soisbault/Dubois), 15th (Zalinge/Lennep) and 16th ("Franc"/Kerguen) – eight Porsches in 20 finishers; ten Porsches in 37 starters!

## Postscript to 1964

Another, albeit minor, success followed in the Rheinland-Pfalz Preis, a 7-lap supporting race to the German Grand Prix at the Nürburgring at the beginning of August. Koch led home the four 904s which dominated the race and won the 2500 cc class, while in the 1600 cc category a brace of 356s finished second and third to a Tubolare Zagato Alfa Giulia. At the last Tourist Trophy held at Goodwood, on August 29th, cars under 2000 cc were banned, but had their own race over 21 laps beforehand. Although Dickie Stoop led for the first three laps, he was caught by later Lotus and B.R.M. Formula One driver Mike Spence with the Chequered Flag's Lotus Elan and Stoop and Mike de Udy had to be content with second and third places for their 904s.

The 1964 season was for Porsche one of considerable and consistent success for the standard 904, but of mediocrity for the 8-cylinder Prototypes. It seemed that the transmission trouble which had plagued these cars for so long had been largely cured, but the engine unreliability had never been overcome. It was in search of a way out of these difficulties and with an eye to future production cars that a 904 powered by the 6-cylinder 911 engine appeared at the Paris 1000 Km race in October. Here the 8-cylinder 904 put up one of its best performances by taking third place with Barth and Davis at the wheel.

In another field, the European Hill Climb Championship, the make Porsche was well to the fore. There could be no greater contrast between the long Continental mountain climbs with their sheer drops at the road edge, their loose surfaces and their narrowness, and the British type of hill climb, usually well surfaced, often artificial and all over in a minute or less. Round One took place at Rossfeld in Southern Germany on June 7th and saw a win by the 1963 Champion Edgar Barth at the wheel of a British Elva (!) with a Porsche engine entered by the Stuttgart factory. The results were decided on the aggregate of two runs over the 6-kilometre course. Barth's time was 6 min 31·18 sec and in second place came Swiss driver Herbert Müller with the 2-litre 8-cylinder Prototype Porsche used by Barth to win the Championship in 1963.

By the next round in the Championship, on June 14th at Mont Ventoux in France, Barth had switched back to his 1963 car and the Elva-Porsche was driven by Müller. Although fastest time was set by Maurice Trintigant's ex-works Formula One B.R.M., Barth was again the victor in the Championship class, while Müller crashed the Elva-Porsche as the result of a suspension breakage. The next two rounds, at Gaisberg in Austria and Trento-Bordone in Northern Italy brought Barth another two wins and enabled him to clinch the Championship with 36 points – although there were three further qualifying rounds.

In the 1964 *Challenge Mondiale de Vitesse*, based on the results of the Sebring, Targa Florio, Nürburgring and Le Mans races, Porsche was the victor – even though Ferrari had scored more points. For, by missing the Targa Florio, the Maranello concern had rendered itself ineligible for victory.

## NINE
# 1965: Another Successful Year For The 904

After the very uncertain footing on which Prototype and Grand Touring racing had got under way in 1962, it had by 1965 achieved a status and following close to matching that of Formula One and this was attributable to the participation of Ford and the ever increasing strength of Ferrari and Porsche. In all there were nearly a dozen major races for these cars during 1965. It was, however, in neither Grand Touring or Prototype racing that a 904 Porsche first appeared in 1965, but in the Monte Carlo Rally. In the absence of works Mercedes-Benz participation, Eugen Böhringer, leading driver for the other Stuttgart concern, teamed up with Rolf Wutherich to drive a 904 GTS, the sort of car that many people thought ought not to be allowed to take part. Starting from Frankfurt, the intrepid German pair brought their hot coupé through to finish second to the Mini-Cooper 'S' of Timo Makinen and Paul Easter – a magnificent performance with a car whose tremendous performance was offset by its lack of suitability for this type of event. There were only 35 finishers out of 227 starters.

As was now usual the season was started off by the Daytona race and the 2000 Km event on 28th February was completely dominated by Ford-powered cars, with GT40s first and third and Cobras second, fourth and sixth. The 904 of Kolb and Heftler was, however, well up with the leaders and took an excellent fifth place to score maximum points in the G.T. Championship. Exactly four weeks later on 27th March was the Sebring 12 Hours race and once again the marque Porsche was well represented by private owners; Huschke von Hanstein was there to supervise operations in the pits and look after the sole works entry, an 8-cylinder car driven by

Linge and Mitter. The race started in boiling hot sunshine and with a duel between Jim Hall's Chaparral and Dan Gurney's Ford-powered Lotus 19, both sports cars and contenders for outright victory only and not Championship points. These two drivers were treating the race as a flat-out sprint, after 20 laps the race average was 100·56 mph, and it was 40 laps before the Lotus broke out on the circuit, letting the Chaparral (now with Hap Sharp at the wheel) into the lead. All this while the Porsches were steadidly droning their way round this flat, characterless circuit and all the time the weather was getting hotter and hotter. As the heat increased, so the sky became blacker and blacker and a storm was inevitable. And von Hanstein was hoping for this more than anybody, as wet conditions would permit the Porsches to make up a lot of ground on the leaders. At 5.25 pm, the storm broke and within minutes the circuit was completely inundated; the leading cars lost ground rapidly as their rain-blinded drivers slithered round the circuit; but the Porsches were splashing the laps off merrily and their shape was such that the windscreens stayed reasonably clear. The rain continued to fall for an hour without respite and while the leading Chaparral managed only a couple of laps, the German's cars were closing rapidly on distance and were constantly lapping their American and Italian rivals. At around 6.30 pm, with $2\frac{1}{2}$ hours racing to go, the rain stopped and although circuit drainage was poor, the cars' tyres soon swept it relatively clear of water. The Pon/Buzzetta and Underwood/Klass 904s were now right on the tail of the leading G.T. car, the Daytona Cobra coupé of Schlesser and Bondurant, but once conditions had improved, the big American coupé was able to forge ahead again. Even so, when the chequered flag fell at 9 pm, the 904s were well up with the leaders as the results reveal:

1st  J. Hall/H. Sharp (Chaparral-Chevrolet), 196 laps (84·72 mph)
2nd  B. McLaren/K. Miles (Ford GT40), 192 laps
3rd  D. Piper/A. Maggs (Ferrari 275LM), 190 laps
4th  J. Schlesser/R. Bondurant (Shelby Cobra), 187 laps
5th  L. Underwood/G. Klass (Porsche 904), 185 laps
6th  B. Pon/J. Buzzetta (Porsche 904), 185 laps

The 904s scored maximum points in the 2000 cc G.T. Championship and the works Prototype, in ninth place with 184 laps to its credit, won its class. A satisfactory outing for the Stuttgart cars in every way.

A fortnight later at the Le Mans Test Week-end, the works turned up at the Sarthe circuit with two Prototype 904 coupés, one with the 8-cylinder engine as had been frequently raced and the other a 6-cylinder car as had appeared briefly at Montlhéry in 1964. The extensively tuned 911 engine had two specially made downdraught Weber carburettors, each having three chokes spaced to match up with the three inlet ports of each bank of air-cooled cylinders. With Mitter at the wheel the 6-cylinder Porsche recorded a time of 3 min 59·4 sec, compared with the fastest lap of 3 min 35·1 sec by John Surtees with the 4-litre Ferrari Prototype.

The European Grand Touring season got under way with the Monza 1000 Km race on 25th April and held on the combined road and very bumpy banked track circuit. Porsche did not enter any works cars, but suffered no loss of Championship points because the make's reputation was very well upheld by private owners. Despite the presence of two Ford GT40s, the race was Ferrari-dominated all the way and the Maranello Prototypes took first two places. Third came the GT40 of Ken Miles and Bruce McLaren and fourth were Ben Pon and Rob Slotemaker with the orange-painted Racing Team Holland Porsche 904 – referred to now by most writers as the 914 because of the disagreement with Peugeot over type numbers containing a middle zero.

*Targa Florio*

It was not until the Sicilian road race on 9th May that the Porsche concern showed its claws in 1965 and fielded a very strong and assorted team. Ferrari was also back again in full strength after giving the race a miss in 1964. This is how the opposing teams lined up:

*Porsche System Engineering:*
Entered in the 1600 cc to 3000 cc Prototype class:
904 with flat-eight 2-litre engine driven by Joakim Bonnier and Graham Hill
904 with flat-six engine driven by Umberto Maglioli and Herbert Linge
New Prototype car with 904 chassis and flat-eight engine, but with very abbreviated open bodywork and humps over the wheels. This was driven by Colin Davis and Gerhard Mitter. It should have been driven by Hill and Bonnier, but having tried it in practice, they concluded that it jumped about the road so badly

that it was unmanageable and refused to handle it. Much of the trouble seemed attributable to the narrow 6-in rims on which the car was running.

2000 cc Grand Touring class:
Normal 904 driven by Baron Antonio Pucci and Günther Klass
*S.E.F.A.C. Ferrari:*
Three 3·3-litre 275/P2 Prototypes driven by Nino Vaccarella/ Luigi Bandini, Lodovico Scarfiotti/Mike Parkes and Jean Guichet/ Giancarlo Baghetti.

In addition a competition version of the 275GTB was entered for Biscaldi and Deserti and a works-supported 275LM driven by de Adamich and Casoni was entered in a special National class.

The roads had been closed to the public by 4 am in preparation for the start four hours later and by that early hour the 44-mile circuit was thronged with thousands of spectators who had ridden and driven out to take up their vantage points. At the end of the first torrid, dusty lap the order on time was Vaccarella-Scarfiotti-Bondurant (with the sole and open GT40 Ford entered)-de Adamich-Maglioli-Herrmann (Abarth). As lap succeeded lap the weather became more and more oppressive, the cars became increasingly battered and increasingly ragged sounding. At the end of lap three many of the runners stopped to refuel, but already Scarfiotti had gone off the road and damaged the steering of his Ferrari and Bonnier had been delayed by throttle cable trouble which meant that Hill took over with a lot of ground to make up. Vaccarella had been travelling fantastically quickly, setting a new lap record of 39 min 32 sec and when he came in to hand over to Bandini, the 275/P2 had a lead of nearly five minutes and the Sciilian received a severe ticking-off from team manager Dragoni for treating the race as a flat-out sprint! The Ford GT lost a lot of time as the result of a wheel coming off and although the Porsches could not match the pace of the Ferraris, once again their consistency was beginning to pay dividends.

Vaccarella took over again from Bandini at the end of lap seven, by when the other remaining 275/P2 of Guichet/Baghetti had disappeared out on the circuit with an electrical short that had caused the battery to run down and Baghetti had started on foot the long trek through the village of Cerda back to the pits. The Davis/Mitter and Maglioli/Linge Porsches were now lying second and third – but without any real hopes of catching the leader – and the Ferrari team was further depleted by the retirement of the 275GTB with transmission trouble. On roads that now had a fine covering of loose gravel, Bondurant lost control of the Ford, tearing off a wheel and suspension when he hit a water trough; Pucci took the chequered flag as leader on the road at the end of the ten laps and then Vaccarella came across the line to bring Ferrari's total of post-war victories to six compared with the five of Porsche. After seven hours of intensive racing, the Davis/Mitter Porsche was $4\frac{1}{2}$ minutes behind and the Porsche team was well satisfied with the performances of their mixed bag of cars and drivers. The final results were:

1st N. Vaccarella/L. Bandini (Ferrari 275/P2), 7 hr 1 min 12·4 sec (63·73 mph)
2nd C. Davis/G. Mitter (Porsche 8-cyl), 7 hr 5 min 34·0 sec
3rd U. Maglioli/H. Linge (Porsche 6-cyl), 7 hr 6 min 58·0 sec
4th J. Bonnier/G. Hill (Porsche 8-cyl), 7 hr 10 min 8·0 sec
5th A. Pucci/G. Klass (Porsche 904), 7 hr 11 min 7·0 sec
6th H. Herrmann/L. Cella (Abarth 1600), 7 hr 17 min 23·0 sec

*Spa 500 Km Race*

In 1965 the Royal Automobile Club of Spa's race on the magnificent circuit in the Ardennes included a class for Prototypes, but the only likely winner in the class was Mike Parkes with the Maranello Concessionaires' 330/P 4-litre Ferrari. The Ferrari led the race with consummate ease until low fuel pressure intervened and then victory went to the Ferrari 275LMs of Mairesse and David Piper, the yellow leading the green – both cars were painted particularly sickly shades of their respective colours. A magnificent third was Ben Pon with his 904 and he defeated Peter Sutcliffe's ex-Piper Ferrari 250GTO.

*Nürburgring 1000 Km Race*

It was Ferraris all the way in the 1000 Km race and the Porsches were never in the picture until retirements and the mechanical derangements of the opposition allowed one of the 8-cylinder cars to move up into third place. The race made it rather obvious that the 8-cylinder Porsche in its existing form was no longer truly competitive, but apart from this the Stuttgart team was noticeably less well organised than usual and everybody in the team had been greatly upset by news of the death of Edgar Barth on the eve of the race after a long illness. Late on the Saturday Gerhard Mitter had crashed and written off the stubby open 8-cylinder car that had gone unexpectedly well in the Targa Florio. The Porsche line-up then consisted of Joakim Bonnier and the young Austrian driver Jochen Rindt with an 8-cylinder coupé, and three 904s with the twin-plug racing version of the 911 engine and driven by Davis/Mitter, Nöcker/Klass and Maglioli/Linge. Just as the 8-cylinder engine was past its best, the 6-cylinder unit was still far from fully developed and, for the time being at least, Porsche had the worst of both worlds. A works 904 in standard Group 4 trim was also entered and driven by Pon and Koch.

The 4-litre Ferrari of Surtees and Scarfiotti and the 3·3-litre of Parkes and Guichet ran away with the race and easily took the first two places; the Ford challenge faded early, but the real sensation of the race was the little V-6 Ferrari Dino, allegedly of only 1600 cc and distinguished by its yellow Formula One wheels, which tenaciously held third place overall after the retirement of the open Ford of Whitmore and Attwood – the 8-cylinder Porsche, admittedly slowed by carburation trouble, was quite unable to catch it. It was only after the Dino had been slowed by a piece of rubber sucked into one of the Webers that Bonnier was able to get ahead of the baby Ferrari. The 6-cylinder cars were no match for the Dino either and it was a rather anxious von Hanstein and Porsche team that returned to Stuttgart with the problem of finding some extra horses in a hurry.

This is how the first six finished:

1st  J. Surtees/L. Scarfiotti (Ferrari 330/P2), 90·66 mph
2nd  M. Parkes/J. Guichet (Ferrari 275/P2)
3rd  J. Bonnier/J. Rindt (Porsche 8-cyl)
4th  L. Bandini/N. Vaccarella (Ferrari Dino 166), 1 lap in arrears
5th  U. Maglioli/H. Linge (Porsche 6-cyl), 1 lap in arrears
6th  P. Nöcker/G. Klass (Porsche 6-cyl), 1 lap in arrears

In the Grand Touring category, the 904 had forged ahead in its class, but the gearbox mountings broke which delayed Pon and Koch in the pits for a long time and when they did restart, they were only able to lap at reduced speed. The class was won by the private 904 of Fischaber and Schütz in 11th place.

*Above:* The 1963 Targa Florio-winning car was overturned in the Nürburgring 1000 Kms race by Phil Hill (*Motor Sport*). *Below:* The first lap of the 1964 Targa Florio was led by this experimental 8-cylinder 2-litre car. Joakim Bonnier retired out on the circuit on the second lap with drive-shaft coupling failure (*Motor Sport*)

*Above:* Victory in the 1964 Targa Florio went to this 904 driven by Colin Davis and Antonio Pucci. The 904 had only just been homologated as a Grand Touring car (*Motor Sport*). *Below:* Private 904 – 'Franc' and Kerguen took 12th place at Le Mans in 1964 with this car

## Le Mans

The 24 Hours race was a battle in which the giants, Ford and Ferrari, destroyed each other; the new 7-litre Mk 2 Fords set an incredibly fast pace, but broke early leaving a new lap record to the credit of Phil Hill in 3 min 37·5 sec; the last of the works Ferraris survived until the Sunday morning and the race then became a battle between two private 275LM Ferraris, the yellow-painted car of Dumay and Gosselin, which led until it burst it right-hand rear tyre and then fell back to finish second, and the red North American Racing Team-entered car of Masten Gregory and Jochen Rindt which covered 2906·23 miles at 121·09 mph. Third was the Ecurie Francorchamps-entered 275GTB of Willy Mairesse and 'Beurlys'. Next came the two surviving Porsches, the expected Dino challenge having faded on lap three when Baghetti brought the sole example entered into the pits with engine trouble. This is how the Porsche entry faired:

H. Linge/P. Nöcker (904 with 6-cylinder engine): finished fourth, having covered 2800·83 miles compared with the winner's 2906·23 miles, and winning the Index of Performance and its class.

C. Davis/G. Mitter (904 with 8-cylinder engine): retired with burnt out clutch.

G. Klass/D. Glempser (904 GTS): retired because of valve trouble.

G. Koch/T. Fischaber (904 GTS): suffered engine trouble in the closing stages of the race, but was pushed over the line to take fifth place, overall, covering 2713·31 miles and winning the Index of Thermal Efficiency.

## Post-Script to The Season

Porsche participated in no further Prototype or Grand Touring races in 1965, but private owners kept the make well to the fore. At the beginning of July, Mike de Udy and Paul Hawkins drove the former's 904 into sixth place in the Rheims 12 Hours race and a fortnight later were the Solitude races. The main event was an 18-lap Formula Two race, but there were two supporting events in which Porsches ran, plus a race for Volkswagen-engined Formula Vee cars. In the 12-lap sports car Preis von Baden Württemberg, two of the 8-cylinder cars of the type used in the European Hill Climb Championship in Group 7 sports/racing trim were driven by Gerhard Mitter and Herbert Linge. These drivers took first and third places, split by Tony Fischaber's Lotus 23 with B.M.W. engine. The 2500 cc G.T. race, the Preis von Stuttgart, was a complete 904 benefit with Ben Pon and Rudolph Stommelen leading home Harder's 2-litre Abarth. At the end of August, Pon won the 125-Km Circuit of Zandvoort. There was no 1000-Km race at Montlhery in 1965, but in the Coupe du Salon 'sprint', Buchet and Meert brought their 904s to the flag behind Ruata's Abarth. The following weekend Stommelen was second to Rindt's Abarth in the Prix du Tyrol at Innsbruck. In short distance races the Italian-built cars of Carlo Abarth were presenting a much strengthened challenge.

In the European Hill Climb Championship, Porsche fielded two of the glass-fibre-bodied flat-eight cars as entered in the Targa Florio and subsequently written off at the Nürburgring. These were driven by Gerhard Mitter and Anton Fischaber and faced stiff opposition from Scarfiotti who drove both open and closed versions of the Dino and Hans Herrmann with a 2-litre Abarth. Mitter was second to Herrmann's Abarth in the 13-mile Mont Ventoux climb in Southern France, but a week later Mitter succeeded in beating the opposition at the German Rossfeld Hill Climb. On 11th July, the Trento-Bordone climb, "the climb of many hairpins", saw the first appearance of the Dino in the hands of the 1962 Champion, Lodovico Scarfiotti. The Italian won this and the next three events in succession. Mitter dropped to third place at Trento-Bordone, beaten by Herrmann's Abarth, and thereafter had to be content to second place to Scarfiotti. The results of the Ollon-Villars climb clinched the Championship for the Italian Ferrari driver.

During the latter months of 1965 Porsche were working feverishly at Stuttgart on a new Grand Touring model that was to strengthen Porsche's hand even further in Group 4 racing the following season.

## TEN
# 1966: Six-Cylinder Competition Cars

*A New Group Four Car*

The Prototype six-cylinder cars raced by Porsche during 1965 had been true prototypes for the new Carrera 6 announced in December of that year, one of the most sophisticated G.T. cars of all time. The power unit was a highly-tuned version of that of the 911 touring car with a capacity of 1991 cc (80 × 66 mm) and a power output of 210 bhp DIN at 8000 rpm – equivalent to an SAE rating of about 240 bhp. Carburation was by a special pair of Weber triple-choke carburettors and the compression ratio was 10·3:1. By racing standards the power range was very wide, between 3500 and 8200 rpm. The engine was mounted immediately behind the driver, well ahead of the rear axle line, and drove through a 5-speed, all-synchromesh gearbox with sliding-spline drive-shafts. A simply enormous range of gear ratios was available and the factory had prepared special sets for the Nürburgring, Le Mans, Monza, aerodrome circuits and hill climbs.

An extremely rigid tubular space-frame chassis was used and the suspension front and rear was typically British Grand Prix-type – double wishbones front and rear, combined coil spring and damper units all round and adjustable anti-roll bars front and rear. The brakes were made by ATE to Dunlop patents, rack-and-pinion steering was fitted and the pressed steel wheels had light alloy rims.

Perhaps the most striking feature of the car was the glass-fibre bodywork. Partly because of the space-frame construction, gull-wing doors were fitted; there was a sharp, clean, penetrating nose-line, a large wrap-round windscreen with the usual Porsche parallelogram single wiper and moulded perspex windows in the door; over the engine was a long, louvred, transparent combined window and cover. At the front there was an air-intake for the alloy oil cooler with its outlet just ahead of the windscreen. The car's overall height was a mere 38½ in – even in 1969 the latest Chevron is 34 in high – and weight, without fuel, at 11 cwt was substantially lower than that of the old 904.

The price of the car ex-factory was 45,000 Dm and by January, 1966 the cars were rolling out of the Stuttgart works. Under the new F.I.A. regulations (referred to below) a production run of 50 was necessary for homologation and these had been completed by May. The first of the production cars went to Porsche Cars Great Britain Ltd, the Aldington Brothers' new Company which had taken over from A.F.N. Ltd all responsibility for Porsches in the United Kingdom. The car was to be driven for the British Concessionaires by Mike de Udy, who had previously raced a 904.

*New Racing Regulations*

Under the F.I.A.'s new Regulations, the term 'Grand Touring' car was supplanted by 'Competition Sports' cars, of which 50 must have been built before homologation. For this category, Group 4, there was a Championship for Manufacturers in three capacity classes: under 1300 cc, 1300-2000 cc and over 2000 cc. In addition there continued to be a Manufacturers' Championship for Group 6 Prototypes, now known as 'Prototype Sports Cars' and not 'Prototype G.T. cars', although they were exactly the same thing. A total of seven races between February (Daytona) and June (Le Mans) – all the established classics – counted towards the Prototype Championship, and so this category of racing was all over by mid-summer. In addition, all these races counted towards two or more classes of the Group 4 Sports Car Championship and after Le Mans a further six Group 4 Championship races were held – but only three of these included the 2000 cc class.

*The American Scene – Daytona and Sebring*

At the beginning of February was the Daytona race, lengthened from 2000 kilometres to 24 hours, which attracted a full team of the very fast and apparently no longer brittle 7-litre Fords. They romped away from the rest of the field – there were no works Ferraris entered – and finished in the three places and fifth. Fourth was the N.A.R.T.-entered Ferrari of Pedro Rodriguez and Mario Andretti. Sixth, but not least, was the new Carrera 6 of Hans

Herrmann, who had returned to the team after a spell with Abarth, and Herbert Linge.

Six weeks later was the Sebring race where a grand total of six works Fords, backed up by seven private cars, were faced by a single works Ferrari, a N.A.R.T-entered Ferrari and two Chaparrals. Next in terms of speed and top in terms of reliability were the Porsches. The single car from Daytona had been joined by another works entry – both had small spoilers at the front – and they were driven by Herrmann/Buzzetta and Mitter/Klass; in addition, three of these new cars were in the hands of private owners. These Carrera 6 entries were backed by a total of five 904s. Porsche's real worry was a solitary Ferrari Dino 206/SP 2-litre car driven by Bandini and Scarfiotti, a very fast and skilful pair of drivers, and this showed its paces in practice by lapping in 3 min and 5 sec, 12th fastest, and faster than all the Stuttgart cars except that of Mitter and Klass, which recorded 3 min 3·6 sec.

And when Governor Haydon Burns of Florida dropped the flag for the Le Mans-type start, it was the amazing Scarfiotti with the amazing Dino that went into the lead and held it for a full half-lap. At lap seven the Dino was still in fourth place, while lower down the field the Porsches droned round with the consistency that was expected to last the full 12 hours. At the end of two hours the Dino was seventh and the highest Porsche ninth. As hour passed hour, so the field depleted; both Chaparrals retired; one of the Comstock-entered Fords crashed, its driver Bob McLean was killed and the other car of the team was withdrawn. The big surprise in the 2-litre class came not from the works Porsches, but from the privately-entered 906 of Patrick and Webster, which was driven with such speed and consistency that it had forged ahead of the Dino to hold fifth place by the six-hour mark. And it was this car that was involved in the worst accident in the 18 years' history of the race. Not long after the circuit had been enveloped in darkness, Mario Andretti spun the N.A.R.T. P2 Ferrari at Webster Turn and bounced off the leading Porsche which was shoved off the track and mowed down a group of spectators who were watching from a forbidden area; four of the onlookers lost their lives.

Shortly afterwards the Dino came into the pits with the gear-lever stuck firmly in top; while this was sorted out its advantage over the first of the works Porsches evaporated from three laps' lead to three laps' deficit. The Dino rejoined the race, but it was unable to make up the deficit. At the finish, although the Klass/Mitter 906 had retired with valve trouble, Porsche, through a combination of speed and reliability, won their class and took four places in the first eight – a strong contrast with the Fords which had fallen by the wayside like swatted flies and had won through sheer weight of numbers.

Results:
1st K. Miles/L. Ruby (Ford Roadster XI), 228 laps (98·631 mph)
2nd W. Hansgen/M. Donohue (Ford Mk. II), 216 laps
3rd P. Revson /S. Scott (Ford GT40), 213 laps
4th H. Herrmann/J. Buzzetta (Porsche 906), 209 laps
5th L. Bandini/L. Scarfiotti (Ferrari Dino), 206 laps
6th C. Voegele/J. Siffert (Porsche 906), 206 laps
7th G. Follmer/P. Gregg (Porsche 904), 205 laps
8th E. Hugus/L. Underwood (Porsche 906), 201 laps

*Monza 1000 Km Race*

As at Sebring, the 906 Porsches had to run in the Prototype class at the Monza race on 25th April as they were not due for homologation until 1st May. Two works 906 cars were backed up by two private cars, and while the Fords and a solitary works 4-litre P3 Ferrari fought out the battle for the top honours, the Stuttgart cars battled out their class with three Dinos. There should have been four of the pretty little Maranello cars which looked like scaled-down versions of their big brothers, the P3s, but Bob Bondurant left the road with one in practice. The race was run in atrociously wet conditions, but the Porsches handled superbly. Although Colin Davis had a minor collision with another competitor on the first lap, and lost time at the pits while the car was checked, the other works 906 driven by Mitter and Herrmann had a completely troublefree run and provided a challenge to the whole field apart from the all-conquering P3 Ferrari of John Surtees and Mike Parkes. Mitter and Herrmann took the chequered flag in fourth place and covered 98 laps of the 6·214-mile circuit compared wth the winner's full 100. Fifth was the private Swiss-entered car of Formula One driver Jo Siffert and Charles Voegele and seventh was the works car of Davis/Glemser. The Dino challenge faded early in the race and the highest placed to finish was the car of Bandini and Scarfiotti in tenth spot.

## The Targa Florio

A charming and enthralling chaos surrounds scrutineering and practice for the Targa Florio and this attained a peak at the 1966 race. For scrutineering was plagued by the necessity that Group 4 cars should be registered for road use, and appear at scrutineering complete with number plates and log books. These rules evoked endless arguments and resulted in the transfer of the Porsche Great Britain 906 driven by Mike de Udy and Peter de Klerk to the Prototype class. There were a total of five works Porsches entered and the team turned up in force with impressive array of transporters, a mobile workshop and a radio communications team for race control. So anxious were Porsche to score a victory that they had visited Sicily a few weeks before the race for an unofficial testing session and to try out the Bosch fuel injection. A new development was a 906 powered by a 2·2-litre flat-eight engine, a development of that used in the 904 Prototypes of 1964-65, and this was driven by Günther Klass and Colin Davis. Two 906s, fitted with fuel injection and running in the Prototype class, were driven by Gerhard Mitter and Joakim Bonnier and Hans Herrmann and Dieter Glemser. In the Sports category ran two normal 906s, the works-entered car of Pucci/Arena and one loaned to the Scuderia Filipinetti, who entrusted it to Mairesse/Müller and also entered two of their own 906s.

With the failure of either Chaparral or Ford to appear, the main opposition came, as usual, from S.E.F.A.C. Ferrari who fielded a 4-litre P3 for Vaccarella and Bandini and 2-litre Dinos for Parkes/Scarfiotti and Guichet/Baghetti. Practice provided consternation for Ferrari, for Targa hero Vaccarella was beaten on time by young Günther Klass with the 8-cylinder Porsche and, to the accompaniment of howling tyres and flying dust and stones, Mike Parkes shot off the road and stuffed the Dino into a clump of trees. This meant a great deal of work for the long suffering Ferrari mechanics, but they managed to get the car ready in time to run.

To make adequate safety precautions on such a long, natural road circuit was out of the question and so the organisers contented themselves with pasting up warning posters all round the circuit with such ominous messages as, "Don't throw fruit or paper on the road – they may cause can accident". In fact the Targa Florio is not a dangerous course for drivers, as most of the very many accidents happen at low speed and are, in the insurance sense, 'damage only' and the local inhabitants have the good sense to watch without getting in the way. Additional hazards in the 1966 race had been the feverish attempts with both shovel and broom and proper tar-laying equipment to carry out re-surfacing while the cars were being scrutineered – but the combination of the hot sun and unofficial practising had largely frustrated the work. Torrential rain on the Saturday, from midday to midnight, had completed the undoing of the circuit preparations and an avalanche of mud and stones had been washed all over the roads. Gangs of labourers were sent out urgently to clear the chaos before the race.

While some of the later starters were still moving off, Mike de Udy had already crashed the brand new British Racing Green 906 of Porsche Great Britain! At the end of the first lap, Vaccarella, as anticipated, was leading on time from the Porsche of Mitter and the Dino of Scarfiotti. Mitter was getting really wound up with the fuel-injection 906 and took the lead on the second lap. After the delays and confusion of refuelling stops, Klass with the 8-cylinder Porsche went into the lead – he had refuelled out in the mountains to avoid the crowded pits area – from Bandini (who had taken over from Vaccarella), Bonnier (from Mitter) and Parkes (from Scarfiotti). Scattered rain was falling round the circuit, the road was treacherously slippery and even those cars that did not bear the scars of contact with solid objects had been battered by flying stones and all were covered with mud.

Parkes had staggered into the Bivio Polizzi "outpost" with petrol pouring out of the tail of the Dino, he took on extra fuel and accelerated away leaving a trail of fuel down the road. Vaccarella was back in the P3 and back in the lead on time – when he handed back to Bandini, the Formula One driver lost ground and the Porsche 8-cylinder went into the lead again. Parkes left the road with the Dino, smashing the rear of the car and buckling a wheel; at Bivio Polizzi the Ferrari mechanics tore off a few bits of battered bodywork and tried, without success, to force the engine cover down; Parkes went off in an attempt to reach the main pits with the Dino, but it was obvious from the way in which the rear end of the car was dancing about that there was something seriously wrong with the suspension. The Dino did not come round again! The next two laps saw the elimination of the two race leaders. On lap seven Bandini with the P3 Ferrari was about to pass a GTO Ferrari when its driver gave him a signal which was supposed to mean "wait", but which, in accordance with normal racing practice, Bandini had interpreted as 'come on'. the inevitable result was that the two cars collided and the P3 shot off the road and into a tree. A bleeding Bandini returned to the pits as a passenger in a very cumpled GTO. A lap later the left-hand rear suspension of the 8-cylinder Porsche tore away from the chassis and the wheel collapsed under the car – the result of a collison between Colin Davis and team-mate Mitter whose 906 was forced off the road!

The race was now, to all intents and purposes, over; Ferrari had failed and Porsche was again the victor. Six Carrera 906 Porsches had started in the Sports class of the 1966 Targa Florio and four had finished – a magnificent performance in this car-destroying race. But the same could not be said for the Prototypes, all three of which had fallen by the wayside and it was as much to Porsche's shame as to their pride that their victory should have been won by the Scuderia Filipinetti team. Who was the least popular man in Sicily that night? Without doubt, Signor Reale, the GTO driver who had put out of the race the car driven by the Sicilians' beloved Nino Vaccarella! Results:

1st W. Mairesse/H. Müller (Porsche 906), 7 hr 16 min 32·6 sec (61·47 mph)
2nd J. Guichet/G. Baghetti (Ferrari Dino), 7 hr 25 min 2·2 sec
3rd A. Pucci/V. Arena (Porsche 906), 7 hr 34 min 8·0 sec
4th E. Pinto/N. Todaro (Alfa Romeo Giulia TZ)
5th R. Bouillot/U. Maglioli (Porsche 906)
6th R. de Lageneste/J. Rosinski (Alpine-Renault 1300 coupé)

*Spa 1000 Km Race*

The 1000 Km race on the very fast Spa-Francorchamps circuit was one of the few races in recent years that have gone seriously wrong for Porsche. A few miles to the east of Liége, the Spa circuit is set in a wooded valley and with its wide roads and fast corners (except for the hairpin at La Source and the bridge a few hundred yards from the start) is one of the fastest circuits in Europe. It was speed that was the downfall of the works 906s of Hans Herrmann/Dieter Glemser (this car was on fuel injection) and Udo Schütz and Gerhard Koch. There should have been a third works car running, but in practice its rear body section came adrift, the car left the road and was completely demolished, and Mitter was lucky to escape with cuts and a fractured knee. In the race the works and private 906s fought furiously with each other and the Dinos instead of following their usual pre-arranged plan of running steadily and the result was almost inevitable. The Schütz/Koch works car broke its engine after being taken a thousand rpm above the limit and Hans Herrmann's car lost a wheel. The race became a complete Ferrari benefit, with outright victory going to the P3 of Parkes and Scarfiotti and the 2000 cc class to the Dino of Attwood and Guichet.

*Nürburgring 1000 Km Race*

The Nürburgring race was the second event in succession in which Porsche results differed substantially from their plans. Five cars were fielded and von Hanstein had a worrying practice session sorting out his drivers. The eventual Porsche line-up was:

906 with 2·2-litre 8-cyl engine: Jochen Rindt/Nino Vaccarella (the Ferrari stalwart was the last man one would expect to see at the wheel of a Porsche!)
906s with fuel injection:
   H. Herrmann/D. Glemser
   O. Schütz/G. Klass
   R. Bondurant/P. Hawkins
Standard 906: J. P. Beltoise (the very successful Matra driver)/P. Nöcker (who used to drive Jaguars with the late Peter Lindner).

Prime contenders for outright victory were the works 4-litre open P3 Ferrari driven by John Surtees and Mike Parkes and the neat, sleek coupé Chaparral 5·3-litre 2D distinguished by its roof-top air scoop and driven by Phil Hill and Joakim Bonnier. The American car was making its European debut and in the hands of such competent *pilotes* its chances of success were high indeed. In the 2-litre class the Porsches faced stiff opposition from three Ferrari Dinos, a works car on fuel injection driven by Scarfiotti and Bandini, the North American Racing Team-owned, but works maintained car of Pedro Rodriguez and Richie Ginther, and the British Maranello Concessionaires' car of David Piper and Dickie Attwood. There were 77 starters and slap in the middle of the line-up arranged according to practice times was a 904 Porsche loaned to a German TV company and driven, complete with TV equipment, by Paul Frère, one-time Ferrari and Jaguar driver. His time of 9 min 36 sec was 26th fastest!

The P3 went straight into the lead on the first lap, two laps later the Chaparral was in second place – and gained the lead when the Ferrari came into the pits to change a collapsed suspension unit. The Porsches were unable to keep up with the second-place works Dino and by half-distance the Stuttgart cars were beginning to crack under the stiff pace of the race. South African Peter de Klerk put the green Porsche Great Britain 906 into a ditch and it was too badly damaged for him to be able to continue; the Filipinetti 906 of Siffert and Voegele broke its chassis; the works 8-cylinder car was falling further and further back because of a slipping clutch and eventually retired brakeless; the Beltoise/Nöcker 906 ploughed through the undergrowth and removed most of its right-hand wheel-arch; and the Schütz/Klass 906 was abandoned out on the circuit with a broken drive-shaft. With three quarters of the race run, rain started to fall and soon the circuit was being inundated by a torrential rainstorm. The works P3 was abandoned with transmission failure and the Chaparral, still in the lead, slithered its way round the long, tortuous circuit, while the mechanics cut some special rain tyres in the pits. When the rain was at its heaviest Glemser put his 906 into a ditch. The Chaparral came into the pits to fit the new tyres and while it did so the second-place Dino made up a lot of ground; but Hill was away, still in the lead and went on to win by a margin of 41 secs. The Dinos were second and third and the highest placed Porsche, the 906 of Bob Bondurant and Paul Hawkins, was in fourth place. Porsche's only real consolation from this sound thrashing was the Group 4 class victory by the orange Racing Team Holland car of the van Lenneps which finished seventh.

*Le Mans*

From the Porsche point of view it was just as well that the main interest at the Sarthe circuit was centred on the struggle between Ford and Ferrari and that the Porsches lacked the speed to challenge for outright victory. There was therefore no encouragement for the drivers to push their cars flat out in an attempt to gain major honours and the chances of another Spa débâcle were much reduced. Zuffenhausen fielded fuel-injection 906s for Davis/Siffert, Linge/Herrmann and de Klerk/Schütz together with a standard 906 for Klass/Stommelen.

The 1966 race was remarkable for the short time in which the Ferrari challenge disappeared. By 5 pm, an hour after the start, Ford were in the first three places and the Porsches were leading the 2-litre class; the highest placed Ferrari was the 330/P3 of Rodriguez and Ginther in fourth position and of the Dinos, two had already retired and the third was on the way out. By 8 am on the Sunday morning, the last of the P3 Ferraris had expired because of an internal water leak and a slipping clutch, Fords were still in the first three places and behind them lay a solid phalanx of five Porsches. At 2 pm rain started to fall and within minutes the circuit was soaking. The entire field eased off no one wanting to risk anything silly happening with so little of the race left to run. With barely $1\frac{1}{4}$ hours to the finish, there was panic in the Porsche pits when the works-assisted 906 of Gregg and Axelson coasted in with a dead engine; the cause was broken valve gear and a failure of this sort was the last thing expected after such a strong display of reliability by the Stuttgart cars. The car rejoined the race on three of its six cylinders, but it was unable to make it to the finish.

Just as the three Fords lined up to take the chequered flag together, so the four remaining Porsches grouped for the finish to take fourth to seventh places in an impressive display of reliability that even bettered any of their previous fine efforts. It was probably the most outstanding display of reliability combined with speed seen in any post-war Le Mans race except for 1953 when the complete Jaguar team finished intact and took first, second and fourth places. The fourth-place car also won the Index of Performance – which meant equal prize money with the winner – and the seventh-place car was the victor in the Group 4 sports category. Results:

1st B. McLaren/C. Amon (Ford Mk 2), 3003·7 miles (126·01 mph)
2nd K. Miles/D. Hulme (Ford Mk 2)
3rd R. Bucknum/R. Hutcherson (Ford Mk 2)
4th C. Davis/J. Siffert (Porsche 906)
5th H. Herrmann/H. Linge (Porsche 906)
6th U. Schütz/P. de Klerk (Porsche 906)
7th G. Klass/R. Stommelen (Porsche 906)
8th R. Pike/P. Courage (Ferrari 275GTB)

*Post-Script To The Season*

Porsche, despite their failures at Spa and the Nürburgring, had won the Prototype Championship outright. Although Porsche with the 906 were undisputed victors in the 2000 cc class of the Group 4

Sports Car Championship, there were still three rounds to be run (including the Nürburgring 500 Km race which was limited to cars of 1300 cc). The first race was the difficult and hazardous Circuit of Mugello held over a distance of 329 miles on 17th July. This long road circuit was fast and dangerous and there were few safety precautions taken to protect drivers, but it was a race very much in the same spirit as the Targa Florio and the lamented Mille Miglia and it was a great shame that it attracted such a poor entry. What entries there were, were further depleted by the withdrawal of the works Ferraris and the Autodelta team of Alfa Romeo saloons because of strikes in Italy. But strikes or not, the organisers were determined to hold the race and some compensation for the paucity of the field was derived by the rather bizarre idea of running a Formula Three race simultaneously with the first two laps of the main event. The race was scheduled to start at 1 pm, the start was put back to 2 pm, brought forward again and finally the first Formula Three car departed at 1.15 pm. And Mugello weather is such that at one stage in the race, the long mountainous circuit was, in different parts, simultaneously bathed in sunshine, soaked by torrential rain and overlaid by a thick mist. Let the fancy, modern tyre experts with their complex compounds sort that one out! Victory went to the works Porsche 906 of Koch and Neerpasch from a pair of privately entered Alfa Romeo Giulia GTA saloons – these were, in fact, Autodelta cars loaned so that the works drivers could run as private entrants and were motoring much faster than could be reasonably expected of any small saloon!

At Zeltweg on 11th September yet another Porsche victory was recorded and 906s took the first three places; Mitter/Herrmann led home Siffert and Schütz/Linge. No works cars as such ran in the Montlhéry 1000 Km race on October 16th, but works mechanics were there to help the private owners. The opening lap of the race was chaotic with sliding cars everywhere, the result of a large pool of oil dropped by someone on the warming up lap and not noticed by the marshals. None of the Porsches was eliminated, although Koch's 906 collided with the Matra-B.R.M. of Beltoise and this Porsche retired with mechanical trouble in the closing laps of the race. Günther Klass, who was sharing a 906 with Buchet, finished up in the back of the car when he put the brakes on hard – the seat was not properly fixed – and crashed. Winners of the race were David Piper and Mike Parkes with the Maranello Concessionaires' Ferrari

275LM, but the 906 Porsche of Jean-Pierre Hanrioud and André Wicky took an excellent second place.

All in all, despite two notable failures, it had been a brilliant season for Porsche and included another victory in the European Hill Climb Championship. Victory in this went to Gerhard Mitter who drove an 8-cylinder car and won outright five of the seasons' seven events. Second place in the Championship went to Scarfiotti at the wheel of a Dino and third was Hans Herrmann who drove both 6- and 8-cylinder Porsches during the hill climb year.

ELEVEN

# 1967: A Season Of Unlimited Success

Since the start of Prototype racing in 1962, the Porsche star had been in the ascendant. 1962 had seen the company bogged down by the problems – practical, technical and administrative – of competing in two categories of racing at the same time and although the abandonment of the Formula One programme at the end of that season had allowed Porsche to concentrate all their efforts on Prototype racing, the 1963 cars had not been the epitome of reliability and had displayed engine and transmission weaknesses not expected of the Stuttgart team. It was with the introduction of the 904 that the almost legendary Porsche reliability of the 'fifties reasserted itself. The rules relating to the homologation of Grand Touring cars were ideally suited to a limited production factory of considerable technical resource and it was a situation of which Porsche took full advantage; the company completely dominated the market for these cars up to 2000 cc and completely dominated their racing category. In 1966, when Stuttgart was racing the 906, the team had enjoyed its best season ever, By 1967 the variations on the 906 theme raced by the works had speed to match their reliability and on all but the fastest circuits they were to be reckoned with as possible overall race winners and 1967 was to prove an even greater year of Porsche triumph.

*Daytona 24 Hours*

Although the Chaparral, complete with high-mounted aerofoil and driven by Phil Hill and Mike Spence, galloped away from the rest of the field at the start of the race, a minor accident as the car was coming off the banking damaged the rear suspension and brought about its retirement. The Fords were plagued by gearbox trouble and Ferraris took the first three places. The performance of the Porsches in this race verged on the fantastic. Fourth overall and winning its class was the new 910 model in the hands of Jo Siffert and Hans Herrmann. This covered 618 laps of the circuit compared with the winning Ferraris' 666. The 910 was a new Prototype based on the 906, and in many ways it was similar to the car used by Mitter to win the 1966 European Hill Climb Championship; the engine had twin overhead camshafts per bank of cylinders; the chassis was much lighter than that of the 906; the body was much lower, and 13 in magnesium wheels were fitted. Two other Porsches were running as Prototypes, both 906s on Bosch fuel injection; that of Jochen Rindt and Gerhard Mitter retired when the German driver damaged the rear suspension in a minor accident – much to the Austrian's unconcealed annoyance; the other Prototype 906, driven by Udo Schütz and Gijs van Lennep, was eliminated by a bent valve after sand had jammed the thottle mechanism. Fifth was the ex-works 906 of Rico Steinemann and Dieter Spoerry, ahead of the Group 4 Ford GT40 of Ickx and Thompson. Magnificent though the performance of the leading Porsche was, it was but a foretaste of the fine performances Porsche Prototypes were to put up during the remainder of the season.

## Sebring 12 Hours

Held on 1st April, slightly later than in previous years, the Sebring race had been made faster by the substitution in the 5·2-mile circuit of a couple of high-speed swerves for the difficult corner known as Webster Turn. Porsche was no longer facing opposition in the 2-litre class only from the Ferrari Dinos, but a team of two of the new V-8 Alfa Romeo Tipo 33 cars was making its debut – and the 33 of de Adamich and Zeccoli was fractionally faster in practice than the fastest of the works Porsches – 3 min 0·6 sec compared with 3 min 1·0 sec. No works Ferraris were entered and after the retirements of the Chaparral team and the Alfas, Porsches filled third, fourth, sixth and seventh places at the finish, behind two 7-litre Fords and split by the Group 4 Ford GT40 of Maglioli and Vaccarella. The second-place Ford came into the pits 30 minutes before the end of the race where a broken camshaft was diagnosed. And there it stayed while the Porsche of Gerhard Mitter and Scooter Patrick drew closer and closer on distance and as the minutes passed seemed increasingly likely to take second place. Although the Ford never

Two prominent Grand Prix drivers who are regular members of the Porsche team are Jo Siffert (*above*) and Vic Elford (*below*) who in 1968 became a member of the Cooper works team (Nigel Snowdon)

*Above:* The Maglioli/Linge Prototype 904 with 6-cylinder engine which took third place in the 1965 race passes through a Sicilian village (*Motor Sport*). *Below:* This 6-cylinder car of Herbert Linge and Peter Nöcker took fourth place in the 1965 Le Mans race (*Motor Sport*)

rejoined the race, it was held by the stewards to have covered a slightly greater distance than the Porsche and retained its second place. This is how the first eight cars finished:

1st B. McLaren/M. Andretti (Ford Mk 4), 238 laps (103·133 mph)
2nd A. J. Foyt/L. Ruby (Ford Mk 2), 226 laps
3rd G. Mitter/S. Patrick (Porsche 910), 226 laps
4th H. Herrmann/J. Siffert (Porsche 910), 223 laps
5th U. Maglioli/N. Vaccarella (Ford GT4O), 223 laps
6th D. Spoerry/R. Steinemann (Porsche 906), 218 laps
7th J. Buzzetta/P. Gregg (Porsche 906), 215 laps
8th W. McNamara/R. Grossmann (Ford GT40), 214 laps

Four works Porsches started, three finished and the make took the team prize. The works car not to take the chequered flag was the 906 of Schütz/van Lennep which hit a large dog and was so badly damaged that it had to be withdrawn.

## The Le Mans Test Days

Of the two days set aside for practice, Saturday the 8th April was dry and cold, but the Sunday was so wet that the cars just splashed round with the drivers looking miserable. Porsche brought along two Prototypes, both with new bodies and known as the 907. The driver sat very close to the centre of the car and the rounded roof was as narrow as possible; this necessitated a very narrow, deep screen and an elaborate double-decker wiper. The rear windows had exceptionally large louvres for fresh air extraction. Both cars were running on Bosch fuel injection, on the one into the ports and the other having the injectors at the entry to the ramming pipes. Of these two cars, one had a brand new and completely untried long tail. A result of this was that the drivers were affected by carbon monoxide poisoning and so long exhaust megaphones were hastily added as an afterthought. The Porsches made no efforts to set up any really fast laps and Mitter's 4 min 23·8 sec was all of 27·1 sec slower than de Adamich with the Alfa Tipo 33.

## Monza 1000 Km Race

Just over three weeks after Sebring, 41 cars set off in a two-by-two rolling start at Monza to race against each other for a fast and furious 1000 kilometres. In the battle for outright victory there were only three serious contenders, the Chaparral and two works P4 Ferraris. The Chaparral retired after an hour's racing and the Ferraris then had the race in the bag. When Nino Vaccarella spun the Ferrari P3/4 he was driving for the Scuderia Filipinetti team, he was passed by the two works Porsche 910s; with three laps to go to the chequered flag, the front suspension of Siffert's 910 collapsed under the pounding it had received from the bumpy banking and Jo struggled to the finish with a car possessing almost non-existent steering. The third-place 910 of Rindt and Mitter was four laps behind the winning Ferraris and Herrmann and Siffert, who finished fifth having lost a place in the last couple of laps to the Filipinetti Ferrari, had covered 95 of the full 100 circuits.

*Spa 1000 Km Race*

For the second 1000-kilometre European race, Porsche again sent along two 910s, but different cars from those raced at Monza. At Spa they were driven by Herrmann/Siffert and Koch/Mitter. Private 906s were in the hands of Swiss drivers Spoerry/Steinemann (this was an ex-works car running in the Prototype class), Roy Pike/Colin Davis (with Mike de Udy's car), Pon/van Lennep (entered by the Racing Team Holland) and Hubert/Peter. The Dutch Porsche, however, non-started because of an unpleasant accident in practice when the tail section blew open, the driver lost control and the car crashed badly. When the small entry of 29 cars lined up for the start, it had been raining all morning, the track was saturated and it continued raining throughout the race. Such conditions certainly favoured Porsche prospects of a high overall placing and the 910 of Siffert/Herrmann was able to stay ahead of even the works P4 Ferrari of Mike Parkes and Scarfiotti. It was, however, no match for the John Wyer-entered Ford Mirage or the Equipe Nationale Belge P3/4 Ferrari both of which had number one drivers who knew the circuit intimately. When Willy Mairesse crashed the yellow Ferrari, the Porsche moved up into second place and that was where it finished, a lap behind the winning Mirage of Ickx and Thompson. Third was the Attwood/Bianchi P3/4 Ferrari of Maranello Concessionaries and fifth the Lola-Chevrolet of Hawkins and Epstein. The other works 910 of Mitter and Koch took seventh place.

## Targa Florio

Porsche were really determined to win the Targa Florio yet again and arrived in Sicily for the 51st race in the series with a total of six cars, three of which were of a type not raced before. These combined the now familiar 910 body and chassis with the 2195 cc flat-eight engine, still based on the old 1962 Grand Prix unit, but much developed and improved, running on Bosch fuel injection and generally as used in the 1966 Prototypes. Externally, the new cars, still typed the 910, could only be distinguished by their single large exhaust in place of the dual exhausts of the sixes and by the behaviour of the drivers. The eights proved comparatively quiet inside the cockpit, whereas the sixes created such a shattering row that the drivers – even wearing ear-plugs – were deafened and for a long time after they had been driving went around shouting at people. The three 8-cylinder cars, running in the unlimited Prototype class, were driven by Mitter/Davis, Herrmann/Siffert and Hawkins/Stommelen. Because of Stommelen's height this car ran with the roof panel removed. Facing the Porsches was a solitary Chaparral in the hands of Phil Hill and Hap Sharp, an equally solitary P4 Ferrari driven by local hero and Targa maestro Vaccarella partnered by Scarfiotti and a Filipinetti-entered P3/4 for Müller and that very skilful, but underrated, French driver Jean Guichet.

In the 2-litre Prototype class Porsche had entered three fuel-injection 910s for Cella/Biscaldi, Neerpasch/Elford and Maglioli/Schütz. Their main opponents were the Scuderia Autodelta-entered Alfa Tipo 33s which were also strong challengers for outright victory. Four of these cars were entered and were making their first real competition appearance, for Sebring had been more in the nature of a test run. These Alfas were running splendidly apart from an unfortunate tendency to discard the front suspension and wheel and so each of the 33s was fitted with a wire-cable safety device to prevent the hub from detaching itself completely. In addition, from Ferrari came an 18-valve, fuel-injection Dino driven by Casoni and the young Günther Klass who had fallen out with the Porsche team.

Two changes had taken place since the 1966 race. A great deal of resurfacing had been done and many of the old bumps had been ironed out – specifically to prevent the faster cars from taking off with all four wheels, a particularly lethal happening in a bend or curve and the cause of many crashes in the past. Practising on the

Friday was compulsory, whereas, in the past, it had been purely optional and the official times revealed what a tough struggle Porsche had if they were to win:

> Vaccarella (Ferrari P4): 37 min 12·4 sec
> Scarfiotti (Ferrari P4): 37 min 53·6 sec
> Klass (Ferrari Dino): 38 min 13 sec – a very fine effort allegedly inspired by the desire to "needle" his former boss Huschke von Hanstein
> Cella (Porsche): 38 min 34 sec
> Hill (Chaparral): 38 min 39·6 sec
> de Adamich (Alfa Romeo): 38 min 46·4 sec

It seemed that nothing would stop the P4 from romping to victory and if the signs dotted on walls and roads all round the course and reading "Viva la P4" were anything to go by, it would be a popular victory. And it was Vaccarella who led on the first lap from Mitter and Müller with the P3/4, but then the Sicilian did it all wrong in the middle of the village of Collesano under the gaze of hundreds of his supporters and crunched the P4 into a low stone wall on a 30 mph hairpin bend. On the same lap Mitter stuffed his 910 into a ditch and the little Swiss driver Herbert Müller found himself in the lead. Already the Porsche pit was in a state of agitation, for Paul Hawkins did not seem at all happy at the wheel of his 8-cylinder car and the Herrmann/Siffert car had been slowed by gear-change trouble. Müller was still dominating the race when he came into hand over to Guichet and by the time Hawkins had handed over to Stommelen he had got the 8-cylinder Porsche really well wound up and had started to close the gap. Guichet was motoring slower than his co-driver and Stommelen drew nearer and nearer. One of the Alfa 33s was out of the race already and the Autodelta leading car was being caught by Schütz' Porsche; seventh was the Chaparral, being carefully driven as the team wanted no accidents before Le Mans.

Then occurred the almost inevitable Targa Florio carnage and three retirements in quick succession gave the Porsches first three places and allowed the Chaparral to move up to fourth spot. By the time Müller had taken over the P3/4 again, it had been caught and passed by the leading Porsche and before he had completed a single lap, the Ferrari ran its back axle and ground its way back to the pits to retire. On lap eight the Porsche of Schütz, which had passed

Rolland's Alfa on time, broke its gearbox and the Tipo 33 went out with the suspension failure that had eliminated the rest of the team. One more lap passed and the Chaparral was out – a rear tyre punctured and by the time Sharp had stopped, all that was left was a mess of rubber tangled round the wheel; as the spare was for the front and would not fit the back, he had no alternative but to retire.

So Porsche were safely ensconced in the first three places and that was how they finished. Towards the end of the race the oppressive heat in the Porsche cockpit had caused Paul Hawkins to feel very unwell, but he was physically sick in the cockpit and then felt a lot better. A particularly fine drive was that of Vic Elford, the rally driver who was taking part in his first serious motor race and who had created just as good an impression with the 910 as he had with a 911 in saloon car races. Results:

1st P. Hawkins/R. Stommelen (Porsche 910 8-cyl), 6 hr 37 min 1 sec (67·61 mph)
2nd L. Cella/G. Biscaldi (Porsche 910)
3rd J. Neerpasch/V. Elford (Porsche 910)
4th V. Venturi/J. Williams (Ferrari Dino)
5th H. Greder/J. M. Giorgi (Ford GT40)
6th H. Herrmann/J. Siffert (Porsche 910 8-cyl)

*Nürburgring 1000 Km Race*

With an aloofness that his prestige, shattered by Ford, hardly justified, Ferrari did not bother to make a proper entry at the Nürburgring, but under pressure from young Günther Klass, anxious to run on home territory, he sent along a 2·4-litre Dino for him to share with Jean Guichet; there were no works Fords entered and by the time the Dino had broken its engine in practice and American Dick Thompson had crashed one of the Mirages, Porsche chances of outright victory had substantially improved! Once again Porsche entered a grand total of six cars and serious opposition was limited to a solitary Chaparral, the remaining Mirage and the Lola-Aston Martin which was making its race debut and was a very unknown quantity. The Porsche entry consisted of three 8-cylinder 910s for Mitter/Lucien Bianchi, Herrmann/Siffert and Stommelen/Ahrens (the latter a steady but unspectacular Formula Two driver) and three 6-cylinder 910s for Schütz/Buzzetta, Neerpasch/Elford and Hawkins/ Koch. From seven German drivers and five foreigners, von Hanstein had carefully arranged his team so that each car had at least one German driver.

Opposition to the 910s in the 2-litre class came only from the Alfa 33s, but even the fastest driver of these, the young bespectacled law student Andreas de Adamich, was not quick enough to beat the Porsche lap times. There *should* have been opposition from another Dino – a works 18-valve 2-litre car on loan – entered by the Scuderia Filipinetti, but it caught fire and was badly damaged in practice.

At the Le Mans start 69 cars were lined up and a few seconds after the starter, who at the Nürburgring takes up a position halfway along the line so that everyone can see him, had dropped the flag, 66 of them were away. The three left on the line were three of the potential winners – Phil Hill who spent a long time strapping himself into the safety harness of the Chaparral, John Surtees because of magneto trouble with the Lola-Aston Martin and Jacky Ickx who was also having safety harness trouble with the Mirage. At the end of lap one it was Porsches in the first five places with the Chaparral, headlamps ablaze, thundering close behind them; on that first lap Hill had overtaken over 30 cars, passing them left and right and on more than one occasion forcing the Chaparral between a pair of slow runners. By the end of lap two Hill had passed three of the leading Porsche team cars and already he had lapped some of the slowest runners. He was ahead of everyone except Siffert at the end of lap four and seemed content to stay there, but the truth of the matter was that Phil had miscounted the number of Porsches he had passed and thought that he was leading the race. He went on deluding himself for several laps and made derisive gestures at the frantic signals displayed by his pit. Hill eventually woke up to the fact that he was wrong and that the pit was right and he took the lead from Siffert at the start of lap nine.

The Porsche team now held second to sixth places plus eighth and were split only by young Belgian Jacky Ickx with the Mirage – and it must be conceded that these high placings were attributable as much to the drivers' intimate knowledge of the circuit, the result of constant testing there, as to the performance of the cars. At the end of lap 11 the Chaparral headed for the pits, but the German spectators' cheers turned to groans when the leading Porsche did the same thing. Mike Spence took over the Chaparral; as the revs of the tremendous 7-litre engine rose and the torque converter transmitted the power to

## 1967: A SEASON OF UNLIMITED SUCCESS

the automatic gearbox, the car gave an explosive bang and stalled; this happened once more and then the car moved off, but Spence realised that the Chaparral had shot its bolt and crept round to the back of the pits to the accompaniment of an excruciating tearing noise from the transmission and the groans of the many thousands of American service-men who had come to watch the race. Herrmann had taken over the leading Porsche from Siffert, but this car had run its race, overtaxed in its efforts to retain the lead, and Herrmann came into the pits to retire with a wrecked engine.

The 5·7-litre Mirage had worked its way up to third place by the time Jacky Ickx, exhausted by the cockpit heat and the strain of controlling this unwieldy brute on the now slippery track, came in to hand over to Dickie Attwood. The Mirage rejoined the race, but 1964 and 1968 B.R.M. driver Attwood could make no impression on the leading Porsches. Lap 30 saw the Mirage expire out on the circuit with two nearside flat tyres and the Lola-Aston had retired long ago because of a broken wishbone. The Porsches were safely holding the first four places, but all was not well with the team. The engine of the leading 910 of Mitter/Bianchi was spluttering and misfiring, the result of a flat battery, and a pit stop was made for this to be changed. This was only the start of the Stuttgart team's troubles, for the Stommelen/Ahrens 8-cylinder car retired with fuel injection trouble and the Neerpasch/Elford 910 slowed right off in the closing laps because of a broken valve and lost a place to teammates Hawkins/Koch – and this car, because of a suspension defect, was handling atrociously! With less than half a lap to the finish the leading 8-cylinder car with Mitter at the wheel expired out on the circuit through rapid discharging of its new battery, but had covered sufficient laps to be classified fourth. Despite this catalogue of mechanical disasters, the Porsche team had scored a magnificent, sweeping victory and had now won the same number of rounds in the Prototype Championship as Ferrari. The privately entered sixth-place 906 won its class and maximum points in the Group 4 GT Championship. Results:

1st U. Schütz/J. Buzzetta (Porsche 910), 44 laps in 6 hr 54 min 12·9 sec (91·41 mph)
2nd P. Hawkins/G. Koch (Porsche 910)
3rd J. Neerpasch/V. Elford (Porsche 910)
4th G. Mitter/L. Bianchi (Porsche 8-cyl 910), 1 lap in arrears

5th A. de Adamich/Nanni "Galli"/R. Bussinello/T. Zeccoli (Alfa Romeo Tipo 33), 1 lap in arrears
6th H. D. Dechent/R. Huhn (Porsche 906), 2 laps in arrears

*Le Mans*

All eyes at Le Mans were centred on the titanic struggle between Ford and Ferrari, a struggle in which the two Chaparrals could well be forceful interlopers. But there were experts who thought that the struggle between the big bangers would be so intense and create such devastating mechanical failure that a Porsche could come through to win. Well aware of their inability to challenge for the lead on such a fast circuit where lap speeds in excess of 140 mph were attained, Porsche did not enter any of the 2·2 litre 8-cylinder cars, but concentrated on security in the 2-litre classes, both Prototypes and Group 4 Sports. This is how the works Porsches entry was made up:

*Prototypes*
Normal 910s (left-hand drive with central gear-change):
Stommelen/Neerpasch
Schütz/Buzzetta
907s (the long-tailed narrow-bodied cars as seen at the test week-end, with right-hand drive and gear-change and, like the 910s, with the latest Porsche magnesium wheels):
Rindt/Mitter
Herrmann/Siffert

*Group 4 Sports Cars*
Normal 906s:
Elford/Pon
Poirot/Koch

With the last-minute withdrawal of the Autodelta team of Alfa 33s and all the Dino Ferraris, opposition was limited to the Matra-B.R.M.s, exceedingly fast cars, but of unproven stamina, and their challenge faded early in the race.

In the opening hours the race was completely dominated by the anticipated Ford-Ferrari struggle and the Chaparral of Phil Hill and Mike Spence was mixing it with them and holding a more than satisfactory seventh place. By 7 pm, three hours after the start, the

*Above:* Sebring, 1966: fourth place went to the 906 2-litre 6-cylinder car of Herrmann and Buzzetta (*Motor Sport*). *Below:* Nürburgring, 1966: fourth place again, for the 906 of Bob Bondurant and Paul Hawkins. This was the best the team could manage and was disappointing for Porsche (Nigel Snowdon)

Porsche gained their seventh win in eleven years in the 1967 Targa Florio. The 910 with 2.2-litre engine of Paul Hawkins and Rolf Stommelen won at record speed (*Motor Sport*)

highest placed Porsche, that of Herrmann and Siffert, was lying in 14th place, lapping with a tireless regularity that suggested that it could still be going round just as fast a week later, and was leading the Index of Performance. All through the night the fight between Detroit and Maranello went on and by 3 am three Fords led the Ferrari of Scarfiotti and Parkes and the Chaparral. As the false dawn flickered just before 4 am and the air had a crispness that penetrated the warmest clothing, disaster struck the Ford team. Mario Andretti, swooping down from the Dunlop Bridge to the Esses, had a brake lock up, spun and hit the wall; Schlesser and McCluskey both crashed their 7-litre Fords into the wall as they took avoiding action. The order was now Ford (Gurney/Foyt) – Ferrari (Scarfiotti/Parkes) – Chaparral (Spence/Hill) – Ferrari (Mairesse/'Beurlys') – Ferrari (Klass/Sutcliffe) – Ferrari (Attwood/Courage) – Ford (McLaren/Donohue) – Porsche (Herrmann/Siffert) – Ford (Hawkins/Bucknum); there were only 24 cars left in the race out of 54 starters, and of those 24 cars, five were Porsches.

Retirement still followed retirement: the P3/4 Ferrari of Attwood/Courage used up all its oil before it was allowed by the Regulations to take on more; the Hawkins/Bucknum Ford went out with a dropped valve; and the Chaparral's automatic transmission packed up yet again. The Porsches were sixth, seventh, eighth and ninth and were still droning round the circuit as inexorably as ever. The Porsches each moved up a place on the Sunday midday when the Klass/Sutcliffe Ferrari was abandoned with fuel pump failure. An overcast sky threatened rain before the finish, but, happily, it was an empty threat and Parkes circulated on and on with the second-place Ferrari because co-driver Scarfiotti was feeling unwell. Then suddenly, or so it seemed to those in the pits, it was five to four and the last-place Abarth, apparently suffering from a severe engine disorder, clanked its way out of the pits to complete its final lap. Fords were first and fourth, Ferraris second and third – both teams were delighted with their efforts, but not more so than Porsche whose cars had put up a fantastic performance, combining speed, reliability and success. In addition to taking fifth to eight places, the Siffert/Herrmann 907 won the Index of Performance and was second to the winning Ford in the Index of Thermal Efficiency, and the make won the 2-litre class in both the Sports and Prototype categories. The two Porsches which retired were the Rindt/Mitter 907 which blew up its engine and the 910 of Schütz/Buzzetta with transmission failure.

Results:

1st D. Gurney/A. J. Foyt (Ford Mk 4), 3250 miles, 132·49 mph
2nd M. Parkes/L. Scarfiotti (Ferrari P4), 3218·2 miles
3rd W. Mairesse/'Beurlys' (Ferrari P3/4), 3159·5 miles
4th B. McLaren/M. Donohue (Ford Mk 4), 3001·7 miles
5th H. Herrmann/J. Siffert (Porsche 907), 3001·7 miles
6th R. Stommelen/J. Neerpasch (Porsche 910), 2942 miles
7th V. Elford/B. Pon (Porsche 906)
8th G. Koch/C. Poirot (Porsche 906)

|  | No. of starters | No. of finishers |
|---|---|---|
| Porsche | 6 | 4 |
| Ford (inc Mirages) | 9 | 2 |
| Ferrari | 7 (plus an outdated P2 model) | 2 |

The above excludes Group 3 Production GT cars (minimum of 500 units) of which one each of Porsche and Ferrari finished the race.

*Rheims 12 Hours – Private Owners To The Fore*

A bare fortnight after Le Mans yet another long-distance Prototype race was held on French soil and the setting was the beautiful city of Rheims, in the cathedral of which French kings from Clovis I to Louis XVI were crowned. The fast circuit situated a couple of miles out of the city attracted very few works entries. For the first few hours, from midnight until 3 am, the race was controlled by the sleek Lola-Chevrolets which were pounding out of the darkness and through the lighted pits area at over 165 mph. Then the Lolas fell out one by one with silly mechanical faults and the lead – and victory – was snatched by the Ford-France-entered 7-litre Mk 2. There were no Porsche factory entries in this race, but in third place Hans Herrmann and Buchet with the latter's private car led home a quartet of private 906s that had performed in a manner that would have done credit to the Zuffenhausen factory team. Fourth were Spoerry/Steinemann, fifth Wick/Bernay, and sixth Elford/Bradley.

*The Circuit of Mugello – Another Sweeping Porsche Victory*

Although one of the oldest European motor races – the first race was held in 1920 and was won by Campari with an Alfa Romeo –

## 1967: A SEASON OF UNLIMITED SUCCESS

the Circuit of Mugello has only taken place spasmodically in recent years. The circuit is near Florence and its length of 66·2 kilometres takes in part of the old Appenines section of the Mille Miglia course including the Futa Pass. The speeds attained by modern competition cars are such that they cannot, with any degree of safety for the drivers, be let loose on ordinary roads without safety barriers, straw bales and other essential forms of protection. The Mugello course was, however, just ordinary roads, even the entrance to the pits was situated in the middle of a dangerous curve, and it was the failure of the organisers to take adequate safety precautions that resulted in the death in practice of one of the most promising young sports car drivers.

As there were good prospects of another outright victory, Porsche made a grand-slam entry which included two of the 2·2-litre 8-cylinder cars. These 910s were driven by Mitter/Schütz and Stommelen/Neerpasch, while a 6-cylinder 910 was entered for Siffert and Herrmann. Group 4 Sports Car 906s were driven by Koch (the winner in 1966)/Glemser and Cella/Biscaldi. In addition Porsche fielded a 911 which had to run in the Prototype class. This was the 911R, a lightened version of the 911S, weighing around 800 kg compared with the 940 of the normal car; it had glass-fibre body panels and plastic windows. On this occasion it was finished in a rather nauseous orange-pink and was handled by Elford and van Lennep.

Facing the Stuttgart team were three of the Autodelta Alfa Romeo Tipo 33s and two Dinos entered by SEFAC Ferrari. One of these was the latest car in the hands of Scarfiotti and Vaccarella, while an older model was driven by Günther Klass and Jonathan Williams. The Scuderia Filipinetti entered a P3/4 Ferrari for Müller and Casoni (winner of the 1965 race) and from Ford-France came the 7-litre Rheims winner.

Practice eliminated nearly all the opposition to the German team. All the Alfas were in trouble with near-dangerous steering caused by a suspension defect and the Dinos were withdrawn after Günther Klass had lost his life in a horrible crash. The Ferrari practice car was that used in hill climbs in Group 7 sports/racing trim. Klass was driving this through a left-hand bend which is followed by a bumpy curve; as he entered the left-hand curve, the car took off over a bump, dropped its nearside wheels off the road on to the grass, and as Klass struggled to maintain control all four wheels went on the grass, the car went sideways and hit a tree at around 60 mph. Just by the cockpit the car was almost bisected and although a helicopter was on the scene within minutes, the talented and very intelligent young German driver died before reaching hospital. The withdrawal of the Dinos was a very natural and understandable act, but it was another unlucky break for Jonathan Williams. The young English teammember was given very few drives by Ferrari during the year, mainly because the Dino Formula Two cars had not yet been developed into a fully raceworthy state. For 1968 Williams signed up to drive for Abarth and the season proved just as wasteful as the previous year because of the failure of the team's Formula One car to reach a competitive state of development.

The Mugello race was run in intensely hot weather and the cars left the start at 10 sec intervals from 1 pm onwards. Mario Casoni had only motored four miles in the Filipinetti P3/4 when he left the road – but without serious damage to the car. He then made his way back to the pits on foot where he complained vociferously about the way the suspension had been set up! First away had been Schütz with the Porsche eight and he was leading on time at the end of lap one; second was Neerpasch and third Schlesser with the vast, hairy 7-litre Ford. Colin Davis brought his Alfa 33 into the pits after three laps with suspension failure and Galli had the suspension on his Tipo 33 collapse out in the mountains! When refuelling took place, under the keen eye of von Hanstein, the Porsches were stopped for less than a minute – and this included checking oil and tyres and changing drivers. In contrast, chaos reigned in the Alfa pits and there was little doubt that one-time Ferrari engineer Carlo Chiti could have learned a few useful lessons on team management from the dapper Baron!

Mitter and Stommelen with the leading Porsches were going just as fast as their co-drivers and seemed to have the race in the bag. For, by the end of lap four, all of the scruffy-looking, ill-prepared Tipo 33 Alfas had retired and the big Ford was rapidly falling back. On the last lap but one the Ford expired out on the circuit and even though it did not make the chequered flag, it was still classified fourth. Probably the finest drive in the race was that of Vic Elford and van Lennep at the wheel of the 911R which was being cornered faster than some of its 'true' Prototype team-mates and took third place after the Koch/Glemser car retired on the last lap with a broken engine. The Siffert/Herrmann 910 was also a casualty, blowing up its engine early in the race. This is how the Porsches finished:

  1st G. Mitter/U. Schütz (8-cyl 910), 4 hr 18 min 59 sec (76·24 mph)
  2nd R. Stommelen/J. Neerpasch (8-cyl 910)
  3rd V. Elford/G. van Lennep (911R)
  4th J. Schlesser/G. Ligier (Ford Mk 2)
  5th L. Cella/G. Biscaldi (906)
  6th C. Facetti/Prince Nicodemi (906)

*B.O.A.C. '500' Race*

Whether a state-owned airline is justified in incurring the expense of sponsoring a motor race is very open to argument, but, certainly, the B.O.A.C. '500' was the best sports car race to be held in Britain since the 1955 Tourist Trophy on the Dundrod circuit. But what a pity the race was not at Oulton Park, without doubt Britain's most interesting circuit – both from a driver's and spectator's point of view. It was understandable that because of a mistake the first B.O.A.C. '500' should be a 6-hours race, but when the same thing happened again in 1968 it seemed just the sort of absurd incongruity that a state transport concern would perpetuate.

The race was the last round in the Prototype Championship and though no works Fords were present, the entry was well worthy of the event. Ferrari fielded three P4s (perhaps ranking with the D-type Jaguar as the most beautiful competition sports cars of all time) and these were driven by Jackie Stewart (having his first drive in a works Ferrari) and Chris Amon, Paul Hawkins and Jonathan Williams, and Lodovico Scarfiotti and Peter Sutcliffe. The works Ferraris were supported by the Maranello Concessionaries' P3/4 of Attwood/Piper. There was a single Chaparral, a single Mirage and three Lolas. Porsche entered a grand total of five cars and clearly had their sights, once again, on outright victory. Flat-eight 910s were driven by works Cooper driver Jochen Rindt partnered by Graham Hill and Jo Siffert partnered by Bruce McLaren – clearly von Hanstein was putting his shirt on the Formula One drivers who knew the circuit intimately. A long-tail 907, but with on this occasion a flat-eight engine, was entrusted to Herrmann and Neerpasch. The remaining two Porsche entries were 6-cylinder 910s driven by Elford and Bianchi, and Schütz and Koch.

Opposition to the 910s in the 2-litre class should have come from a team of Alfa Tipo 33s, but these were withdrawn at the last moment.

There were, however, three of the Bolton-built Chevrons. These superbly made, space-frame rear-engined coupés were travelling sufficiently fast in practice for von Hanstein to give them a very searching scrutiny. Brian Redman and Chris Williams with a 2-litre V-8 B.R.M.-powered car recorded 1 min 41 ·4 sec compared with the 1 min 41 ·0 sec of Elford/Bianchi – the slowest of the Porsche team. A humorous side of practice – humorous at least for Ferrari – was that the timekeepers lost track of who was driving what and Jackie Stewart was able to record good times for all three cars of the Maranello team. This is how the first three rows of the starting grid were formed:

| | | |
|---|---|---|
| Spence/Hill | Surtees/Hobbs | Hulme/Brabham |
| (Chaparral) | (Lola-Chevrolet) | (Lola-Chevrolet) |
| 1 min 37 ·4 sec | 1 min 36 ·6 sec | 1 min 36 ·6 sec |
| | Hawkins/Williams | Scarfiotti/Sutcliffe |
| | (Ferrari P4) | (Ferrari P4) |
| | 1 min 37 ·8 sec | 1 min 37 ·8 sec |
| Siffert/McLaren | Hill/Rindt | Stewart/Amon |
| (Porsche) | (Porsche) | (Ferrari) |
| 1 min 38 ·2 sec | 1 min 38 ·2 sec | 1 min 38 ·2 sec |

The traffic jam on the first lap as the 36 cars moved off together round the tight circuit was almost frightening to watch and there was hardly a single car that did not bear the scars of a minor prang. The pack gradually sorted itself out by dint of taking corners three or even four abreast, passing on both sides and by faster cars squeezing between pairs of slower cars. By the end of the first hour the order was Chaparral (Spence) – Ferrari (Scarfiotti) – Porsche (Siffert) – Mirage (Rodriguez) – Ferrari (Hawkins) – Porsche (Schütz). Already the B.R.M.-engined Chevron had broken its crown wheel-and-pinion and Denis Hulme had brought his Lola into the pits for a broken rocker to be changed. And Graham Hill had had his Porsche jump out of gear, causing the engine to over-rev and break a valve. Pit stops caused changes in the order, but as the fourth hour approached all three Lolas were out of the running and the order was Ferrari (Stewart/Amon), Chaparral (Spence/Hill) and Porsche (Siffert/McLaren). Then Hawkins spun his P4 at Clearways, crumpling the tail, and dashed into the pits for emergency repairs. The leading Ferrari, calling in for its scheduled pit stop, arrived moments later. For a while chaos reigned as Mauro Forghieri steamed up his glasses in his efforts to maintain order in the midst of crowds of marshals, photographers and rubbernecks. The Hawkins/Williams car roared back into the race, its tail firmly held down with wire, and two minutes later the Stewart/Amon car was back on the course – but it had fallen back to third place behind the Chaparral and the Siffert/McLaren Porsche. The Elford/Bianchi 910, which had risen through the field to fourth place, went out with broken valve gear. The second-place Porsche dropped back one place at its last refuelling stop and failed to regain it when the Ferrari made *its* final stop. Which was crucial for Porsche, as before this race the two makes were separated by only a single point in the Prototype Championship and so victory in this went to Ferrari. Everyone, however, was delighted that the Chaparral team had scored an important win after so much frustration and failure earlier in the season. Results:

1st M. Spence/P. Hill (Chaparral 2F), 211 laps (93·08 mph).
2nd J. Stewart/C. Amon (Ferrari P4), 211 laps
3rd J. Siffert/B. McLaren (Porsche 910), 209 laps
4th H. Herrmann/J. Neerpasch (Porsche 907), 206 laps
5th L. Scarfiotti/P. Sutcliffe (Ferrari P4), 206 laps
6th P. Hawkins/J. Williams (Ferrari P4), 204 laps

*Post-Script To The Season*

Although the Group 4 Championship had already been decided in favour of Ford and Porsche who had scored maximum points in their classes, there were still two rounds to be run, the 500 Km race at Zeltweg in Austria and the Nürburgring 500 Km race limited to 1300 cc cars. Rindt was especially anxious to drive a Porsche on home territory, so the factory supplied a 906 for the Zeltweg race and he entered this in his own name. In 1966 the works 906s of Mitter and Siffert had set a new lap record of 1 min 10·49 sec and the fiery Rindt was all out to beat this. In Friday practice he tried rather too hard and when a Ford got in the way spun the white Porsche into the straw bales. This meant a night's hard work for the mechanics, but the car was sorted out in time for Rindt to have another go on the Saturday when he managed 1 min 9·59 sec. In the race Rindt lost a great deal of time while a defective damper was sorted out in the pits, victory went to the Ford GT40 of Paul Hawkins and the

Porsche in second place was the 906 of Bill Bradley which he was sharing with Dickie Attwood.

For the Paris 1000 Km race it was Hans Herrmann who was loaned a car by the works, a 910 which he shared with Udo Schütz and which was looked after by the works mechanics. The 910 was down on power and was never able to challenge for the lead. Even so it was driven consistently and survived the bumps of Montlhéry to finish third behind the Mirage of Ickx and Hawkins and the Ferrari P3/4 of Bianchi and 'Beurlys'.

Works Porsches did not race again in 1967, but two long-distance events far away from European shores attracted private 906 owners. November 4th was the date of the tenth International *Rand Daily Mail* Nine Hours race at Kyalami near Johannesburg. The entry ranged from a Mirage, Lolas and Ferraris to the 906s of the Racing Team Holland and British driver Tony Dean and to a really ancient RSK Porsche. First and second places went to two of the fire-spitting monsters, the Mirage of Jacky Ickx and Brian Redman and the Lola of Paul Hawkins and John Love, both running on Firestone tyres, 400 of which had been air-freighted to South Africa at a cost of £7,500! Tony Dean, co-driving with Basil van Rooyen, one of South Africa's most successful saloon car drivers, finished a very satisfactory fourth.

Six weeks later on 16th December was the Lourenco Marques Three Hours race. Lourenco Marques is one of the largest towns in the Portuguese state of Mozambique. The race did not start until 5 pm and so, with practice finished on the Friday, most of the drivers spent the day having a long lie-in and then lazed in the sunshine. Lola and one-time Porsche driver Mike de Udy put the Saturday to good use by having a much-needed haircut and Rollo Fielding spent the day with his mechanic re-assembling the engine of his 275LM Ferrari, having discovered a bent valve in practice. The almost flat, 2·1-mile circuit consisted of a long straight forming part of the main coastal road and 1·6 miles of very narrow roads and a host of slow, banked corners. Tony Dean's 906 was well suited to the circuit and despite gear-selection trouble had worked his way up to second place by just before the half-way mark. When he stopped to refuel, Dean handed over to Basil van Rooyen. Only 15 laps later the 906 came to rest out on the circuit with broken throttle cable. Eventually the Porsche got back to the pits where a makeshift hand-operated wire cable was fitted. A further pit stop became necessary when the cable stretched and the car was still suffering from gear-

Le Mans, 1967: the long-tailed Porsche 907s of Mitter/Rindt and Siffert/Herrmann follow the Ferrari of Rodriguez and Parsons. No. 41 took fifth place overall, won the Index of Performance and took equal prize money to the winner (Nigel Snowdon)

All four wheels off the ground. The 3-litre car of Elford and Siffert which won the 1968 Nürburgring 1000 Km race (Nigel Snowdon)

## 1967: A SEASON OF UNLIMITED SUCCESS

selection trouble. Despite all this it was lapping within three seconds of its potential and finished sixth.

1967 had been another magnificent year for Porsche, even though many of the make's finer performances had been overshadowed by the struggle between Detroit and Maranello. If on some circuits Porsche could defeat their rivals of much larger capacity by using engines of only 2 and 2·2 litres, it looked very much as though Prototype racing in 1968 with a capacity of 3 litres would be completely scooped by the low, long white coupés. In one other field in 1967 the Porsches were well to the fore – the European Hill Climb Championship. All seven rounds from the Rossfeld climb in Germany in June to the Gaisberg event in Austria in September were won by the 8-cylinder Porsches with four victories to Stommelen, who won the Championship, and three to Mitter.

## TWELVE
# 1968: Porsche Versus Ford

*The International Line-Up*

The announcement by the Federation Internationale de l'Automobile, not made in 1967 until after Le Mans, that in 1968 Group 6 Prototypes would be limited in capacity to 3 litres and Group 4 Sports Cars to 5 litres came like a thunderbolt out of the blue and it was at once obvious that two teams, Chaparral and Ferrari, would not be racing in Group 6 in 1968 unless they brought out completely new cars – which neither was willing to do. Ford also announced their intention of withdrawing from racing and it became clear that the strongly French-influenced F.I.A. had reached their decision after the Ford decision had become known to them and with a view to giving the French constructors, Alpine and Matra, a substantial advantage over their rivals in 1968. In any case, because of the vast capital expenditure incurred in any worthwhile racing project, the new Regulations came into effect with unreasonable rapidity. As it happened, the Alpine proved uncompetitive and the Matra missed most of the season's racing and was out of luck at Le Mans. It was very much to the credit of Porsche that Huschke von Hanstein announced that his company was opposed to the 3-litre limit, for there was no doubt that Porsche now stood an excellent chance of success in 1968 Group 6 races and that a 3-litre Porsche would be built to take advantage of what was a *fait accompli*.

With the initial rumpus over, constructors made the best of the situation and a varied assortment of cars took part in the season's racing. This was the prospective line-up of Porsche's rivals:

*France*

*Alpine:* the 3-litre V-8 Renault-sponsored cars built at Dieppe and with an engine designed by Amédée Gordini were generally reliable, but lacked the speed to challenge for top honours.

*Matra:* Matra Sports raced only one car during the year, a development of the existing V-8 B.R.M.-powered coupé of unconventional and aerodynamically very efficient lines and powered by the team's 79·7 × 50 mm 3-litre Grand Prix engine.

*Great Britain*

*Mirage:* John Wyer's Gulf Petroleum-sponsored J.W. Automotive team built a new 3-litre Prototype powered by the B.R.M. V-12 engine; this was crashed in July at Snetterton by Robin Widdows and was not raced during the year. Throughout 1968 the team relied on their distinctive blue and orange-painted Group 4 4·7-litre GT40 Fords; these possessed an exceptionally fine performance, the result of careful development work, and Wyer had a team of drivers second to none in this class of racing. It was the Gulf Fords that brought about the downfall of Porsche's Prototype Championship hopes and achieved far greater success than many observers of the racing scene anticipated.

*Chevron:* Derek Bennett's 2-litre B.M.W.-powered coupés were not contenders for outright honours, but throughout the season they displayed fantastic roadholding and dominated their class in minor events; they were homologated as Group 4 cars and although production is now well over the fifty mark, there was a little tolerance in the granting of homologation. One Chevron *was* aimed at Group 6 honours; this was John Woolfe's car powered by a Repco-Brabham 3-litre single cam per bank Grand Prix engine (originally it was intended to fit a Martin V-8 engine) and which had a slightly lengthened chassis. The weakness of this car was persistent cylinder head gasket failure and for this reason it must be regarded as being completely unsuccessful.

*Lola:* Eric Broadley's T.70 Mk III coupé was homologated with the 5-litre Chevrolet engine in Group 4. The F.I.A. was sufficiently understanding about the difficulties faced by small constructors to permit cars built with engines both below and above 5 litres capacity to count for homologation purposes. Although the Lolas were very fast – every bit as fast as the Gulf Fords and the works Porsches – they were plagued once again by minor troubles and, in any case, were rarely seen in major events with top-line drivers at the wheel. The most successful Lola was that owned by Sid Taylor, but its successes were limited to comparatively unimportant races.

*Marcos:* Jem Marsh of Marcos, the make famed for its wooden chassis construction and its gloriously beautiful lines, built a superb looking car with the Repco V-8 engine (in this case it was originally intended to use a V-12 B.R.M. unit, but financial reasons may well have prevented this). The body, designed by Denis Adams who was responsible for the touring cars, was distinguished by both its angular lines and enormous "greenhouse" top. The car, known as the Mantis, was entered at Le Mans, but after a trial appearance at Spa it was not again raced. The cause was the work necessary to recover from severe flooding of the small Marcos works at Bradford-on-Avon in Wiltshire.

*Ford:* Although Ford of America had withdrawn from racing, Ford of Great Britain appeared with a new Group 6 challenger. This was the work of Ford's Len Bailey and was built in the Alan Mann workshops. Alan Mann was also team manager for the new car. Power unit was the Cosworth-Ford V-8 Grand Prix unit of 2993 cc (85·7 × 64·8 mm) developing 420 bhp at 9000 rpm, driving through a Hewland or ZF 5-speed gearbox and mounted centrally. The basis of the car was a full monocoque with riveted and bonded light-alloy panels. The wheelbase was only 7 ft 3 in – notably shorter than that of Grand Prix single seaters using the same engine. The car was plagued by handling problems and had a serious crash at the Nürburgring with Chris Irwin at the wheel – it may well be that the handling problems are insuperable. The P68 Ford was certainly the fastest of the 1968 Prototypes and had a maximum speed of close to 200 mph.

*Italy*

*Alfa Romeo:* After a season of failure Carlo Chiti's Autodelta team began to find their feet with the Tipo 33s which for 1968 were given coupé bodywork; a version enlarged to 2·5 litres was also raced. It was common knowledge that a 3-litre engine (also suitable for Grand Prix racing) was extensively tested. Series Two coupés were also entered by the Belgian Racing Team V.D.S.

*Panther:* This car was sponsored by Umberto Maglioli's Scuderia Brescia Corse and was exhibited at the Geneva Salon in March, 1968. The body was a magnificent styled coupé by Bertone, but its appearance was rather marred by the prevalent contagious rash of aerofoil building – in this case a high-mounted hydraulically operated aerofoil and it was only to be hoped that the designer knew a little more about aerodynamic effects than some of the Grand Prix car constructors seemed to. The chassis was a very rigid monocoque with extensive use of titanium at high stress areas and the power unit was to be a B.R.M. V-12 driving through a 5-speed Hewland DG gearbox. It was planned to build six of these cars, but unfortunately none reached the starting line in 1968.

## United States

*Howmet:* The only American Prototype to racing in 1968, the Howmet TX was powered by a Continental gas turbine engine developing 330 shp at 37,000 rpm. By the F.I.A.'s complex Formula to equate gas turbine and piston engines the TX came out with an equivalent capacity of 2960 cc. The gearbox had only two positions, neutral and forward, and reverse was gained electrically and operated off the starter motor. A multi-tubular space-frame was used and the body was similar to that of the Chaparral 2D raced in 1966. Two cars were entered by the team in 1968, but there were plagued by teething troubles.

## The Porsche Offensive

In December, 1967 Porsche held a press display at the Hockenheim circuit and Huschke von Hanstein was able to reveal both the strength of the team's offensive and how advanced in time the team was with its preparations. The drivers were to be: Jo Siffert (the Swiss driver who handled Formula One cars for Rob Walker and was probably among the World's top six drivers); Vic Elford (who became in 1968 a member of the Cooper works team); Rolf Stommelen; Lodovico Scarfiotti ('Lulu' had changed his allegiance now that Ferrari had withdrawn from Prototype racing); Hans Herrmann (who by virtue of his works Porsche and Mercedes drives in 1954 has been competing in major International events far longer than any other driver except Italian Umberto Maglioli); Gerhard Mitter; and Jochen Neerpasch.

Porsche intended competing with a very varied range of cars:

*907:* The narrow ultra-light (600 kg) car which in 2195 cc (80 × 54 mm) 8-cylinder form had a power output of 270 bhp at 8600 rpm. Bosch fuel injection was fitted, the compression ratio was 10·2:1 and the crankshaft ran in nine main bearings. As on all the

Prototype Porsche models, transmission was by a 5-speed gearbox. The glass-fibre body had gull-wing doors, space-frame construction was used and there was still torsion bar suspension – by wishbones and MacPherson struts at the front and trailing arms at the rear. Light alloy wheels with 5·25 × 13 front and 7·00 × 13 rear tyres were used. The fuel tank had a capacity of 110 litres. Lighting was by four quartz-iodine units, each pair enclosed in plexiglass shields.

*907 Langheck* ('long-tail'): This was mechanically identical to the normal 907, but had a long, tapering tail squared off at the trailing edge through which the exhausts emitted and above which was a narrow, adjustable spoiler running right across the tail. Maximum speed in this form was approximately 185 mph.

*907 Berg:* This was the extremely light (450 kg) car intended for use in Group 7 sports/racing form in the European Hill Climb Championship with Scarfiotti and Mitter as drivers. Because of the 2-litre capacity limit in the Championship, the flat-eight engine was in 1981 cc form and in sprint tune developed 272 bhp at 9000 rpm. The body was an abreviated open 2-seater with a small roll-over bar behind the cockpit, a cut-off tail and rear adjustable spoiler. A small capacity 15-litre tank was fitted.

*908:* This was the 3-litre car to which von Hanstein made no reference in December and which was first raced at Monza in April. During the 1968 season there were strong rumours that Porsche would be offering a 3-litre production car, but, recently, von Hanstein has denied this – which is just as well, for one has only to compare a DB2 Aston Martin of the early 'fifties (which then represented everything that a 911 Porsche does today) with the current DB6 and DBS to see the folly of a policy of constant engine enlargements.

*910:* The existing 910, which had a slightly narrower track than the 907, were to be raced with 6-cylinder engines by works-assisted private owners.

*911R:* The 850 kg lightweight version of the 911 touring car which had performed so well at Mugello in 1967 was to be used when there was a suitable event. Light alloy wheels and a 5-speed gearbox were fitted. Power output was 210 bhp at 8000 rpm and twin electric pumps drew from a 100-litre tank. Maximum speed was 150 mph.

## Daytona 24 Hours Race

As was inevitable after the change in the Regulations, the first major race of 1968 was a mere shadow of the struggle seen in 1967 between Ford, Ferrari and Chaparral. Porsche took the race very seriously and in December, 1967 sent along a 907 for a series of tests, but these came to an abrupt end when Neerpasch had a spectacular crash – fortunately, without injuring himself. At the race in February Porsche fielded four 907s with 2·2-litre flat-eight engines and the opposition came from two main sources. J.W. Automotive fielded two GT40 Fords, one a brand new car and the other a Mirage rebuilt to GT40 specification. These were driven by Ferrari Grand Prix driver Jacky Ickx and Brian Redman, and by Paul Hawkins and David Hobbs (who had the former Mirage). Since 1967 the Alfa Romeo challenge had been much strengthened. The 2-litre V-8s had new bodies of typical Prototype coupé concept and new chassis; the oil and water radiators had been transferred from the front to either side in front of the rear wheels; power output was 260 bhp at 8300 rpm. A single Howmet was entered for Dick Thompson and Lowther. The fastest practice times for each of the four makes were:

Ford GT40 (Ickx/Redman): 1 min 54·91 sec
Porsche 907 (Stommelen/Mitter): 1 min 57·31 sec
Howmet TX (Thompson/Lowther): 2 min 1·19 sec
Alfa Romeo Tipo 33 (Schütz/Vaccarella): 2 min 2·21 sec

At Daytona the cars form up in a two-by-two grid and then do $1\frac{1}{2}$ pace laps before the flag drops on the back straight before the fastest banking. The two Fords, heading the line-up, pulled slightly away from the Porsches, but after only three laps Hawkins shot into the pits for a loose plug lead to be re-attached. With one hour of the 24 gone, the Fords were first and sixth, the four Porsches sandwiched between them, and the Howmet was out of the race. The jet car had displayed a distinct lack of stability through corners and had run into the retaining wall where the road circuit meets the banking; although the car was not severely damaged, it was enough to put it out of the race.

Just as darkness was closing in on the circuit, Brian Redman abandoned his GT40 out on the circuit and walked to the pits to report to team manager David Yorke that the gearbox had packed in. The lead was then assumed by the other Ford of the Gulf team. An epidemic of punctures had been caused by sharp sea shells being thrown up and on to the road from the hard, sandy verges. On the shallow banking opposite the pits a Ford Mustang blew up its engine and dropped a trail of oil along the track. This was the starting point of a horrifying spectacle in front of the pits. Mitter, whose car had just punctured a tyre, braked at the usual point halfway round the banking and as a result of the leaking tyre started to lose control; the Porsche struck the oil trail, shot on to the grass in front of the pits, a wheel dug into the ground, the car rolled over on to its roof and careered on towards the next corner in a shower of sparks; on seeing the sparks, Masten Gregory, at the wheel of a Ferrari 275LM of the North American Racing Team, braked hard, right on the patch of oil, and collided with the private 907 of Spoerry. The Ferrari, still travelling at close to 160 mph, shot up in the air, bounced and rolled over and over. Next on the scene was Vic Elford with his 907 but he managed to avoid both the oil and Spoerry's Porsche which hit the retaining wall. Although Mitter had received a very severe shaking, none of the three drivers suffered any actual injuries. But quite a number of the pit staff needed a stiff drink to recover from the shock!

The GT40 of Hawkins and Hobbs thundered round in the lead until midnight when it fell back to third place because of a long pit stop to remove the brake backing plates which had become rough after being worn down to the metal. The Ford started to make up the deficiency, but when it was refuelled at 6 am, a large puddle formed in the road as the fuel went in and it was retired with a split tank. The Porsches were now completely unassailable despite long pit stops by the two leading cars with a broken throttle link and a burnt-out dynamo respectively. In the closing stages of the race von Hanstein decided to ring the changes with his drivers. The Elford/Neerpasch car was now in the lead and he sent it out in turn with the drivers of the second-place Porsche and Stommelen who had been Mitter's co-driver. The nonsensical situation arose that the same drivers appeared in the results for both the winning and second-place cars. The Porsches lined up to finish three-abreast in a race that had been of greater interest for its incidents than for the intensity of the competition. The reliability of the Alfas made a striking contrast with their 1967 performances:

1st V. Elford/J. Neerpasch/J. Siffert/R. Stommelen/H. Herrmann (Porsche 907), 2565·69 miles (106·69 mph)

2nd J. Siffert/H. Herrmann (Porsche 907)
3rd J. Buzzetta/J. Schlesser (Porsche 907)
4th J. Titus/R. Bucknum (Ford Mustang)
5th U. Schütz/N. Vaccarella (Alfa Romeo Tipo 33)
6th M. Andretti/L. Bianchi (Alfa Romeo Tipo 33)
7th G. Biscaldi/M. Casoni (Alfa Romeo Tipo 33)

*Sebring 12 Hours Race*

Again, this was one of the less exciting races in the series and Porsche fielded four cars as at Daytona, except that they had the shorter tails and had a very novel form of driver cooling. This worked by means of a large block of ice inserted in a receptacle by the left headlamps and an electric pump that forced water into a suit of underclothes threaded with fine plastic capillary tubes which carried coolant to all parts of the body. Despite its Emmet-like conception, the drivers were very enthusiastic about the system. Porsche's opposition was limited to the J.W. Automotive Fords with the same collection of drivers as at Daytona, a rather rag-tag assortment of Lolas, a single Howmet and the Alpine 3-litre that displayed no more speed than it had at Montlhéry in 1967.

The race started in cool, overcast weather that made the Porsche cooling system unnecessary and at the Le Mans start there was an official stationed by each car to check that the driver fastened his seat belt. Siffert took the lead at the start, but the Lola of Patrick and Jordan got ahead for a short while until its front suspension broke; happily for Porsche, the J.W. Fords were out of luck. Redman spun off and damaged the clutch of the car he was sharing with Ickx, and Hawkins, while leading the race, was all "crossed-up" by a woman Rambler driver and collided with a Porsche 911; the front of the Ford was badly damaged and a lot of time was lost, in the first place patching the nose and then swapping it for that of the retired car; the Ford was back in the race and nicely wound up again when a front wishbone broke. The Porsches of Mitter/Stommelen and Scarfiotti/Buzzetta both broke their engines, but the other two cars were securely entrenched in first two places until near the end of the race when Elford brought his car into the pits with wheel bearing trouble. The mechanics stripped the complete suspension upright and replaced it with one from one of the retired cars. Herrmann and Siffert won from Elford and Neerpasch and the poor calibre of the entry in this race was revealed by the fact that two Chevrolet Camaros finished third and fourth.

## The B.O.A.C. '500'

The six hour-race on the full Brands Hatch circuit attracted a much better entry than had been seen at either Daytona or Sebring. J.W. Automotive fielded only one GT40 with the special Gurney-Weslake cylinder heads, but there were five of these cars altogether, including Paul Hawkins' private car which he shared with David Hobbs. *The* Ford in the race, however, was the new Alan Mann-entered 3-litre model driven by Bruce McLaren and Mike Spence– there should have been two running, but one broke its engine in practice, and the one that did run had spoilers running across the tail to keep the rear wheels on the ground; it seemed that the much publicised vortex-creating tail (an idea used by John Cooper on his "Manx"-tailed sports cars as long ago as 1955) was not all that it was cracked up to be. Autodelta fielded their Tipo 33 coupés, there were three Lolas and two Chevron-B.M.W.s. A single Howmet again ran. Hotly tipped to win were the three Porsche 907 entries for Siffert/ Herrmann, Mitter/Scarfiotti and Elford/Neerpasch. In addition the factory team was looking after three privately entered 910s. Jochen Rindt should have driven instead of Scarfiotti, but the week before the race he and von Hanstein decided that it would be better if the Austrian and Porsche parted company.

When the flag fell at twelve noon, McLaren shot ahead from the centre of the front row of the grid, only to have a bout of fuel pump trouble, and all the works Porsches and much of the rest of the field went past. McLaren soon worked his way through to hold third place behind the leading Porsches of Elford and Siffert; as the leaders strove to hold off McLaren, and Mitter endeavoured to stay with the Ford, the Porsches were snaking wildly under acceleration from Druids bend. The Ford closed right up on Elford, squeezed its way past and time and time again the two cars swapped places. The J.W. Ford was holding a watching brief in fifth spot and after less than a quarter of an hour's racing the Howmet had come to an abrupt halt by clouting the bank at Druids. The Ford succeeded in getting through into the lead, but was boxed back into third place when the leaders were lapping slower cars. Once again McLaren fought his way to the front and the 907s kept up the chase, but shortly after Spence had taken over, the Ford coasted to a halt opposite the pits – the left-hand inner drive-shaft coupling had broken.

After the confusion of the first refuelling stops, the Elford/Neerpasch Porsche led from the J.W. Ford of Ickx and Redman. By 2.30 pm the Siffert/Neerpasch Porsche was back in the lead and, despite an unexpected pit stop for new front brake pads by the Elford/Neerpasch car, it seemed inevitable that one of the low, white German cars, distinguished by the harsh, raucous note of the 8-cylinder engines, would win. Then Siffert with the leading Porsche came into the pits for brake pads; these were changed, the Porsche accelerated away – and then dived back into the pits again by way of the back entrance; the right-hand front wheel was jamming and when the hub and front brake were dismantled, the damage was found to be too severe to rectify. At the same time Scarfiotti stopped for brake pads and without anyone in the Porsche pit realising that it had happened, the pale blue GT40 was in the lead and the Porsches were second and third. When the Ford made its last refuelling stop, Mitter closed right up and then caught the Ford after it had rejoined the race. If the Porsche was to win, Mitter had to open up a substantial lead for the Stuttgart car needed another pit stop. Alas, by the time the Porsche had stopped and left the pits, its lead had become a deficiency of 45 sec. Scarfiotti, who had taken over, was unable to regain ground at more than second a lap, and the Porsche finished 22 sec in arrears. A private 910 won the 2-litre class, but second in the class was the Chevron-B.M.W. of Digby Martland and Brian Classick which defeated two other 910s. A disappointing outing for Porsche! Results:

1st J. Ickx/B. Redman (Ford GT40), 218 laps (95·96 mph)
2nd G. Mitter/L. Scarfiotti (Porsche 907)
3rd V. Elford/J. Neerpasch (Porsche 907)
4th P. Hawkins/D. Hobbs (Ford GT40)
5th P. Rodriguez/R. Pierpoint (Ferrari 275LM)
6th J. Bonnier/S. Axelsson (Lola T.70 Mk III)

*Monza 1000 Km Race*

Again a fortnight passed and the works Porsches were in action, at Monza where the team fielded the new 3-litre model first seen at the Le Mans Practice Week-end. The flat-eight engine had a capacity of 2924 cc (84 × 66 mm), developed 310 bhp and was in fact a development of the 6-cylinder engine rather than the 2·2-litre 8-

cylinder design. The twin overhead camshafts were driven by gears and chains from the front of the engine, whereas the old eights had the drive by a shaft and bevel gears from the crankshaft and required a great deal of skill to set up properly. The 908s were still very much in the experimental stage and had slightly different means of valve operation. Transmission was by a 6-speed gearbox with, on one of the two cars entered, the four-plate clutch mounted on the end of the gearbox – as with former Ferrari Prototype practice and, on the other, a wet multi-plate clutch between the engine and the gearbox. The gearbox had its own lubrication system complete with filter. The body and chassis were similar to the 907 apart from heavier springs and dampers and with the long tail it weighed 700 kg. The 908s were driven by Siffert/Herrmann and Scarfiotti/Mitter and a 907 was entered for Stommelen/Neerpasch. In addition the factory fielded in the Gran Turismo class a 911T for the dashing Jean-Claude Killy, the French International ski champion, and Jean Guichet. Killy is treated on the Continent like the Beatles and 'Stones are in Britain and the crowds that constantly mob him must make his motor racing rather tedious. A 6-cylinder 2-litre 907 was loaned to the Swiss Hart-Ski team for Spoerry and Steinemann to drive, but Spoerry wrote it off in practice.

Although the Automobile Club of Milan had received 75 entries for the race, there were after non-appearances and practice mishaps only 35 starters. Porsche's opposition was limited to the J.W. Automoitve Fords and the race was a straightforward duel between the two. The early laps witnessed a fierce scrap between the German and Anglo-American cars, with the Fords having a slight edge and young Jacky Ickx leading for most of the time. The average speed of the leading cars was close to 125 mph and they were attaining around 175 mph along the straights. After only 19 laps, Siffert rushed into the pits, his 908 emitting clouds of smoke and a foul smell of burning plastic and rubber. The wire-wound flexible tube that carried air from the tail scoop to the left-hand rear brake had become detached and caught up in the open half-shaft; the result was a horrible mess of tangled and torn piping and the mechanics set to work to sort it out. Seven laps later the other 908 came in with a misfiring engine – one of the fuel injection pipe unions had come loose – and this left the Fords in complete command of the race. Suddenly there was a bang from the leading Ford as it passed the pits and next time round Ickx brought it into the pits; an exhaust pipe had broken through on the sharp bend after the port and the mechanics desperately tried to wire it back on. Both the Ford and the 3-litre Porsches rejoined the race, but all these were well down the field, and so the Hawkins/Hobbs Gulf Ford led from the 907 Porsche of Stommelen/Neerpasch. This Porsche was suffering from battery trouble caused by alternator regulator system failure and two battery changes were made. Von Hanstein was not in the Porsche pits at this race and the result was chaos and near desperation. Not only was the team's leading car ailing, but even when it was fit it lacked the speed to match the Ford and the works 911T was being led by the private car of Glemser and Kelleners. To add to their troubles, the weary mechanics had to set to work again on the 908 of Scarfiotti/Mitter which came back in again with its clutch toggle mechanism almost falling off. Even at the end of the race Porsche were still in trouble, for Siffert made a last-minute pit stop because the single wheel-nut was loose and the wheel had nearly fallen off, and Mitter completed his last lap with a flat offside front tyre. It was an exhausted and very despondent team of mechanics that returned to Stuttgart to explain their misfortunes to their Competitions Manager! This is how the Porsches finished:

2nd R. Stommelen/J. Neerpasch (907)
10th J-C. Killy/J. Guichet (911T)
11th L. Scarfiotti/G. Mitter (908)
19th J. Siffert/H. Herrmann (908)

*The Targa Florio*

It was clear that the Autodelta team of Alfa Romeos had been withdrawn from Monza so as to concentrate all their efforts on the Sicilian race; these cars had been steadily improving in both speed and stamina and it was evident that even without Ferrari there was plenty of opposition for the Porsches. The rivalry was intensified because former Ferrari driver Vaccarella was in the Alfa team and Scarfiotti in the Porsche and on the first lap of practice on the Friday there was a tremendous fight between the two drivers which resulted in the Porsche leaving the road and writing itself off. Fortunately Porsche had a hack practice car which they were able to put into shape for the race. This is how the two teams were formed:

*Porsche:*
2.2-litre 8-cyl 907s:
   H. Herrmann/J. Neerpasch

V. Elford/U. Maglioli (this car had an open top to accommodate the very tall Italian).
J. Siffert/R. Stommelen
L. Scarfiotti/G. Mitter
2-litre 6-cyl 910 loaned to the Valvoline Racing Team.
R. Steinemann/R. Lins
   2-litre 6-cyl 910:
A. Nicodemi/C. Facetti
Alberti/Mardesi
   entered by the Swiss Piccionaia Racing Team and looked after by the works

*Alfa Romeo*

2·5-litre Tipo 33:
   N. Vaccarella/U. Schütz
2-litre Tipo 33:
   G. Baghetti/G. Biscaldi
   I. Giunti/"Nanni" Galli
   L. Bianchi/M. Casoni
2-litre Tipo 33s:
   T. Pilette/R. Slotemaker
   Trosch/G. Gosselin
      entered by the V.D.S. Belgian team and looked after by the Autodelta team.

Right on the first lap Porsche were in trouble, for the centre-lock nut on the right rear wheel of Elford's car came undone and the wheel slid off the driving pins; Vic brought the car to a quiet halt and tightened the nut with the enormous socket spanner carried in the nose of the car together with the spare wheel; when he reached the Bivio Polizzi "outpost", he stopped to have a new nut fitted. This was not the end of Elford's – or Porsche's – troubles, for the new hub nut on the same wheel worked its way loose again on a fast bend and the loss of drive caused the car to hit a rock with the right-hand front wheel and burst a tyre. It was determination rather than natural skill that had made Vic Elford a first-class racing driver and whatever anyone else might have done, he had no intention of giving in. He tightened up the wheel nut, fitted the spare wheel and made his way back to the pits with the tools jingling on the passenger seat. Siffert was already in the pits, for the outer taper-roller race on the right-hand front stub axle had seized up, and the mechanics were changing the upright and hub assembly. By the time Elford rejoined the race, he was 18 minutes behind schedule.

Lap two saw Scarfiotti increase his lead over Vaccarella to 28·3 sec, but the 2-litre class was being led by the Alfa 33 of Giunti which had a sender, three-second advantage over the works 910 and was in third place overall. While most of the other drivers were stopping to refuel and hand their cars over to their co-drivers, Elford, who had refuelled during his emergency stop, was pressing on and his third-lap time of 36 min 2·3 sec chopped nearly a minute off the lap record. Nino Vaccarella had handed over to Udo Schütz, but forgot to warn him about a corner, the surface of which had completely broken up; the result was that Schütz lost control on the loose gravel and wrecked the Alfa Romeo against a wall. Mitter had the drive-shaft rubber "doughnut" split and so he stopped at the pits to have a new drive-shaft fitted. Mitter succeeded in rejoining the race sufficiently quickly to regain the lead from Giunti's Alfa and as a result of his furious driving Elford had worked his 907 back to seventh place by the time he handed over to Maglioli.

More troubles were to follow for the Porsche team, for at the end of five laps, the half-way mark, Mitter brought the leading Porsche into the pits with sticking front brakes and a loss of engine power. The brake trouble was quickly cured, but the power loss was due to the broken half-shaft having flattened one of the exhaust tail pipes and to fit a new one on to the hot expanded metal of the exhaust system was a slow, difficult job. While the minutes ticked past, the Alfas of Galli/Giunti and Casoni/Bianchi moved up into first and second places and there was nothing that the highest placed Porsches could do about it; for the Herrmann/Neerpasch 907 was handling atrociously and the drivers were having great difficulty in keeping it on the road, while the Steinemann/Lins 910 had an inoperative self-locking differential. The 907 rejoined the race, but the flattened pipe had caused the engine to overheat and the car died out on the circuit near the village of Cerda. All this while Maglioli was making up ground and when Elford took over at the end of lap seven, he had only $2\frac{1}{2}$ minutes to make up on the leader and three laps to do it in. Giunti tried his hardest to stay ahead with the Alfa, but it was to no avail, for Elford turned in two very fast and consistent laps, within two seconds of each other, and this put him in the lead. The 910 of Steinemann/Lins moved up to third place ahead of the Alfa 33 of

Casoni/Bianchi which was suffering from falling oil pressure, but then the Porsche broke a half-shaft on its last lap.

Although victory had been achieved, Porsche reliability had once again been notable by its absence and the Alfas were clearly going to provide stiff opposition on all but the very fastest circuits – and there the J.W. Fords would do the Porsche-baiting. The winners were perhaps the most exceptional members of the Porsche team. Vic Elford was renowned for his ambition, determination and sheer guts and epitomised the modern image of the racing driver as "the working boy made good", while Umberto Maglioli was a hangover from the traditional Italian school of gentlemen drivers. His career in International racing was even longer than that of Hans Herrmann and back in 1953 he had driven a works Grand Prix Ferrari at Monza; in 1954 he had won the Carrera Panamericana Mexico road race with a 4·9-litre Ferrari and this was his third win in the Targa Florio – the first was in 1953 when he won with a Lancia D.20 sports/racing coupé. Results:

1st V. Elford/U. Maglioli (Porsche 907), 69·04 mph
2nd N. Galli/I. Giunti (Alfa Romeo Tipo 33)
3rd M. Casoni/L. Bianchi (Alfa Romeo Tipo 33)
4th H. Herrmann/J. Neerpasch (Porsche 907)
5th T. Pilette/R. Slotemaker (Alfa Romeo Tipo 33)
6th G. Baghetti/G. Biscaldi (Alfa Romeo Tipo 33)

One of the results of the F.I.A.'s new Regulations was the combination of the Group 4 and Group 6 Championships into a World Manufacturer's Championship. This was how the scores stood after the Targa Florio:

1st Porsche, 39 points
2nd Ford, 18 points
3rd Alfa Romeo, 9 points

*Nürburgring 1000 Km Race*

Although there were 113 entries for the German race, eventually only 76 drivers ran to their cars at the fall of the flag. Many entrants simply failed to turn up and practice crashes ravaged the entry list. The most serious of these involved Chris Irwin whose 3-litre Ford Prototype left the road at the Flugplatz and the young Englishman received severe head injuries. In a season when the death toll among

Private owners and the 906 in 1968 – (*above*) Tony Dean at Silverstone and (*below*) Bill Bradley, who won the R.A.C. Sports Cars Championship, in the Tourist Trophy at Oulton Park (Guy Griffiths)

*Above:* Neck and neck in the 1968 B.O.A.C. '500' at Brands Hatch – Spoerry and Steinemann with their 910 and the works 907 of Scarfiotti and Herrmann (Nigel Snowdon). *Below:* Porsche idea of an aerofoil on the Siffert/Herrmann 3-litre car at Le Mans, 1968. How it works is explained in the text (Nigel Snowdon)

drivers was so tragically and inexplicably high, Irwin must have felt thankful that Providence had looked upon him less severely than it might. Even before this crash nasty rumours were circulating about the poor roadholding and instability of the Fords and journalists were beginning to have a hard look at the motives of drivers who were willing to handle them. The fight for outright victory lay between eight cars:

Porsche 908 (works):
  J. Siffert/V. Elford: 9 min 35·9 sec in practice (the poor time was because of injection trouble)
  G. Mitter/L. Scarfiotti: 8 min 40·1 sec
Porsche 907 2·2-litre (works):
  H. Herrmann/R. Stommelen: 8 min 32·8 sec
  J. Neerpasch/J. Buzzetta: 8 min 52·1 sec
Ford GT40 (J.W. Automotive):
  J. Ickx/P. Hawkins: 8 min 37·4 sec
  D. Hobbs/B. Redman: 9 min 3·7 sec
Ford 3-litre (Alan Mann Racing):
  F. Gardner/R. Attwood: 8 min 42·5 sec
Alfa Romeo Tipo 33 2½-litre:
  U. Schütz/L. Bianchi: 8 min 42·2 sec (entered diplomatically for this race, like the rest of the Autodelta Cars, by Alfa Romeo Deutschland)

Porsche again had entered a 911 for Killy and Guichet and there were several 910s in the hands of friends of Zuffenhausen which the works team was keeping an eye on.

One of the most striking aspects of the Nürburgring is the large number of American servicemen who come to watch races. They arrive by the horde in vast coaches with small windows that look more like security vans than a comfortable form of transportation and it may be a reflection on the tensions of American life that once they are released from their khaki cages, they run amok. The general aim seems to be to get inebriated as quickly as possible (which takes a lot of bottles of German beer) and when it rains – as it did during the 1968 race – and the spectator area turns into sodden, squelching bogs, many of the Americans take off their shoes and plop about in the mud bare-footed. When their shirts become soaked, these come off too. Groups of service-men stagger about, supporting each other and wolfing large, over-juicy sausages. And at times the commentator has to appeal to spectators not to throw bottles on the track. The German spectators try to behave as though the Americans were not there and push out their paunches even further in their attempts to remain dignified and aloof.

Siffert, who was well back down the line of starters, made a magnificent getaway and shoved his Porsche through the dense traffic jam, while the J.W. Ford drivers were still struggling to do up their seat belts, and was in fourth position by the end of the first lap. At this stage Mitter was leading the race, but Siffert went ahead on lap two. The 907s were running with the consistency of a Circle Line train on the London Tube system and held third and fourth places. The 3-litre Ford was in trouble right from the start, for on the first lap the retaining clip on the right-hand front brake calliper fell off and the brake pads with it. On the car's second lap, the driver's door came open and the air pressure twisted it out of shape and in addition a tyre punctured; when this was all sorted out, the car managed only a few laps before the engine died out on the circuit. The next of the leading contenders to be in trouble was the 3-litre Porsche of Mitter/Scarfiotti which started to dart sideways when the brakes were applied and just about every detachable component was changed without improving matters and the car was retired with a suspected broken chassis. The Alfa 2·5-litre car challenged the Porsche 907s strongly until the alternator driving belt broke and this meant a long pit stop and a time loss too great to overcome. Both the J.W. Fords ran well, but an unfortunate choice of driver pairings prevented them from challenging the leading Porsches. On the strength of his knowledge of the Nürburgring Paul Hawkins was paired with Jacky Ickx, but unfortunately his lap times were much slower and whenever he was at the wheel, their car lost ground. In the other Ford were Brian Redman and David Hobbs who were not expected to match the Porsche lap times, but Redman, despite not having driven at the Nürburgring previously, learned the circuit very quickly and if he had been partnering Ickx, Ford might very well have won the race outright. As it was, Porsche, as at Daytona and Sebring, had things very much their own way. Results:

1st J. Siffert/V. Elford (Porsche 908), 95·05 mph
2nd H. Herrmann/R. Stommelen (Porsche 907)
3rd J. Ickx/P. Hawkins (Ford GT40)

4th J. Neerpasch/J. Buzzetta (Porsche 907)
5th N. Galli/I. Giunti (Alfa Romeo Tipo 33 2-litre)
6th D. Hobbs/B. Redman (Ford GT40)

*Spa 1000 Km Race*

Clearly Porsches had a stiff battle on their hands if they were to win the Spa race, for, being a fast circuit, it favoured the Fords' superior top end performance, Belgian driver Jacky Ickx was completely at home on the circuit whatever the conditions and Brian Redman was such an improved driver that he was close to matching Ickx' lap times. Porsches arrived with four cars and six drivers and discarded the long-tail 908 as its extra speed along the straights was offset by its wandering under braking. Accordingly short-tailed 908s were fielded for Elford/Neerpasch and Herrmann/Stommelen, together with a 907 for Mitter/Schlesser (the driver who was to lose his life at the wheel of the air-cooled Honda at the French Grand Prix). On the Sunday morning of the race, the circuit was saturated by the so frequent Ardennes downpour and Ickx streaked away at the start with the GT40 Ford pursued by three Porsches and at the end of 12 laps had doubled the whole field apart from the two leading Stuttgart cars. The Porsche to be lapped was Elford's 908 which had the throttle linkage come apart and was now streaking through the field after its pit stop. By lap 25 Elford was back in fourth place ahead of the J.W. Ford of Hawkins/Hobbs. When Redman took over from Ickx, the rain was slackening and Brian had no difficulty in maintaining his lead. On lap 36 Hobbs was right behind the 908 of Neerpasch and as the pale blue Ford, enveloped in a cloud of spray, closed up on the Porsche, it went out of control – apparently because of a structural defect – and spun viciously; it bounced from bank to bank and Neerpasch was quite badly injured. Ickx took over for his final stint on lap 46 and the race ran its distance over a rapidly drying track without any changes of place amongst the leaders. Porsche had been beaten fair and square and there was nothing they could do to prevent it from happening again. For the Fords, which were still being carefully developed at Slough, were as fast as a 5-litre push-rod Prototype was likely to be (if such were allowed) and the combination of the Ford's speed and Ickx' skill was more than a 2·2 or 3-litre could cope with.

This race also saw the debut of the Marcos Mantis, which was plagued by a succession of minor troubles including wet electrics – but the event had been intended to form part of the model's development testing. The new 3-litre Matra, the sole 3-litre Ford entered and the Belgian Team V.D.S. Alfa 33s were also afflicted by problems with soaked electrical equipment – but which both Porsche and J.W. Automotive avoided by coating the electrical system with a generous layer of jelly. Results:

1st J. Ickx/B. Redman (Ford GT40), 122·11 mph
2nd G. Mitter/J. Schlesser (Porsche 907)
3rd H. Herrmann/R. Stommelen (Porsche 908)
4th P. Hawkins/D. Hobbs (Ford GT40)
5th G. Koch/R. Lins (Porsche 910)
6th D. Spoerry/R. Steinemann (Porsche 910)

*Watkins Glen Six Hours*

The postponement of Le Mans because of the strikes in France gave the teams a little breathing space in which to carry out some development work and it ensured that at least Porsche and J.W. Automotive turned up to support the Watkins Glen race. Two Howmets and John Woolfe's new Chevron-Repco were entered, but otherwise the entry was of much the same calibre as can be seen at Silverstone any weekend during the Club racing season.

Since the Nürburgring the Porsche 908s had been modified by fitting an air scoop on top of the left-hand wing to cool the oil tank and by two stabiliser flaps at the rear. These were a foot wide and seven inches high and pivoted on rods attached to the body and slightly to the rear of the suspension. A short horizontal arm and a long rod connected them with the lower suspension members. On the straights the flaps were raised at an angle of 35 degrees and acted simply as spoilers, but the linkage was arranged so that when the car was cornered, the angle of the flap of the loaded wheel on the outside of the corner was reduced, thereby reducing the aerodynamic pressure on that side of the car, while the angle of the flap of the wheel on the inside of the corner was raised. Vic Elford expressed the view that the flaps probably helped on fast sweeping bends, but that they were almost certainly useless on slow bends. Four short-tail 908s were driven at Watkins Glen by Siffert/Elford, Herrmann/Attwood, Patrick/Ikuzawa and Buzzetta/Follmer. Tetsu Ikuzawa was a Japanese driver who had put in several seasons of Formula Three racing in Britain and had raced a 906 in Japan.

The only change to the J.W. Automotive Fords was the fitting of 5-litre engines, still with Gurney-Weslake cylinder heads, instead of the former 4·7-litre units. Only 28 starters moved off when the green flag fell in excessively hot conditions and Siffert led until lap 13 when Ickx went ahead with the Ford. The young Belgian stayed in front until lap 37 and then the Porsche forged past again. A bare hour of racing had elapsed when the Porsche shot into the pits with a seized front wheel bearing. While the mechanics were labouring to change this, Herrmann appeared at the Porsche box because the alternator of his 908 was overcharging (this car had been running badly since the start of the race) and Patrick brought the second-place Porsche in; the American driver, half-conscious from the heat, stumbled out of the cockpit and Attwood took his place; Ikuzawa took over Herrmann's car, But it was all to no avail, for, as Vic Elford pointed out after the race, there was a very bad bump slap in the middle of one of the fastest corners and this was putting an excessive strain on the left-hand front wheel. Both Attwood and Elford brought their cars in to retire with wheel bearing failure – there was neither time nor point in changing the bearings. Herrmann's car, with which Siffert also had a go, was delayed by a succession of pit stops for battery changes and for the throttle linkage to be repaired, and finished sixth. The Fords, in the order Ickx/Bianchi and Hawkins/Hobbs, easily took first and second places with the Howmet of Thompson/Heppenstall in third spot. Taking into account the best five finishes so far, Porsche still led Ford in the Championship by 42 points to 40 and as the results of the Austrian Grand Prix counted for only half-points, the final outcome would not be known until after Le Mans. When asked about the Porsche failure in this race, von Hanstein smiled whimsically and attributed the failure to the luck of racing.

### A Lull In Championship Racing

Before the 24 Hours race on the Sarthe circuit, Porsches appeared in a number of less important races. The Circuit of Mugello provided the first ever victory for the Alfa Romeo Tipo 33, but it was hardly a convincing victory, for only one car finished out of four starters and after a month's training on the circuit. Second and third were

Porsches of the Swiss Hart-Ski team. Second was the 910 of Jo Siffert and Rico Steinemann. This was leading until Steinemann rushed into the pits to hand over to his co-driver, found that Siffert was sleeping in the back of the tender car in a semi-undressed state and had to do another lap. Third was a 911R – it looked suspiciously like the same car as Porsche had used at the press day at Hockenheim the previous December – driven by Dieter Spoerry and Ben Pon. It was Hart-Ski to the fore again at the Enna Cup held on 15th August on a circuit bordering Lake Pergusa in Sicily. The 150-mile race was easily won by Jo Siffert at the wheel of the team's 910 from the Serenissima which was making its debut in the hands of Jonathan Williams.

The J.W. Automotive Fords were not entered in the Austrian Grand Prix at Zeltweg airfield circuit on 25th August so the race was a complete Porsche benefit. The three 908s were on the front row of the grid together with Mauro Bianchi's 3-litre Alpine and these stayed in the first three places until Elford's car had the rod which operates the fuel metering unit and throttles break and made his way back to the pits with the engine on tick-over. So the 157-lap race ran out with Siffert's 908 leading home the similar car shared by Herrmann and Kurt Ahrens. Elford restarted to finish eighth. Privately entered 910s took the first three places in the 2-litre class. After the race the 'tell-tale' on the Herrmann/Ahrens car showed that it had been taken up to 10,500 rpm – the red line is at 8,500 rpm!

*Le Mans*

The Panther woman, the wall of death riders, the prize fighters in the side-shows, the greasy smell of cooking and the gendarmes were just the same at Le Mans in 1968 as in past years, but in some intangible way the race, held at the end of September, had a very different atmosphere from usual years when it was held in June. The combination of the 3 and 5-litre capacity limits, the start and finish of the race at 3 pm, the long hours of darkness, and the new Ford chicane before the pits so that the cars had to brake heavily after White House and negotiate two 45 mph corners before accelerating away up the hill past the pits had worked a transformation. No longer was Le Mans *the* fascinating spectacle of speed and entertainment, but just another motor race. Unkind critics (but, quite possibly, truthful ones) had suggested that the Ford Company had financed the new chicane so that their lap record would never be broken – indeed, if the chicane was needed, it was needed more in 1967 when lap speeds were higher.

The race was clearly going to be a straight duel between Porsche and the J.W. Automotive Fords – but there were some interesting interlopers. It was a sad reflection on Zuffenhausen fortunes that the Slough cars were the favourites in terms of both speed and reliability. The Porsches had been extensively tested and von Hanstein was keeping his fingers crossed and hoping that it was the Fords – and not the Porsches – that broke, just as they had at Daytona and Sebring.

*The Porsche Offensive*

*Entered by Porsche System Engineering:*
908, 2996 cc (capacity increased by larger bore of 85 mm), long-tail:
    Jo Siffert/Hans Herrmann
    Gerhard Mitter/Vic Elford
    Rolf Stommelen/Jochen Neerpasch
    Scooter Patrick/Joe Buzzetta
*Porsche Supporting Cars* (loaned by the works):
907, 2196 cc:
    Alex Soler-Roig (entrant)/Rudi Lins
    Gianrico Steinemann/Dieter Spoerry (entered by Squadra Tartaruga)
    Herbert Linge/Robert Buchet (entered by Philippe Farjon)
*Porsche Supporting Cars* (owned and entered by private owners):
906: Christian Poirot (entrant)/Pierre Maublanc
910: Jean-Pierre Hanrioud (entrant)/André Wicky
*Porsche Group 3 Grand Touring Cars:*
911T:
    Roger Vanderschrick/Jean-Pierre Gaban (entrant)
    Guy Chasseuil/Claude Ballot-Lena (entered by Auguste Veuillet, the 1951-52 1100 cc class winner)
    Willy Meier/Jean de Mortemart (entered by André Wicky)
    Claude Laurent (entrant)/Jean-Claude Ogier

*The Main Opposition*

Ford GT40, 4942 cc, entered by J.W. Automotive Engineering Ltd:

Pedro Rodriguez/Lucien Bianchi
David Hobbs/Paul Hawkins
Jackie Oliver/Brian Muir

*Outsiders*

Howmet TX, 2960 cc, entered by the Howmet Corporation:
Dick Thompson/Ray Heppenstall
Bob Tullius/Hugh Dibley
Matra 630, 2992 cc, entered by Matra Sports:
Johnny Servoz-Gavin/Henri Pescarolo
Alpine-Renault A-220, 2996 cc, entered by Société des Autombiles Alpine
Gerard Larrousse/Henri Grandsire
Jean Guichet/Jean-Pierre Jabouille
Alain de Cortanze/Jean Vinatier
Alpine-Renault A-220, 2996 cc, entered by Ecurie Savin Calberson:
Mauro Bianchi/Patrick Depailler

The 2-litre class was very much an Alfa Romeo Tipo 33 benefit with a grand total of six of these cars entered.

When Signor Agnelli, head of the Fiat organisation, dropped the flag to start the race, there was a momentary hush before the crowd roared as the drivers ran across the wet track to their cars. The Porsches were first away and it was Porsche-Porsche-Porsche-Porsche as the field swept down from the Dunlop Bridge to the Esses. The Fords moved through to hold the next three places and were circulating in a tight group – it only needed the leader, Brian Muir, to make a slight mistake and all three cars could have piled up. The fate of the works Jaguars in the 1956 event showed how easily this can happen. All three Fords were on wet weather tyres and were unable to get to grips with the Porsches on the rapidly drying track. With less than 35 minutes of the race run, Paul Hawkins brought his Ford in with a badly chunked rear tyre, a full change was made and the car rejoined the race on dry weather tyres; Rodriguez came in for a change shortly afterwards. Poor Brian Muir had a bad moment under braking for Mulsanne and ended up with the Ford deeply embedded in the sand bank. Desperately he tore down advertisement hoardings and pushed them under the rear wheels of the car, but it was all to no avail. By dint of almost three hours' digging he managed to extricate the car, but then it had to be withdrawn as the constant reversing had weakened the clutch and, under the minimum distance rule, it was likely to be disqualified for having covered insufficient laps.

At the end of two hours' racing Porsches were still first and second, but Neerpasch had been delayed with clutch trouble on his car and the Fords were third and fourth. Already the field had been depleted by retirements; the Climax-powered Healey SR had retired when the clutch splines jammed out on the circuit and the Dibley/ Tullius Howmet had broken its rear suspension and was destined for early retirement. All the time the Fords were forging closer and closer to the leaders. Towards the end of the fourth hour the Porsche team suffered their greatest set-back. Siffert, at the wheel of the leading Porsche, disappeared out on the circuit; after a long interval 'Seppe' reached the pits on foot to report that he had lost the drive when the car was travelling at close to 180 mph on the Mulsanne Straight and thought that the clutch had gone; at once a mechanic was sent out to the Porsche to find out exactly what had gone wrong as it would be a pointer to the potential weaknesses of the cars still running. Clutch trouble was the official diagnosis. By 7 pm the Fords were first and second, while mechanical troubles had caused the Stommelen/ Neerpasch car to lose seven laps, but it was still soldiering on. Stops y the Fords for fuel and tyres had put the Buzzetta/Patrick 908 back in the lead by 9 pm, the quarter-distance mark. The Ford of Rodriguez/ Bianchi was second, Mitter/Elford third and the Matra had risen to a menacing fourth. The Hawkins/Hobbs Ford was stationary in the pits with clutch trouble. To the cheers of the crowd, the Ford rejoined the race after an hour, but all the mechanics' work was in vain, for the car ground to a halt at Mulsanne not long afterwards with engine trouble. One Ford was left in the race and Porsche troubles were about to start in earnest.

The Stommelen/Neerpasch car was in constant trouble with its engine cooling fan; the Mitter/Elford 908 was throwing alternator belts and finally Ferdinand Piëch in the Porsche pit decided to take the plunge and change the alternator. The replacement of this component was strictly forbidden and it was just hoped that the vigilant commissaires would not notice. Porsche had nothing to lose for the car would have had to be retired anyway. Despite von Hanstein's vociferous protests the car was disqualified and the same fate befell the 907 of Buchet/Linge which had been bothered with starter soelnoid trouble and had the whole unit changed. The

Buzzetta/Patrick 908 was still in second place, but at around 10.30 pm it too started to throw alternator belts and after a 40-minute pit stop it was pushed into the paddock. Porsche's misfortunes had resulted in the sole remaining Ford leading from the Matra by three laps; the highest placed Porsches were the 907s of Steinemann/ Spoerry and Soler-Roig/Lins in third and fourth spots. A vivid reminder of Zuffenhausen reliability of the past were the Alfa Romeo Tipo 33s holding fifth, sixth, seventh and eighth places. The sole surviving 3-litre Porsche of Stommelen/Neerpasch had now been cured of its cooling fan problems and was being driven like the hammers of hell to make up lost ground – but it was too far behind to have any hopes of regaining the lead.

In the early hours of Sunday morning the rain cascaded down on the circuit, driving soaked spectators back to the cars, coaches and tents and forming light-reflecting pools all round the circuit. Just as it started Lucien Bianchi lost the Ford in a big way at the chicane – in full view of team manager David Yorke – but without hitting anything and motored on unabashed. In recent years the race has never been run in such bad conditions. At the height of the storm the very consistent running, brutal-looking 7-litre Chevrolet Stingray of Sylvain Garant hit the bank so hard at the Dunlop Turn that it disintegrated. The race came almost to a standstill as the drivers snaked their way through the wreckage. At around 5 am the rain stopped abruptly – as did the Matra with wiper trouble, but without losing its second place. With six hours to the finish the highest placed Porsches were fourth (Steinemann/Spoerry) and fifth (Stommelen/ Neerpasch), but they were seven and twelve laps behind the leading Ford and a lap and six behind the Matra and Alfa 33 in second and third places. During the night hours the Soler-Roig/Lins 907 had been forced out by a broken cam-follower.

Just after 11 am occurred the most horrifying incident in the race. As Mauro Bianchi swooped down from the Dunlop Bridge to the Esses, his Alpine had a tyre blow out, went sideways with the driver desperately trying to regain control and side-swiped the straw bales. There was an explosive bang, flames shot into the air and on both sides of the track, the panic-seized crowd, perhaps mindful of the 1955 disaster, scrambled up the slopes away from the fences; women fell into the mud and men tripped over them and left them there; a dense cloud of smoke rose from the burning car, straw bales on both sides of the track were ablaze and the competing cars came to a halt, the road completely blocked. When the hoses were brought out to fight the blaze, one running across the track had to be raised by a *pompier* so that the cars could pass beneath. It seemed impossible that the driver could have escaped from this inferno alive, but escape he did, unharmed apart from minor burns while all that was left of the Alpine was a charred mess of bent tubing.

As a result of mechanical trouble with the second-place Alfa, the Matra moved back into second place, but then punctured on debris from the Alpine wreckage. Pescarolo limped back towards the pits, but the damaged wheel caused so much vibration that the battery broke away from its mountings and set the rear of the car on fire. Pescarolo jumped unhurt from the low blue car which had raised so high French hopes of victory in their most important race. Porsches were now second and third, but with no hopes of catching the leading Ford; Lucien Bianchi continued to lap consistently despite his fears as to the fate of his younger brother. Porsche troubles were still not over, for two laps from the end the Chasseuil/Ballot-Lena 911, assured of 14th place and a class third, dropped a valve. At 3 pm a large bottle of champagne celebrated Ford's victory in the race for the third year in succession and John Wyer's defeat of Zuffenhausen's ambitions both at the Sarthe circuit and in the World Championship. Results:

1st P. Rodriguez/L. Bianchi (Ford GT40), 2727·02 miles (115·29 mph)
2nd R. Steinemann/D. Spoerry (Porsche 907)
3rd R. Stommelen/J. Neerpasch (Porsche 908)
4th I. Giunti/"Nanni" Galli (Alfa Romeo Tipo 33)
5th C. Facetti/S. Dini (Alfa Romeo Tipo 33)
6th M. Casoni/G. Biscaldi (Alfa Romeo Tipo 33)
7th R. Attwood/D. Piper (Ferrari 275LM)
8th A. de Cortanze/J. Vinatier (Alpine A-220 3-litre)

*World Manuafacturers' Groups 4 and 6 Championship*
1st Ford: 45 points
2nd Porsche: 42 points
3rd Alfa Romeo: 15½ points
4th Howmet, Alpine-Renault and Chevrolet: 4 points each
7th Ferrari: 2 points
8th Lola: 1 point

*World Manufacturers' Group 3 Grand Touring Championship*
1st Porsche: 45 points
2nd Chevrolet: 26 points
3rd M.G.: 7 points
4th Lancia: 4 points

*Non-Championship Races*

Both before and after Le Mans works Porsches raced in non-Championship events. On the 15th September Hans Herrmann scored a victory in the 203-km Nation Preis at Hockenheim from the Ferrari P3/4 of David Piper and the Ford GT40 of Paul Hawkins. A fortnight after Le Mans was the 1000-km sports car race at the Montlhéry circuit, 17 miles south of the centre of Paris. The 4·85-mile circuit consisted of several link roads and one side of the now almost derelict banked track. Straw bale chicanes were used to slow the cars at the start of the banking, in the middle and at the end opposite the pits. This was a direct result of the 1964 accident when Peter Lindner's Jaguar collided with Patria's Abarth and resulted in the deaths of both drivers – the remains of the E-type are still in pound with the Paris police. Fastest in practice was the 4·3-litre P3/4 Ferrari of David Piper and shared with Dickie Attwood, but next fastest were the three works Porsche 908s and the 3-litre Matra driven by Jean-Pierre Beltoise and Johnny Servoz-Gavin.

The Porsches led away from the start, but David Piper's 4·3-litre Ferrari, a Prototype no longer eligible to run in Championship events, proved there was no substitute for litres by howling past into the lead on lap two and stayed there; all Vic Elford's efforts to keep the Ferrari in sight were to no avail and merely resulted in a vicious spin. The beautifully prepared green Ferrari led until shortly after Attwood had taken over when it came into the pits to retire with a broken radiator mounting. Early in the race a broken oil pipe had been the downfall of the Matra and the two leading Porsches were now unchallenged. Hans Herrmann and Rolf Stommelen won at 100·24 mph from Vic Elford and Rudi Lins. The third car of the team driven by Buchet and Linge ran slowly throughout the race and after a pit stop to cure an oil leak finished a poor twelfth.

*The European Hill Climb Championship*

There were eight rounds in the Championship from the Montseny climb in Spain on 2nd June to the Mont Ventoux climb in France on 22nd September. Every one of these rounds, except the Abarth-dominated Trento-Bordone climb, was won by Gerhard Mitter and his 907 'Berg'. Mitter was undisputed Champion, but his victory was marred for Porsche by the tragedy that struck Scarfiotti at the German Rossfeld climb in June. Lodovico Scarfiotti was a member of both the Porsche team and the Cooper-B.R.M. Formula One team and as the Rossfeld climb was the same weekend as the Belgian Grand Prix, he was forced to miss the Spa race. "Lulu" or "Dodo", as he was known to his friends, the son of a cement manufacturer in Ancona, started racing in 1953 with a Fiat when he was just 20. He drove Ferraris on many occasions and his finest victory and his only Grand Prix win was in the Italian race at Monza in 1966. He had won the European Hill Climb Championship for Ferrari in both 1962 and 1965 and at Rossfeld, having made fastest practice, he crashed with fatal results. Scarfiotti was married and had two children.

*Post-Script*

The 1968 season had not brought the rewards in Prototype racing that Porsche had sought and had been expected to gain, for the cars had been plagued by completely uncharacteristic minor weaknesses. Competing in Prototype racing, rallying and the European Hill Climb Championship combined with the expanding production side and outside design work had strained Porsche's resources to the limit. Already Porsche had made it known that their rallying efforts in 1969 would be restricted to one car.

Late in 1968 Huschke von Hanstein ceased to be Racing Manager and became Press Officer which was his original role when he first joined the Company in 1951. Von Hanstein, who started racing motor cycles in the 1930s and won the 1940 closed circuit Mille Miglia at Brescia with a B.M.W. 328 coupé, has been outstandingly successful as Porsche's Racing Manager. With his sleek silver hair, thick glasses and neat brown suits, the quick-talking von Hanstein (with a superb command of English) gives the initial impression that he might be a rather voluble Black Forest clock maker, but his combination of personal racing experience, intimate knowledge of racing and his cars and his exceptional administrative ability having made him a team manager ranking with the 'greats' of this branch of motor racing – Neubauer of Mercedes-Benz, John Wyer of Aston Martin and Ford, David Yorke of Vanwall, Bertocchi of Maserati and, of course, Enzo Ferrari himself.

Von Hanstein's place has been taken by Rico Steinemann, editor of the Swiss magazine "*Powerslide*" and very successful driver of works-supported 907s and 910s. Helmuth Boll remains head of the racing department, while Ferdinand Piëch, son of Professor Porsche's sister, at the age of 31 is now the racing director and amongst his very successful designs have been the 906, 908 and 910. His complex task is aided by an IBM computer which speeds development by work on such matters as camshaft design, bearing loads and choice of gear ratios for known circuits.

For 1969 the 6-cylinder four-cam 910 has been homologated as a Group 4 car now that the necessary 25 have been built and throughout 1968 these were raced by private owners. Porsche had completed 15 of the 3-litre 908s by December, 1968, as it is the team's practice to build new cars for each important race. Two 908s, however, were written off on 13th December at Monza during tests when Gerhard Mitter and Karl von Wendt (successful driver of private Porsches) crashed, The aim for 1969 was to field three or four 908s in Prototype races driven by Jo Siffert, Gerhard Mitter, Vic Elford, Rolf Stommelen, Udo Schütz (after a year with the Autodelta team), Hans Herrmann, Dickie Attwood, Brian Redman and Kurt Ahrens. Jochen Neerpasch retired to become Competitions Manager of Ford-Germany.

At the Hockenheim circuit on 8th January, 1969, new team manager Steinemann and Huschke von Hanstein (deputising for Ferry Porsche) revealed their offensive for the coming season. Once again the cars were very varied and full of technical interest:

*908:* There were three versions of the 2997 cc car which now had a power output of 350 bhp at 8400 rpm on a compression ratio of 10·4:1 All 908s have a wheelbase of 7 ft 6·55 in:

*Normal coupé:* This had an overall length of 13 ft 1·48 in and was generally similar to the cars raced in 1968, Maximum speed was 185 mph. Weight was 12 cwt 108 lb.

'*Lang*' *coupé:* The long-tailed streamlined version of the 908 with a maximum speed of 200 mph. This model had a length of 15 ft 10 in and weighed 13 cwt 40 lb.

'*Spyder*': To take advantage of the 1969 Group 6 Regulation which dispense with minimum windscreen heights, Porsche had introduced this open car derived from their experience with the hill climb models. The length was only 13 ft 2·27 in and the car weighed 12 cwt 42 lb. Maximum speed was 175 mph and the model was raced mainly on the more tortuous circuits. The Spyder had a 5-speed gearbox and the coupés a 6-speed.

*909 'Berg'*; The 1981 cc (54·6 × 76 mm) flat eight Group 7 hill climb car with a power output of 275 bhp at 9000 rpm and a weight of only $8\frac{1}{2}$ cwt. Porsche did not compete in the 1969 European Hill Climb Championship, but the car may well be entrusted to a private owner for suitable events.

And what of the future? The post-war years have seen the rise and decline of many of the smaller manufacturers including Bristol, Aston Martin, Maserati and Borgward (the Bremen concern went into liquidation) and very often the decline has been the result of withdrawing from competition work which is so important for the image of a maker of sporting cars. Porsche's future rests in the hands of their directors and as long as they maintain the enthusiasm for motor sport, the flair for design and attention to detail which they have displayed over the last 21 years, we, the enthusiasts who love Porsche cars so much, need have no fears.

## THIRTEEN
# 1969: Resumé of the Season

*Racing in Florida*

Having so easily dominated the Daytona race in 1968, Porsche, with Rico Steinemann in charge and a team of five 908 *Lang* coupés turned up full of confidence at the Florida banked track for the 24 Hours' race held on 1st–2nd February. Opposition came from two Ford GT40 cars entered by JW Automotive and four Lola T70-Chevrolet cars. At the end of the first hour the Porsches held the first five places and their victory seemed certain. But it was not to be and the team's troubles started during the third hour when Redman came in, overcome by fumes from cracked exhausts; these were changed, the car rejoined the race and the same trouble affected all but one of the other cars. The car not affected was that of Attwood/Buzzetta, but this was the first to retire – after nine hours' racing – with a broken intermediate gear between the crankshaft and one bank of camshafts. During the night all remaining four cars of the team fell out with the same trouble, both JW Automotive Fords were eliminated and first two places at the finish went to Lolas with a Pontiac Firebird running in the Trans-Am Class third.

At Sebring Porsche once again fielded five cars, but they were 908 *Spyders*. The engines now had a new firing order giving smoother running in an effort to overcome the Daytona troubles and the intermediate idler shaft in the drive train had changed from alloy to steel. As the drivers were unable to detect whether the suspension-connected twin-flippers at the rear of the bodywork were disconnected or not, these were discarded. Since Daytona the opposition had been much strengthened and apart from the JW Fords, there was a single example of the new and very fast 3-litre Tipo 312 Ferrari – based on the team's Grand Prix car – driven by Chris Amon and Mario Andretti and three of the new, open 3-litre Alfa Romeo Tipo 33-3 cars. These Alfas were all eliminated during the first two hours of the race by the failure of the glue-assembled radiators, but the Ferrari put up a magnificent performance, harrying the Porsches and eventually finishing second to the Ford GT40 of Ickx and Oliver. It was another unhappy race for Porsche, as Elford, co-driving with Attwood, lost 40 min while a damaged wing was replaced, the cars of Herrmann/Ahrens and Siffert/Redman retired with fractured chassis cross-members and although the same trouble occurred on the Mitter/Schütz car – when leading the race – a bodge-up with steel bars enabled it to continue on to finish fifth. The highest placed 908 was that of Buzzetta/Stommelen which finished third and Soler-Roig/Lins took fourth place with a 907.

## The European Races

The B.O.A.C. '500' provided a complete Porsche benefit. The 908 *Spyders* had only one serious opponent, the Ferrari Tipo 312, which finished fourth, slowed by a stretched throttle cable. Siffert/Redman, the star combination of the 1969 season, were the winners at 100·2 mph from Elford/Attwood and Mitter/Schütz with Herrmann/Stommelen sixth; the latter pair were delayed by a 20-minute pit stop after running over wreckage from Bonnier's crashed Lola.

At the Monza 1000 Km race held over the combined road and track circuit four Porsche 908 *Lang* coupés were fielded. These had full-width aerofoils mounted on vestigial tail-fins with adjustable twin-tabs at each end and operated by links coupled to the suspension. Facing the Stuttgart cars were two of the Ferraris driven by Amon/Andretti and Rodriguez/Schetty and only Siffert of the Porsche team could match their speed. Andretti was delayed by tyre trouble and this car blew up its engine in a spectacular manner after putting up a tremendous fight; Rodriguez spun and crashed his Ferrari as a result of the tail-section disintegrating after a minor accident. Of the Porsches, Siffert/Redman and Herrmann/Ahrens were first and second, but the Schütz/Mitter car broke its engine – gear-selection trouble and a missed 'change resulted in over-revving – and Elford crashed the car he was sharing with Attwood after a tyre burst. Third was the 907 of Koch/Dechent.

The absence of works Ferraris and any cars from JW Automotive meant that Porsche had things completely their own way in the Targa Florio. The only serious challenger, the 2½-litre Autodelta Alfa 33 of Vaccarella and de Adamich, retired with engine trouble.

Porsche fielded six 908 *Spyders* and took the first four places in the order Mitter/Schütz, Elford/Maglioli, Herrmann/Stommelen and von Wendt/Klausen. Larrousse/Lins were classified 21st after gear-selection trouble, Redman/Attwood retired with drive-shaft failure and a works 911R driven by Spoerry/Toivonen caught fire.

Just before the Geneva Show in March Porsche had announced the new Type 917 car with a 4495 cc flat-twelve and, as usual, air-cooled engine developing 520 bhp (DIN) at 8000 rpm. General design principles followed those successfully employed with the 907 and 908, transmission is by a 5-speed gearbox and the car was designed for use with long or short tail. For it to be eligible for Championship racing Porsche had to construct 25 examples of the 917 and this they did immediately. The cars were offered at a price of £14,000. Clearly the 917 was a rush job and it seemed that Porsche were determined to possess a team of cars that could more than match the speed of the JW Automotive Fords – in 1968 the Slough-prepared cars had proved as fast as the 908s. But it is one thing to build a car like the 917 and another and longer undertaking to develop it into a race-winning state. The line-up of 25 cars that Porsche had so proudly presented for homologation in Group 4 all had to be rebuilt and in its first few races the 917 appeared to be almost uncontrollable.

At the Spa 1000 Km race Porsche had two 917s, but only Mitter and Schütz drove one in the race and this retired early on with engine failure. The sole 312 Ferrari was superbly driven into second place by Rodriguez and David Piper, but on this difficult and very fast circuit only Siffert had the legs of the Maranello car and although Redman was slower, the Swiss driver was able to keep the long-tailed 908 sufficiently far ahead for it not to be caught when his team-mate was at the wheel. Third and fourth were the similar 908s of Elford/Ahrens and Stommelen/Herrmann. It was Porsche all the way in the Nürburgring 1000 Km race and the winning drive of Siffert/Redman clinched the team's victory in the Sports Car Championship. Their car and the 908s that took the next four places were 908 *Spyders*, but three of the cars had redesigned bodywork and faired-in cockpits. Mitter/Schütz were seriously delayed by wheel bearing failure and finished at the tail of the field. Again only a single 917 ran, driven by Frank Gardner and David Piper, and handling atrociously as at Spa it finished eighth.

It has been said that Porsche's bid to win Le Mans cost £500,000, but little joy did it bring the Stuttgart concern. The race was marred by the fatal crash on the first lap of John Woolfe with the first 917 to be delivered to a private owner; the vast armada of works cars proved lacking in reliability; and the JW Automotive Fords had a stamina and speed that resulted in the final laps turning into the most exciting finish in the history of the race. Jacky Ickx took the chequered flag a mere 100 yards ahead of Hans Herrmann after the two cars had swapped places a dozen times in almost as few minutes. This is how the works Porsches fared:

917: Stommelen/Ahrens: led early in the race, but retired with an oil leak on the Sunday morning.

917: Elford/Attwood: was leading the race less than three hours before the finish when it retired with transmission failure. Elford set a new lap record of 145·42 mph, bettering the pre-Ford Chicane record.

908 *Lang:* Schütz/Mitter: Schütz crashed when in second place early on Sunday morning.

908 *Lang:* Herrmann/Larrousse: took second place after a long pit stop caused by front wheel bearing failure.

908 *Lang:* Lins/Kauhsen (works car entered in the name of the Hart-Ski Team): retired with clutch failure on Saturday evening when in second place.

908 *Spyder:* Siffert/Redman: this car, which had two high tail-fins, led after four hours, but retired with gearbox damage caused by an oil leak.

After long arguments the 917s were permitted to run at Le Mans with their aerofoils fully operating because they had been homologated with these, but the 908s ran with their full-width flaps in a fixed position. Porsche vastly exceeded their racing budget in the early part of 1969 and after Le Mans the size of their entries was much reduced!

For the 1969 Can-Am series of races Porsche produced a *Spyder* version of the 917 known as the PA (Prototype America). The design was sponsored by the Audi division of V.W.

# APPENDIX ONE
# Specification of Porsche Cars

## 356 PRODUCTION MODELS, 1953

**ENGINE**
*General design:* 4-cylinder horizontally opposed push-rod overhead valve with air cooling through blower.

|  | *1·1-litre* | *1·3-litre* | *1·5-litre* | *1500 Super* |
|---|---|---|---|---|
| *Bore:* | 73·5 mm | 80 mm | 80 mm | 80 mm |
| *Stroke:* | 64 mm | 64 mm | 74 mm | 74 mm |
| *Capacity:* | 1086 cc | 1286 cc | 1488 cc | 1488 cc |
| *Power output:* | 40 bhp at 4200 rpm | 44 bhp at 4400 rpm | 55 bhp at 4400 rpm | 70 bhp at 5000 rpm |
| *Comp. ratio:* | 6·5 : 1 | 6·5 : 1 | 7 : 1 | 8·2 : 1 |

*Camshaft drive:* spiral-toothed spur wheels
*Crankshaft:* running in four light alloy slide bearings
*Firing order:* 1–4–3–2
*Carburettors:* twin Solex downdraught 32 PBI

**TRANSMISSION**
*Clutch:* single dry-plate
*Gearbox:* 4-speed all-synchromesh, with ball, socket and rod-operated gear-lever and ratios of 1st, 3·15; 2nd, 1·76; 3rd, 1·13; and top, 0·815 : 1.
*Final drive:* spiral bevel with conical wheel compensating gear

**CHASSIS**
*Frame:* welded pressed-steel box-frame
*Front suspension:* independent by parallel links and square laminated torsion bars
*Rear suspension:* individual torsion bars for each wheel
*Steering:* worm gear with divided track rod
*Brakes:* hydraulic to all four wheels

*Wheelbase:* 6 ft 11 in    *Front track:* 4 ft 2¾ in
*Rear track:* 4 ft 1¼ in    *Length:* 12 ft 5½ in
*Width:* 5 ft 5¼ in    *Height:* 4 ft 3¼ in
*Dry weight:* 1640 lb

**Porsche 356 Model Distinctions**

TYPE 356

*1·1-litre* (40 bhp at 4000 rpm)
Original type that first appeared in 1948. The engine was typed the 369 and the car was in production from 1950–54 with steel body by Reutter.

# APPENDIX 1: SPECIFICATION OF PORSCHE CARS

*1·3-litre* (44 bhp at 4200 rpm)
As 1·1-litre, except that it did not appear until 1951. The engine was typed the 506. The early cars had an overbored 1100 cc engine with the same 64 mm stroke, but the 74 mm stroke of the 1500 was adopted in 1953 and the engine was then known as the Type 506/1.

*1500* (60 bhp at 5000 rpm)
As 1·1-litre, except that it did not appear until October, 1951. Both this and the 1500 'Damen' were often referred to in catalogues as the 1·5-litre. The engine was the first in a Porsche to have a roller-bearing crankshaft and it was typed the 527.

*1500 'Damen'* (55 bhp at 4400 rpm)
In 1952 the range was sub-divided and this was the 'cooking' model with reduced power output and plain bearing crankshaft. The engine was known as the Type 546; it was the first Porsche model to have an all-synchromesh gearbox.

*1500 'Super'* (70 bhp at 5000 rpm)
The higher performance model introduced simultaneously with the 'Damen'. The engine was known as the Type 528.

*1500 'America'*
A run of 15 cars to 'Super' specification built with open bodywork in 1952.

*1300 'Super'*
Higher-performance 1300 model with engined typed as the 589 and introduced in 1953. This engine had roller main bearings, alloy cylinders and the standard 74 mm stroke.

*1300 'Normal'* (44 bhp at 4200 rpm)
Revised version of the ordinary 1300 with 74 mm stroke which was in production from 1954 to 1957.

*Speedster*
Open version available in both 1300 and 1500, Normal and Super forms from 1954 and 1600 form until 1958.

TYPE 356A
(The 356A had a slightly 'cleaner' body, was a little heavier and had fractionally increased track. Engine capacity was increased to 1582 cc (82·5 × 74 mm)).

*1600 'Normal'* (60 bhp at 4500 rpm)
The engine was typed the 616/1 and the model remained in production from October, 1955 until 1959.

*1600 'Super'* (75 bhp at 5000 rpm)
The engine was typed the 616/2 and the model remained in production from October, 1955 until 1959.

*1500GS 'Carrera'* (100 bhp at 6200 rpm)
High-performance model powered by the 1498 cc four overhead camshaft 'Spyder' engine in production from October, 1955. From 1957 the 'Carrera' was offered in de luxe (100 bhp) and GT (110 bhp) forms.

*1600 'Carrera'*
From 1958 the 'Carrera' was also increased to 1600 cc and continued to be available in two degrees of tune.

*Convertible D*
Built by the Drauz body works and fitted with wind-up windows, the model was available from 1958 in 1600 'Normal' and 'Super' forms.

## TYPE 356B

(The 356B had raised bumpers and headlamps, rear seats, an enlarged windscreen, improved drum brakes and a shorter gear-lever. The Convertible D was replaced by the Roadster.)

*60* (60 bhp at 4500 rpm)
In production from late 1959 until July, 1963.

*'Super' 75* (75 bhp at 5000 rpm)
In production from late 1959 until July, 1963.

*'Super' 90* (90 bhp at 5500 rpm)
In production from late 1959 until July, 1963. There were larger Carrera carburettors and larger inlet ports and claimed maximum speed was 115 mph.

*'Carrera' 2* (130 bhp at 6200 rpm)
The 356 fitted with the 92 × 74 mm version of the 2-litre four overhead camshaft competition engine and the first production Porsche with disc brakes. It entered production in 1962.

## TYPE 356C

(The body was far more comfortable, more vertical headlamps were fitted and the model could be distinguished from the 356B by the larger rear window and twin instead of a single air vent in the tail.)

*1600* (75 bhp at 5200 rpm)
Standard version made from July, 1963 until May, 1965.

*1600SC* (95 bhp at 5800 rpm)
Higher performance made from July, 1963 until May, 1965.


550 'SPYDER', 1955

ENGINE
*Capacity:* 1498 cc (85 × 66 mm)
*No. of cylinders:* four, horizontally opposed
*Valves:* two per cylinder
*Valve actuation:* twin overhead camshafts per bank of cylinders
*Carburation:* twin Solex or single Weber 40 DCM instrument
*Cooling:* air-cooled
*Compression ratio:* 9·5 : 1
*Lubrication:* dry sump
*Power output:* 110 bhp at 6200 rpm

TRANSMISSION
*Clutch:* hydraulically operated single-plate
*Gearbox:* 4-speed all-synchromesh with overall ratios of 1st, 13·92; 2nd, 7·72; 3rd, 4·94; and top, 3·56 : 1
*Final drive:* ZF with splash lubrication

**CHASSIS**
*Frame:* multi-tubular
*Front suspension:* independent by trailing arms and torsion bars
*Rear suspension:* independent by swing axles and torsion bars
*Fuel capacity:* 20 gallons
*Tyre size:* front: 5·00 × 16; rear: 5·25 × 16
*Wheelbase:* 6 ft 10¾ in                *Front track:* 4 ft 2¾ in
*Rear track:* 4 ft 1¼ in                *Overall length:* 11 ft 9¾ in
*Overall width:* 5 ft 1 in              *Overall height:* 3 ft 4 in
*Dry weight:* 13½ cwt


## 718 RSK, 1958

**ENGINE**
*Capacity:* 1587·5 cc (87·5 × 66·0 mm)
*No. of cylinders:* four, horizontally opposed
*Valves:* two per cylinder at an angle of 90 degrees and operated through rocking fingers
*Valve actuation:* twin overhead camshafts per bank of cylinders driven by spiral bevel gears and shafts to the lower, exhaust camshafts and then upwards to the inlet mechanism
*Crankshaft:* counter-balanced and running in three roller and one ball-bearing
*Crankcase:* heavily finned, light alloy
*Cylinder barrels:* cast separately and with hard aluminium bores
*Cylinder heads:* light alloy, cast in pairs

*Carburation:* two twin-choke Weber IDM instruments
*Ignition:* twin plugs per cylinder and twin distributors
*Lubrication:* dry sump with the force-feed and scavenge pump assembly driven by gears at the base of the magneto drive
*Cooling:* centrifugal blower, belt-driven from the crankshaft
*Compression ratio:* 9·8 : 1
*Power output:* 165 bhp at 8000 rpm


**TRANSMISSION**
*Clutch:* single dry-plate
*Gearbox:* 5-speed with synchromesh on the upper four ratios, in unit with the final drive and with Elektron casting
*Final drive:* ZF differential with splash lubrication


**CHASSIS**
*Frame:* small-diameter multi-tubular space-frame
*Body:* light alloy
*Front suspension:* torsion bars, radius arms, trailing arms and anti-roll bar
*Rear suspension:* fabricated swing-axles pivoted on cross-member below the gearbox casing, fore and aft location by Watts linkage and coil springs
*Steering gear:* ZF
*Brakes:* ATE 11 in drum
*Fuel tankage:* fuel tanks above spare wheel in nose and alongside the passenger seat giving a capacity of 28½ gallons
*Wheels:* 16 in five-stud, bolt-on pressed aluminium

*Tyres:* front: 5·00 × 16; rear: 5·25 × 16
*Wheelbase:* 6 ft 10¾ in
*Rear track:* 4 ft 1¼ in
*Overall width:* 4 ft 10¼ in
*Ground clearance:* 5 in

*Front track:* 4 ft 2¾ in
*Overall length:* 12 ft 5¾ in
*Overall height:* 2 ft 10¾ in
*Dry weight:* 10¼ cwt

## CARRERA 2, 1962–65

ENGINE
*Capacity:* 1966 cc (92 × 74 mm)
*No. of cylinders:* four, horizontally opposed
*Valves:* two per cylinder
*Valve actuation:* twin overhead camshafts per bank of cylinders
*Carburation:* twin Solex instruments
*Cooling:* air-cooled
*Compression ratio:* 9·5 : 1
*Power output:* 130 bhp at 6200 rpm

TRANSMISSION
*Gearbox:* 4-speed all-synchromesh with overall ratios of 1st, 13·69; 2nd, 7·82; 3rd, 5·01; and top, 3·78 : 1
*Final drive:* spiral bevel with ratio of 4·43 : 1

CHASSIS
*Frame:* welded pressed steel box-frame
*Front suspension:* twin trailing arms, two square-section torsion bars and anti-roll bar
*Rear suspension:* swing-axles with a round-section torsion bar per wheel
*Steering:* cam and peg
*Brakes:* 11 in disc
*Tyre size:* 5·90 × 15 in
*Wheelbase:* 6 ft 11 in
*Rear track:* 4 ft 2 in
*Overall width:* 5 ft 5 in

*Front track:* 4 ft 2¾ in
*Overall length:* 13 ft 2 in
*Kerb weight:* 2227 lb

## FORMULA ONE CAR, 1962

ENGINE
*Capacity:* 1494 cc (66 × 54·6 mm)
*No. of cylinders:* eight, horizontally opposed
*Valves:* two per cylinder
*Valve actuation:* twin overhead camshafts per bank driven by a series of shafts and bevel gears.
*Crankshaft:* running in nine main bearings
*Cylinder block and crankcase:* Elektron alloy
*Cylinder heads:* aluminium alloy
*Carburation:* four 38 mm twin-choke downdraught Weber instruments
*Ignition:* twin plugs per cylinder, four coils and twin distributors
*Lubrication:* dry sump system with oil radiator mounted low down at the front and lower chassis members serving as oil pipes.
*Cooling:* air-cooled with glass-fibre horizontal fan driven by shafts and bevel gears
*Power output:* 180 bhp at 9300 rpm

## APPENDIX 1: SPECIFICATION OF PORSCHE CARS

**TRANSMISSION**
*Clutch:* mechanically operated single dry-plate
*Gearbox:* 6-speed with synchromesh on the upper five ratios, a right-hand gear change and in unit with the final drive

**CHASSIS**
*Frame:* multi-tubular space-frame constructed from mild steel tubing, with wall thickness of 1 mm and diameter ranging from 15 to 30 mm
*Front suspension:* wide-based bottom wishbones, narrow-based cantilever-type top wishbones pivoting on the chassis and acting on adjustable longitudinal torsion bars, top radius arms, inboard-mounted dampers and anti-roll bar
*Rear suspension:* narrow-based bottom and top wishbones, the upper acting on longitudinal torsion bars, inboard-mounted dampers and anti-roll bar
*Fuel tankage:* main tank alongside and behind the seat with supplementary tanks in the nose and above the driver's knees
*Wheelbase:* 7 ft 6½ in
*Front track:* 4 ft 3¼ in
*Rear track:* 4 ft 5½ in


### CARRERA 904 GTS, 1964

**ENGINE**
*Capacity:* 1966 cc (92 × 74 mm)
*No. of cylinders:* four, horizontally opposed
*Valves:* two per cylinder
*Valve actuation:* twin overhead camshafts per bank of cylinders
*Carburation:* two 46 mm twin-choke downdraught Weber instruments
*Cooling:* air-cooled with centrifugal fan
*Compression ratio:* 9·8 : 1
*Power output:* 180 bhp at 7000 rpm (racing) and 155 bhp at 6400 rpm (standard)

**TRANSMISSION**
*Clutch:* single dry-plate
*Gearbox:* 5-speed all-synchromesh with overall ratios of 1st, 11·7; 2nd, 7·46; 3rd, 5·39; 4th, 4·26; and top, 3·36 : 1 (racing); and 1st, 11·7; 2nd, 7·46; 3rd, 5·39; 4th, 3·94; and top, 3·00 : 1 (standard)
*Final drive:* by solid drive-shafts with joggled Hooke joints at the inboard end to take up vibrations in length due to the suspension geometry.

**CHASSIS**
*Frame:* box-section ladder-type
*Front suspension:* independent by double wishbones, co-axial coil spring and damper units and anti-roll bar
*Rear suspension:* independent by double transverse links and radius arms, co-axial coil spring and damper units and anti-roll bar
*Steering:* rack-and-pinion
*Brakes:* Porsche-ATE dual circuit disc front and rear
*Wheels:* 15 in pressed steel disc
*Tyres:* 5·50 × 15 front and 6·00 × 15 rear (racing)
*Wheelbase:* 7 ft 6·75 in
*Rear track:* 4 ft 3·6 in
*Overall height:* 3 ft 5·5 in
*Front track:* 4 ft 3·6 in
*Overall length:* 13 ft 6 in
*Overall width:* 5 ft 0·75 in

## 911, 1965

**ENGINE**
*Capacity:* 1991 cc (80 × 66 mm)
*No. of cylinders:* six, horizontally opposed
*Valves:* two per cylinder
*Valve actuation:* single overhead camshaft per bank of cylinders
*Crankshaft:* running in eight main bearings
*Cylinder barrels and heads:* machined from light alloy castings
*Carburation:* two triple-choke 40 mm Solex instruments
*Lubrication:* dry sump
*Cooling:* air-cooled
*Compression ratio:* 9·0 : 1
*Power output:* 145 bhp at 6100 rpm

**TRANSMISSION**
*Clutch:* single dry-plate
*Gearbox:* 5-speed baulk-ring synchromesh with overall ratios of top, 3·64; 4th, 4·26; 3rd, 5·39; 2nd, 7·87; 1st, 12·57 : 1
*Final drive:* spiral bevel with ratio of 4·428 : 1

**CHASSIS**
*Frame:* steel unit body and chassis
*Front suspension:* independent by Macpherson struts, single lower wishbones and torsion bars, with anti-roll bar and telescopic dampers
*Rear suspension:* independent by triangulated trailing links and torsion bars, with telescopic dampers

*Steering:* rack-and-pinion
*Brakes:* disc with swept area of 365 sq in, 10·6 in diameter at front and 11 in at rear
*Fuel tankage:* 13·6 imp gallons
*Wheels:* perforated steel disc
*Tyre size:* 165 × 15
*Wheelbase:* 7 ft 3 in
*Rear track:* 4 ft 3·7 in
*Overall width:* 5 ft 3·5 in
*Ground clearance:* 6 in
*Front track:* 4 ft 4·5 in
*Overall length:* 13 ft 8 in
*Overall height:* 4 ft 4 in
*Kerb weight:* 19·1 cwt

## 906 CARRERA 6, 1966

**ENGINE**
*Capacity:* 1991 cc (80 × 66 mm)
*No. of cylinders:* six, horizontally opposed
*Valves:* two per cylinder
*Valve actuation:* single overhead camshaft per bank of cylinders
*Carburation:* two triple-choke Weber 46 IDA 3c instruments
*Cooling:* air-cooled
*Compression ratio:* 10·3 : 1
*Power output:* 210 bhp at 8000 rpm (DIN)—equivalent to approx. 230 bhp SAE

**TRANSMISSION**
*Clutch:* single dry-plate
*Gearbox:* 5-speed all-synchromesh
*Final drive:* to wheels by sliding spline drive-shafts

## APPENDIX 1: SPECIFICATION OF PORSCHE CARS

**CHASSIS**
*Frame:* multi-tubular space-frame
*Body:* glass-fibre with hinged and quickly detachable rear section and gull-wing doors
*Front suspension:* double wishbones, combined coil spring and damper units and adjustable anti-roll bar
*Rear suspension:* double wishbones, combined coil spring and damper units and adjustable anti-roll bar
*Steering:* rack-and-pinion
*Brakes:* Dunlop-ATE disc on all four wheels and mounted outboard
*Wheels:* 15 in pressed steel with light alloy rims, 7 in at front and 9 in at rear
*Wheelbase:* 7 ft 6½ in
*Front track:* 4 ft 3 in
*Rear track:* 4 ft 7 in
*Overall length:* 13 ft 5 in
*Overall height:* 3 ft 2½ in
*Weight* (without fuel): 11 cwt 3 lb

## 908 NORMAL COUPE, 1968

**ENGINE**
*Capacity:* 2996 cc (85 × 66 mm)
*No. of cylinders:* eight, horizontally opposed
*Valves:* two per cylinder
*Valve actuation:* twin overhead camshafts per bank of cylinders
*Carburation:* Bosch indirect fuel injection
*Cooling:* air-cooled
*Compression ratio:* 10·3:1
*Power output:* 310 bhp at 8000 rpm

**TRANSMISSION**
*Clutch:* dry multi-plate
*Gearbox:* 6-speed all-synchromesh

**CHASSIS**
*Frame:* multi-tubular space-frame
*Body:* glass-fibre
*Front suspension:* double wishbones, combined coil spring and damper units and adjustable anti-roll bar
*Rear suspension:* double wishbones, combined coil spring and damper units and adjustable anti-roll bar
*Steering:* rack-and-pinion
*Brakes:* Dunlop-ATE disc on all four wheels and mounted outboard
*Wheelbase:* 7 ft 6½ in
*Front track:* 4 ft 8·3 in
*Rear track:* 4 ft 7·1 in
*Overall length:* 13 ft 5½ in
*Overall height:* 3 ft 2·6 in
*Weight* (without fuel): 12 cwt

# APPENDIX TWO
# Porsche Competition Performances

SPORTS CAR PERFORMANCES, 1951-61

*1951*
Le Mans 24 Hours,            *20th, A. Veuillet/E. Mouche (356 1100)
23rd-24th June

*1952*
Mille Miglia,            1st (1500 cc Gran Turismo class), Count
3rd-4th May,            Lurani/Count Berckheim (356), 65·14 mph
972 miles

Le Mans 24 Hours,            *11th, A. Veuillet/E. Mouche (356 1100),
14th-15th June            Retired, H. von Hanstein/P. Müller (brake failure, 356 1100)

*1953*
Le Mans 24 Hours,            *15th, R. von Frankenberg/H. von Hanstein
13th-14th June            16th, H. Glöckler/H. Herrmann (both cars were push-rod 1500 cc, tubular chassis prototype coupés)

Carrera Panamericana Mexico,    Retired, K. Kling (engine trouble, 550
19th-23rd November,            'Spyder')
1,934 miles            Retired, H. Herrmann (front suspension trouble, 550 'Spyder')

*1954*
Mille Miglia,            *6th, H. Herrmann/H. Linge (550 'Spyder')
1st-2nd May,
992 miles

Le Mans 24 Hours,            *12th, J. Claes/P. Stasse (550 'Spyder'),
12th-13th June            *14th, A. Duntov/G. Olivier (550 'Spyder' 1100),
           Retired, H. Herrmann/H. Polensky (burnt piston, 550 'Spyder'),
           Retired, R. von Frankenberg/H. Glöckler (burnt piston, 550 'Spyder')

Rheims 12 Hours Race,            *8th, H. Polensky/R. von Frankenberg (550
4th July            'Spyder'),
           13th, A. Veuillet/G. Olivier (550 'Spyder')

* denotes class winner

APPENDIX 2: PORSCHE COMPETITION PERFORMANCES 181

| | |
|---|---|
| Silverstone, Combined 1500 and 1100 cc sports car race, 17th July, 50 miles | 3rd in 1500 cc class, H. Herrmann (550 'Spyder'), 1st in 1100 cc class, H. von Hanstein (550 'Spyder') |
| Rheinland Cup 1500 cc sports car race, Nürburgring, 1st August, 99 miles | 1st, H. Herrmann (550 'Spyder'), 76·37 mph, 2nd, R. von Frankenberg (550 'Spyder'), 3rd, H. Polensky (550 'Spyder'), 4th, H. von Hanstein (550 'Spyder') |
| Carrera Panamericana Mexico, 19th-23rd November, (1500 cc Sports Category), 1,908 miles | 1st, H. Herrmann (550 'Spyder'), 2nd, J. Juhan (550 'Spyder') |

*1955*

| | |
|---|---|
| Sebring 12 Hours, 13th March | 8th, H. von Hanstein/H. Linge (550 'Spyder') |
| Mille Miglia, 30th April-1st May, 992 miles | *8th, W. Seidel (550 'Spyder') |
| Le Mans 24 Hours, 11th-12th June | *4th, H. Polensky/R. von Frankenberg (550 'Spyder'), 5th, W. Seidel/A. Milhoux (550 'Spyder'), 6th, H. Glöckler/J. Juhan (550 'Spyder'), *13th, A. Duntov /A.Veuillet (550 'Spyder' 1100) |
| Kristianstad Series Production Sports Car Race, Sweden, 7th August, 65 miles | 1st, R. von Frankenberg (550 'Spyder') |
| Goodwood Nine Hours Race, 20th August | 10th, W. Seidel/R. D. Steed (550 'Spyder'), Crashed, S. Moss/H. von Hanstein (550 'Spyder') |
| Nürburgring 500 Km Race, 28th August | 2nd, R. von Frankenberg (550 'Spyder'), 6th, H. Linge (550 'Spyder') |
| Tourist Trophy, Dundrod, 17th September, 623 miles | *9th, C. Shelby/M. Gregory (550 'Spyder'), 12th, H. Glöckler/W. Seidel (550 'Spyder'), 16th, R. von Frankenberg/H. Linge (550 'Spyder') |
| Avusrennen, 25th September, 155 miles | 1st, R. von Frankenberg (550 'Spyder') 122·78 mph |

*1956*

| | |
|---|---|
| Sebring 12 Hours Race, 8th April | *6th, H. Herrmann/W. von Trips (550 'Spyder'), 7th, E. McAfee/P. Lovely (550 'Spyder) |
| Mille Miglia, 28th-29th April, 992 miles | Retired, H. Herrmann (valve trouble, 550 'Spyder'), Retired, G. Bracco (brake failure, 550 'Spyder') |

| | |
|---|---|
| Nürburgring 1000 Km Race, 27th May | *4th, W. von Trips/U. Maglioli (RS), 6th, H. Herrmann/R. von Frankenberg (RS) |
| Targa Florio, 10th June, 447 miles | *1st, U. Maglioli/H. von Hanstein (RS), 56·37 mph |
| Rheims 12 Hours Race (1500 cc cars), 30th June-1st July | 1st, R. von Frankenberg/C. Storez (RS), 102·26 mph, 2nd, C. Goethals/P. Goethals (550 'Spyder') |
| Le Mans 24 Hours, 28th-29th July | *5th, R. von Frankenberg/W. von Trips (RS), Retired, H. Herrmann/U. Maglioli (valve trouble, RS) |
| Rheinland Cup 1500 cc sports car race, Nürburgring, 5th August, 98 miles | 1st, H. Herrmann (RS), 81·09 mph, 4th, R. von Frankenberg (RS), 5th, U. Maglioli (RS), Retired, W. von Trips (engine failure, RS) |

*1957*

| | |
|---|---|
| Mille Miglia, 12th May, 992 miles | *5th, H. Herrmann (RS), *16th, P. Strahle/H. Linge (Carrera) |
| Nürburgring 1000 Km Race, 26th May | *4th, U. Maglioli/E. Barth (RS), 7th, R. von. Frankenberg/E Schulze (RS) |
| Le Mans 24 Hours, 22nd-23rd June | Crashed, U. Maglioli/E. Barth (RSK), Retired, H. Herrmann/R. von Frankenberg (piston failure, RS), Retired, C. Storez/E. Crawford (broken crankshaft, RS) |

*1958*

| | |
|---|---|
| Buenos Aires 1000 Km, 26th January | *3rd, S. Moss/J. Behra (1600 cc RS), 5th, E. Barth/R. Mieres (RS) |
| Sebring 12 Hours, 22nd March | *3rd, H. Schell/W. Seidel (RS), 10th, H. von Hanstein/H. Linge (RS) |
| Targa Florio 11th May, 626 miles | *2nd, J. Behra/G. Scarlatti (RSK), *6th, A. Pucci/H. von Hanstein (Carrera), Retired, E. Barth/G. Scarlatti (broken driveshaft, RS) |
| Nürburgring 1000 Km Race, 1st June | *11th, R. von Frankenberg/C. G. de Beaufort/ E. Barth (RSK), 12th, P. Frère/H. Schell (RSK), Retired, J. Behra/E. Barth (valve trouble, RSK) |
| Le Mans 24 Hours, 21st-22nd June | *3rd, J. Behra/H. Herrmann (RSK 1600), *4th, E. Barth/P. Frère (RSK), 5th, C. G. de Beaufort/H. Linge (RSK), Crashed, R. von Frankenberg/C. Storez (RSK 1600) |
| Rheinland Cup, Nürburgring, 3rd August, 85 miles | 1st, J. Behra (RSK), 85·75 mph, 3rd, E. Barth (RSK) |

APPENDIX 2: PORSCHE COMPETITION PERFORMANCES   183

| | |
|---|---|
| Zeltweg 1500 cc sports cars,<br>15th August,<br>99 miles | 1st, W. von Trips (RSK),<br>2nd, J. Behra (RSK),<br>3rd, E. Barth (RSK) |
| Tourist Trophy,<br>Goodwood,<br>13th September,<br>four hours | *4th, J. Behra/E. Barth (RSK),<br>8th, C. G. de Beaufort/B. Heins (RSK) |
| Avusrennen,<br>21st September,<br>200 miles | 1st, J. Behra (RSK), 128·62 mph,<br>3rd, E. Barth (RSK) |

*1959*

| | |
|---|---|
| Sebring 12 Hours,<br>21st March | *3rd, W. von Trips/J. Bonnier (RSK 1600),<br>5th, J. Fitch/E. Barth (RSK),<br>11th, H. von Hanstein/C. G. de Beaufort (RSK 1600) |
| Spa Grand Prix,<br>3rd May,<br>132 miles | 1st, C. G. de Beaufort (RSK) |
| Targa Florio,<br>24th May,<br>447 miles | *1st, E. Barth/W. Seidel (RSK), 56·74 mph,<br>*3rd, A. Pucci/H. von Hanstein (Carrera),<br>Retired, U. Maglioli/H. Herrmann (engine failure, RSK 1600),<br>Retired, J. Bonnier/W. von Trips (rear suspension failure, RSK 1600) |
| Nürburgring 1000 Km,<br>7th June | *4th, U. Maglioli/H. Herrmann (RSK 1600),<br>7th, W. von Trips/J. Bonnier (RSK 1600),<br>10th, H. J. Walter/P. Strahle (Carrera exp.),<br>13th, R. Rodriguez/L. Levine (push-rod exp),<br>Retired, E. Barth/C. G. de Beaufort (engine failure, RSK) |
| Le Mans 24 Hours,<br>20th-21st June | Retired, H. Herrmann/U. Maglioli (engine trouble RSK 1600),<br>Retired, J. Bonnier/W. von Trips (engine trouble, RSK 1600),<br>Retired, E. Barth/W. Seidel (engine trouble, RSK) |
| Berlin Grand Prix,<br>Avus,<br>1st August,<br>129 miles | 1st, W. von Trips (RSK), 121·73 mph,<br>2nd, J. Bonnier (RSK),<br>3rd, H. J. Walter (RSK) |
| Tourist Trophy,<br>Goodwood,<br>5th September,<br>6 Hours | *2nd, J. Bonnier/W. von Trips (RSK 1600),<br>12th, U. Maglioli/E. Barth (RSK 1600),<br>Crashed, H. Herrmann/C. Bristow (RSK 1600) |

*1960*

| | |
|---|---|
| Buenos Aires 1000 Km,<br>31st January | *3rd, G. Hill/J. Bonnier (RSK 1600),<br>7th, M. Trintignant/H. Herrmann (RSK 1600),<br>10th, Bohnen/H. von Hanstein (Carrera),<br>Retired, E. Barth/O. Gendebien (RSK 1600) |

| | |
|---|---|
| Sebring 12 Hours<br>26th March | *1st, O. Gendebien/H. Herrmann (RSK 1600), 84·93 mph |
| Targa Florio,<br>8th May,<br>447 miles | *1st, J. Bonnier/H. Herrmann (RS60 1630), 59·24 mph<br>3rd, O. Gendebien/H. Herrmann (RS60 1630),<br>*5th, E. Barth/G. Hill (RS60 1600),<br>Crashed, A. Pucci/H. von Hanstein (Carrera) |
| Nürburgring 1000 Km,<br>22nd May | *2nd, J. Bonnier/I. Gendebien (RS60 1630), 4th, H. Herrmann/M. Trintignant (RS60 1630), 7th, H. Linge/J. Greger (Carrera-Abarth exp), 19th, H. Schulze/Graf Einseidel (push-rod exp), Crashed, G. Hill/E. Barth (RS60 1600) |
| Le Mans,<br>25th-26th June | 12th, E. Barth/W. Seidel (RS60 1500),<br>Retired, J. Bonnier/G. Hill (blown cylinder head joint, RS60 1630),<br>Retired, M. Trintignant/H. Herrmann (piston failure, RS60 1630) |
| Circuit of Auvergne,<br>Clermont Ferrand,<br>10th July,<br>Six hours | 1st, J. Bonnier (RS60 1600), 70·38 mph |
| Tourist Trophy,<br>Goodwood,<br>20th August,<br>Three hours | *4th, G. Hill (Carrera-Abarth),<br>11th, J. Bonnier (Carrera-Abarth) |

*1961*

| | |
|---|---|
| Sebring 12 Hours,<br>25th March | *5th, R. Holbert/R. Penske (RS61 1600),<br>Retired, J. Bonnier/D. Gurney (engine failure, RS61 1600),<br>Retired, H. Herrmann/E. Barth (engine failure, RS61 1600) |
| Targa Florio,<br>30th April,<br>447 miles | *2nd, J. Bonnier/D. Gurney (RS61 2000),<br>3rd, H. Herrmann/E. Barth (RS61 1700),<br>7th, H. Linge/P. Strahle/H. von Hanstein (Carrera-Abarth),<br>Retired, S. Moss/G. Hill (final drive failure, RS61 1700 nominally entered by the Camoradi team) |
| Nürburgring 1000 Km,<br>28th May | *8th, H. Linge/S. Greger/S. Moss/G. Hill (Carrera exp),<br>10th, D. Gurney/J. Bonnier (RS61 1700),<br>Retired, E. Barth/H. Herrmann (leaking cylinder head joint, RS61 1700),<br>Retired, S. Moss/G. Hill (RS61 1700 nominally entered by the Camoradi team) |
| Le Mans 24 Hours,<br>10th-11th June | *5th, M. Gregory/R. Holbert (RS61 2000),<br>7th, E. Barth/H. Herrmann (RS61 1600),<br>*10th, B. Pon/H. Linge (Carrera-Abarth),<br>Retired, J. Bonnier/D. Gurney (clutch failure, RS61 1600) |

Tourist Trophy, \*6th, G. Hill (Carrera-Abarth),
Goodwood, Retired, H. Linge (transmission failure,
19th August, Carrera-Abarth)
Three hours

## FORMULA TWO RACE PERFORMANCES, 1957–60

*1957*
German Grand Prix, 12th overall and 1st in class, E. Barth (1500
(Formula Two Class), RS Spyder), 82·46 mph,
4th August, 14th overall and 3rd in class, C. de Beaufort
312 miles (1500RS Spyder),
Retired, U. Maglioli (broken stub axle, RS)

*1958*
Coupe de Vitesse, Rheims, 1st, J. Behra (RSK Spyder), 116·43 mph
Rheims,
7th July,
155 miles

German Grand Prix, 6th overall and 2nd in class, E. Barth (RSK
(Formula Two Class), Spyder)
3rd August,
213 miles

Berlin Grand Prix, Avus, 1st, M. Gregory (RSK Spyder), 126·08 mph
21st September,
206 miles

*1959*
Monaco Grand Prix, Crashed, W. von Trips
10th May,
195 miles

Coupe de Vitesse, Rheims, 3rd, J. Bonnier,
5th July, 5th, W. von Trips (RSK Spyder)
129 miles

*1960*
Syracuse Grand Prix Retired, S. Moss (entered by R. R. C. Walker,
19th March, engine trouble)
191 miles

Brussels Grand Prix, 2nd, S. Moss (entered by R. R. C. Walker),
10th April, Retired, J. Bonnier (in heat one with engine
Aggregate of two trouble)
99-mile heats

Pau Grand Prix, 3rd, O. Gendebien (entered by Equipe
18th April, Nationale Belge)
154 miles

Aintree '200', 1st, S. Moss (entered by R. R. C. Walker),
30th April, 88·41 mph,
150 miles 2nd, J. Bonnier,
3rd, G. Hill

| | |
|---|---|
| Solitude Grand Prix,<br>24th July,<br>142 miles | 2nd, H. Herrmann,<br>3rd, J. Bonnier,<br>4th G. Hill,<br>5th, D. Gurney,<br>Retired, J. Surtees (entered by R. R. C. Walker, spun and stalled) |
| German Grand Prix,<br>South Nürburgring,<br>31st July,<br>154 miles | 1st, J. Bonnier, 80·28 mph,<br>2nd, W. von Trips,<br>4th G. Hill,<br>5th, H. Herrmann,<br>6th, E. Barth |
| Italian Grand Prix, Monza,<br>4th September,<br>311 miles | 6th, H. Herrmann,<br>7th, E. Barth |
| Circuit of Zeltweg,<br>18th September,<br>117 miles | 1st, S. Moss (entered by R. R. C. Walker), 87·62 mph<br>2nd, H. Herrmann,<br>3rd, E. Barth |
| Modena Grand Prix,<br>2nd October,<br>148 miles | 1st, J. Bonnier, 87·55 mph,<br>4th, H. Herrmann,<br>5th, E. Barth |

## FORMULA ONE RACE PERFORMANCES, 1961-62

*1961*

| | |
|---|---|
| Brussels Grand Prix,<br>9th April,<br>Results decided on the aggregate of three 62-mile heats | Retired, D. Gurney (broken gear-change mechanism),<br>Crashed, J. Bonnier |
| Syracuse Grand Prix,<br>25th April,<br>191 miles | 2nd, D. Gurney,<br>3rd, J. Bonnier |
| Monaco Grand Prix,<br>14th May,<br>195 miles | 5th, D. Gurney,<br>9th, H. Herrmann,<br>12th, J. Bonnier (not running at end of race) |
| Dutch Grand Prix,<br>Zandvoort,<br>22nd May,<br>195 miles | 10th, D. Gurney,<br>11th, J. Bonnier,<br>14th, C. G. de Beaufort,<br>15th, H. Herrmann |
| Belgian Grand Prix,<br>Spa,<br>18th June,<br>263 miles | 6th, D. Gurney,<br>7th, J. Bonnier,<br>11th, C. G. de Beaufort |
| French Grand Prix,<br>Rheims,<br>2nd July,<br>268 miles | 2nd, D. Gurney,<br>7th, J. Bonnier,<br>Retired, C. G. de Beaufort (engine trouble) |
| British Grand Prix,<br>Aintree,<br>15th July,<br>225 miles | 5th, J. Bonnier,<br>7th, D. Gurney,<br>16th, C. G. de Beaufort |

## APPENDIX 2: PORSCHE COMPETITION PERFORMANCES 187

| | |
|---|---|
| Solitude Grand Prix,<br>23rd July,<br>177 miles | 2nd, J. Bonnier,<br>3rd, D. Gurney,<br>6th, H. Herrmann,<br>8th, E. Barth,<br>Retired, C. G. de Beaufort (engine trouble) |
| German Grand Prix,<br>Nürburgring,<br>5th August,<br>213 miles | 7th, D. Gurney,<br>13th, H. Herrmann,<br>14th, C. G. de Beaufort,<br>Retired, J. Bonnier (engine trouble) |
| Karlskoga,<br>20th August,<br>56 miles | 2nd, J. Bonnier |
| Modena Grand Prix,<br>3rd September,<br>148 miles | 2nd, J. Bonnier,<br>3rd, D. Gurney |
| Italian Grand Prix,<br>Monza,<br>10th September,<br>267 miles | 2nd, D. Gurney,<br>7th, C. G. de Beaufort,<br>Retired, J. Bonnier (vibration following minor crash) |
| Circuit of Zeltweg,<br>17th September,<br>159 miles | 3rd, J. Bonnier |
| United States Grand Prix,<br>Watkins Glen,<br>8th October,<br>230 miles | 2nd, D. Gurney,<br>6th, J. Bonnier |

Drivers' Championship: 3rd (equal with Stirling Moss), Dan Gurney, 21 points
Constructor's Championship: 3rd, 18 points

*1962*

| | |
|---|---|
| Dutch Grand Prix,<br>Zandvoort,<br>20th May,<br>208 miles | 7th, J. Bonnier<br>Retired, D. Gurney (gear linkage trouble) |
| Monaco Grand Prix,<br>3rd June,<br>195 miles | 5th, J. Bonnier (4-cylinder car),<br>Crashed, D. Gurney |
| French Grand Prix,<br>Rouen,<br>8th July,<br>219 miles | 1st, D. Gurney, 101·89 mph,<br>Retired, J. Bonnier (engine trouble) |
| Solitude Grand Prix,<br>15th July,<br>177 miles | 1st, D. Gurney, 100·72 mph,<br>2nd, J. Bonnier |
| British Grand Prix,<br>Aintree,<br>21st July,<br>225 miles | 9th, D. Gurney,<br>Retired, J. Bonnier (gearbox trouble) |

*denotes class winner

| | |
|---|---|
| German Grand Prix,<br>Nürburgring,<br>5th August,<br>213 miles | 3rd, D. Gurney,<br>7th, J. Bonnier |
| Italian Grand Prix,<br>Monza,<br>16th September,<br>307 miles | 6th, J. Bonnier,<br>Retired, D. Gurney (crown wheel-and-pinion failure) |
| United States Grand Prix,<br>Watkins Glen,<br>7th October,<br>230 miles | 5th, D. Gurney,<br>13th, J. Bonnier |

## GRAND TOURING AND PROTOTYPE RACE PERFORMANCES, 1962–69

*1962*

| | |
|---|---|
| Targa Florio<br>6th May,<br>447 miles | *3rd, N. Vaccarella/J. Bonnier (2-litre 8-cyl),<br>*6th H. Herrmann/H. Linge (Abarth-Carrera),<br>10th, A. Pucci/E. Barth (Abarth-Carrera),<br>Retired, D. Gurney/J. Bonnier (crash damage, 2 litre 8-cyl),<br>Retired, U. Maglioli/T. Spychiger (gearbox trouble, RS61) |
| Nürburgring 1000 Km,<br>27th May,<br>624 miles | *3rd, G. Hill/H. Herrmann (2-litre 8-cyl),<br>*6th, E. Barth/H. Linge (Carrera-Abarth),<br>Retired, D. Gurney/J. Bonnier (gearbox trouble, 2-litre 8-cyl) |
| Le Mans,<br>23rd-24th June | *7th, E. Barth/H. Herrmann (Carrera-Abarth),<br>Retired, B. Pon/H. Walter (back axle failure, Carrera-Abarth) |

*1963*

| | |
|---|---|
| Targa Florio<br>5th May,<br>447 miles | *1st, J. Bonnier/C. M. Abate (2-litre 8-cyl), 64·57 mph<br>*3rd, H. Linge/E. Barth (2-litre Carrera),<br>5th, P. Strahle/A. Pucci (2-litre Carrera-Abarth),<br>7th, U. Maglioli/G. Baghetti (2-litre 8-cyl) |
| Nürburgring 1000 Km,<br>19th May,<br>624 miles | *4th, H. J. Walter/B. Pon/H. Linge/E. Barth (2-litre Carrera),<br>10th, G. Koch/P. Strahle (1·6 litre Carrera-Abarth),<br>Retired, E. Barth/H. Linge (rear axle failure, 2-litre 8-cyl),<br>Crashed, J. Bonnier /P.Hill (2-litre 8-cyl) |
| Le Mans,<br>15th-16th June | *8th, H. Linge/E. Barth (2-litre 8-cyl),<br>Crashed, J. Bonnier/A. Maggs (2-litre 8-cyl) |

*1964*

| | |
|---|---|
| Daytona 2000 Km,<br>Florida,<br>16th February | *6th, E. Barth/H. Linge (904) |

## APPENDIX 2: PORSCHE COMPETITION PERFORMANCES

| | |
|---|---|
| Targa Florio<br>24th April,<br>447 miles | *1st, A. Pucci/C. Davis (904), 62·28 mph,<br>2nd, H. Linge/G. Balzarini (904),<br>6th, E. Barth/U. Maglioli (904 8-cyl),<br>Retired, J. Bonnier/G. Hill (2-litre 8-cyl, broken drive-shaft coupling) |
| Spa 500 Km<br>17th May | *5th, E. Barth (904) |
| Le Mans,<br>20th-21st June | *10th, G. Koch/H. Schiller (904),<br>Retired, E. Barth/H. Linge (engine trouble, 904 8-cyl),<br>Retired, C. Davis/G. Mitter (engine trouble, 904 8-cyl) |
| Paris 1000 Km, Montlhéry,<br>11th October | *3rd, E. Barth/C. Davis (904 8-cyl) |

*1965*

| | |
|---|---|
| Sebring 12 Hours,<br>27th March | *9th, H. Linge/G. Mitter (904 8-cyl), |
| Targa Florio,<br>9th May | *2nd, C. Davis/G. Mitter (8-cyl prototype),<br>3rd, U. Maglioli/H. Linge (904 6-cyl),<br>4th, J. Bonnier/G. Hill (904 8-cyl),<br>*5th, G. Klass/A. Pucci (904) |
| Nürburgring 1000 Km,<br>23rd May | *3rd, J. Bonnier/J. Rindt (904 8-cyl),<br>5th, U. Maglioli/H. Linge (904 6-cyl),<br>6th, P. Nöcker/G. Klass (904 6-cyl),<br>9th, C. Davis/G. Mitter (904 6-cyl),<br>25th, B. Pon/G. Koch (904) |
| Le Mans,<br>19th-20th June | *4th, H. Linge/P. Nöcker (904 6-cyl),<br>5th, G. Koch/A. Fischaber (904),<br>Retired, C. Davis/G. Mitter (clutch failure, 904 8-cyl),<br>Retired, G. Klass/Glemser (engine failure, 904) |
| Preis von Baden-Württemberg,<br>Sports Car Race, Solitude,<br>18th July,<br>85 miles | 1st, G. Mitter (8-cyl prototype), 104·33 mph,<br>3rd, H. Linge (8-cyl prototype) |

*1966*

| | |
|---|---|
| Daytona 24 Hours,<br>5th-6th February | *6th, H. Herrmann/H. Linge (906) |
| Sebring 12 Hours,<br>26th March | *4th, H. Herrmann/J. Buzzetta (906),<br>Retired, G. Klass/G. Mitter (valve trouble, 906) |
| Monza 1000 Km,<br>25th April | *4th, G. Mitter/H. Herrmann (906),<br>7th, C. Davis/D. Glemser (906) |

| | |
|---|---|
| Targa Florio, 8th May | *1st, W. Mairesse/H. Müller (906, works car entered by Scuderia Filipinetti), 61·47 mph, 3rd, A. Pucci/V. Arena (906), Retired, G. Klass/C. Davis (suspension failure, 8-cyl 906), Crashed, D. Glemser/H. Herrmann (906), Crashed, G. Mitter/J. Bonnier (906) |
| Spa 1000 Km, 22nd May | Retired, U. Schütz/G. Koch (engine failure, 906), Retired, H. Herrmann/D. Glemser (loss of wheel, 906) |
| Nürburgring 1000 Km, 5th June | *4th, R. Bondurant/P. Hawkins (906), 11th, J-P. Beltoise/P. Nöcker (906), Retired, J. Rindt/N. Vaccarella (brake failure, 8-cyl 906), Retired, O. Schütz/G. Klass (broken driveshaft, 906), Crashed, H. Herrmann/D. Glemser (906) |
| Le Mans, 18th-19th June | *4th, C. Davis/J. Siffert (906), 5th, H. Herrmann/H. Linge (906), 6th, U. Schütz/P. de Klerk (906), 7th, G. Klass/R. Stommelen (906) |
| Circuit of Mugello, Florence, 17th July | *1st, G. Koch/J. Neerpasch (906), 66·72 mph |

*1967*

| | |
|---|---|
| Daytona 24 Hours 4th-5th February | *4th, J. Siffert/H. Herrmann (910), Retired, J. Rindt/G. Mitter (suspension damaged in crash, 906), Retired, U. Schütz/G. van Lennep (valve trouble, 906) |
| Sebring 12 Hours, 1st April | *3rd, G. Mitter/S. Patrick (910) 4th, H. Herrmann/J. Siffert (910), *6th, D. Spoerry/R. Steinemann (906), Retired, U. Schütz/G. van Lennep (Accident, 906) |
| Monza 1000 Km, 25th April | *3rd, J. Rindt/G. Mitter (910), 5th, H. Herrmann/J. Siffert (910) |
| Spa 1000 Km, 1st May | *2nd, J. Siffert/H. Herrmann (910), 7th, G. Mitter/G. Koch (910) |
| Targa Florio, 14th May | *1st, P. Hawkins/R. Stommelen (8-cyl, 910), 67·61 mph 2nd, L. Cella/G. Biscaldi (910), 3rd, J. Neerpasch/V. Elford (910), 6th, H. Herrmann/J. Siffert (8-cyl 910), Crashed, G. Mitter/C. Davis (8-cyl 910), Crashed, U. Maglioli/U. Schütz (910) |

APPENDIX 2: PORSCHE COMPETITION PERFORMANCES 191

| | |
|---|---|
| Nürburgring 1000 Km,<br>28th May | *1st, U. Schütz/J. Buzzetta (910), 91·41 mph,<br>2nd, P. Hawkins/G. Koch (910),<br>3rd, J. Neerpasch/V. Elford (910),<br>4th, G. Mitter/L. Bianchi (8-cyl 910),<br>Retired, H. Herrmann/J. Siffert (engine trouble, 8-cyl 910),<br>Retired, R. Stommelen/K. Ahrens (fuel injection trouble, 8-cyl 910) |
| Le Mans,<br>10th-11th June | *5th, J. Siffert/H. Herrmann (907),<br>6th, R. Stommelen/J. Neerpasch (910),<br>*7th, V. Elford/B. Pon (906),<br>8th, G. Koch/C. Poirot (906),<br>Retired, J. Rindt/G. Mitter (engine failure, 907),<br>Retired, U. Schütz/G. Buzzetta (transmission failure, 910) |
| Circuit of Mugello,<br>Florence,<br>23rd July | *1st, G. Mitter/U. Schütz (8-cyl 910), 76·24 mph,<br>2nd, R. Stommelen/J. Neerpasch (910),<br>3rd, V. Elford/G. van Lennep (911R),<br>*5th, L. Cella/G. Biscaldi (906),<br>Retired, J. Siffert/H. Herrmann (engine failure, 910),<br>Retired, G. Koch/D. Glemser (engine failure, 906) |
| B.O.A.C. '500',<br>Brands Hatch,<br>30th July | *3rd, J. Siffert/B. McLaren (8-cyl 910),<br>4th, H. Herrmann/J. Neerpasch (8-cyl 907),<br>11th, U. Schütz/J. Rindt (910),<br>Retired, J. Rindt/G. Hill (engine failure, 8-cyl 910),<br>Retired, V. Elford/L. Bianchi (engine failure, 910) |
| *1968*<br>Daytona 24 Hours,<br>3rd-4th February | *1st, V. Elford/J. Neerpasch/J. Siffert/R. Stommelen/H. Herrmann (907 8-cyl), 106·69 mph,<br>2nd, J. Siffert/H. Herrmann (907 8-cyl),<br>3rd, J. Buzzetta/J. Schlesser (907 8-cyl),<br>Crashed, G. Mitter/R. Stommelen (907 8-cyl) |
| Sebring 12 Hours,<br>23rd March | *1st, H. Herrmann/J. Siffert (907 8-cyl), 101·59 mph,<br>2nd, V. Elford/J. Neerpasch (907 8-cyl),<br>Retired, G. Mitter/R. Stommelen (engine trouble, 907 8-cyl),<br>Retired, L. Scarfiotti/J. Buzzetta (engine trouble, 907 8-cyl) |
| B.O.A.C. '500',<br>Brands Hatch,<br>7th April | *2nd, G. Mitter/L. Scarfiotti (907 8-cyl),<br>3rd, V. Elford/J. Neerpasch (907 8-cyl),<br>Retired, J. Siffert/H. Herrmann (stub axle failure, 907 8-cyl) |

| | |
|---|---|
| Monza 1000 Km,<br>25th April | *2nd, R. Stommelen/J. Neerpasch (907 8-cyl),<br>10th, J-C. Killy/J. Guichet (911T),<br>11th, L. Scarfiotti/G. Mitter (908),<br>19th, J. Siffert/H. Herrmann (908) |
| Targa Florio,<br>5th May,<br>447 miles | *1st, V. Elford/U. Maglioli (907 8-cyl), 69·04 mph,<br>4th, H. Herrmann/J. Neerpasch (907 8-cyl),<br>9th (not running at the finish), G. Steinemann/R. Lins (910 6-cyl),<br>18th, J. Siffert/R. Stommelen (907 8-cyl),<br>49th (not running at the finish), L. Scarfiotti/G. Mitter (907 8-cyl) |
| Nürburgring 1000 Km,<br>19th May | *1st, J. Siffert/V. Elford (908), 95·04 mph,<br>2nd, H. Herrmann/R. Stommelen (907 8-cyl),<br>4th, J. Neerpasch/J. Buzzetta (907 8-cyl),<br>25th, J-C. Killy/J. Guichet (911T),<br>Retired, G. Mitter/L. Scarfiotti (suspected broken chassis, 908) |
| Spa 1000 Km,<br>3rd June | 2nd, G. Mitter/J. Schlesser (907 8-cyl),<br>3rd, H. Herrmann/R. Stommelen (908),<br>Crashed, J. Neerpasch/V. Elford (908) |
| Watkins Glen Six Hours,<br>14th July | 6th, H. Herrmann/J. Siffert/T. Ikuzawa (908),<br>Retired, J. Buzzetta/G. Follmer (engine failure, 908),<br>Retired, J. Siffert/V. Elford (seized wheel bearing 908),<br>Retired, S. Patrick/R. Attwood (seized wheel bearing, 908) |
| Nation Preis, Hockenheim,<br>15th August | 1st, H. Herrmann (908), 126·76 mph) |
| Austrian Grand Prix,<br>Zeltweg,<br>25th August | *1st, J. Siffert (908), 106·86 mph<br>2nd, H. Herrmann/K. Ahrens (908),<br>8th, V. Elford (908) |
| Le Mans 24 Hours,<br>28th-29th September | 3rd, R. Stommelen/J. Neerpasch (908),<br>Retired, J. Siffert/H. Herrmann (clutch failure, 908),<br>Disqualified, G. Mitter/V. Elford (change of alternator, 908),<br>Retired, J. Buzzetta/S. Patrick (alternator failure, 908) |
| Paris 1000 Km,<br>Montlhéry,<br>13th October | 1st, H. Herrmann/R. Stommelen (908), 100·24 mph,<br>2nd, V. Elford/R. Lins (908),<br>12th, R. Buchet/H. Linge (908) |

APPENDIX 2: PORSCHE COMPETITION PERFORMANCES 193

*1969*

Daytona 24 Hours,
1st-2nd February

Retired, J. Siffert/H. Herrmann,
Retired, R. Attwood/J. Buzzetta,
Retired, V. Elford/B. Redman,
Retired, G. Mitter/U. Schütz,
Retired, R. Stommelen/K. Ahrens
(All 908 *Lang* cars eliminated by broken camshaft drives)

Sebring 12 Hours,
22nd March

3rd, J. Buzzetta/R. Stommelen,
5th, G. Mitter/U. Schütz,
7th, V. Elford/R. Attwood,
Retired, J. Siffert/B. Redman (broken chassis cross-member),
Retired, H. Herrmann/K. Ahrens (broken chassis cross-member)
(All 908 *Spyder* cars)

B.O.A.C. '500',
Brands Hatch,
13th April

1st, J. Siffert/B. Redman, 100·22 mph,
2nd, V. Elford/R. Attwood,
3rd, G. Mitter/U. Schütz,
6th, H. Herrmann/R. Stommelen
(All 908 *Spyder* cars)

Monza 1000 Km,
25th April

1st, J. Siffert/B. Redman, 128·39 mph,
2nd, H. Herrmann/K. Ahrens,
16th, V. Elford/R. Attwood (crashed and not running at the finish),
Retired, G. Mitter/U. Schütz (engine failure)
(All 908 *Lang* cars)

Targa Florio,
4th May,
447 miles

1st, G. Mitter/U. Schütz, 72·99 mph,
2nd, V. Elford/U. Maglioli,
3rd, H. Herrmann/R. Stommelen,
4th, K. von Wendt/W. Kauhsen,
21st, G. Larrousse/R. Lins,
Retired, B. Redman/R. Attwood (drive-shaft failure)
(all 908 *Spyder* cars),
Retired, D. Spoerry/P. Toivonen (fire, 911R)

Spa 1000 Km,
11th May

1st, J. Siffert/B. Redman, 139·29 mph,
3rd, V. Elford/K. Ahrens,
4th, R. Stommelen/H. Herrmann
(all 908 *Lang* cars),
Retired, G. Mitter/U. Schütz (917)

Nürburgring 1000 Km,
1st June

1st, J. Siffert/B. Redman, 102·77 mph,
2nd, R. Stommelen/H. Herrmann,
3rd, V. Elford/K. Ahrens,
4th, R. Attwood/R. Lins,
5th, W. Kauhsen/K. von Wendt,
31st, G. Mitter/U. Schütz
(all 908 *Spyder* cars),
8th, F. Gardner/D. Piper (917)

Le Mans 24 Hours, 14th-15th June

2nd, H. Herrmann/G. Larrousse,
Retired, H. Schütz/G. Mitter (crash),
Retired, R. Lins/W. Kauhsen (clutch failure), (all 908 *Lang* cars),
Retired, J. Siffert/B. Redman (gearbox failure, 908 *Spyder*),
Retired, R. Stommelen/K. Ahrens (oil leak),
Retired, V. Elford/R. Attwood (clutch failure), (both 917)

# Index

## A

Abarth cars, 25, 106, 129, 132
Adams, D., 140
Aintree '200' race, *1960*, 49
Aldington, W. H., 14
Alfa Romeo cars, 120, 121, 123, 126, 133, 140, 146, 149, 150, 157, 169
Alpine cars, 138, 162, 163
Andretti, M., 129
Aston Martin cars, 36, 38, 39, 76, 95
A.T.S. cars, 59, 86
Austrian Alpine Rally, *1950*, 21; *1967*, 70
Austrian-Daimler Company, 15–16
Austrian Grand Prix, *1968*, 158
Autoar car, 19
Autodelta Racing Team, 117, 123, 128, 131, 140, 146, 149
Auto-Sports Team, 59
Auto Union cars, 17–18
Auvergne, Circuit of, *1960*, 41
Avusrennen, *1955*, 31–2; *1958*, 36

## B

Baghetti, Giancarlo, 53, 55
Bailey, L., 140
Bandini, L., 84, 113
Barth, E., 34, 35, 104
Behra, J., 46, 47, 48
Behra-Porsche car, 47, 48, 50
Belgian Grand Prix, *1961*, 54
Bentley cars, 16
Berlin Grand Prix, *1958*, 46; *1959*, 39
Bertone coachbuilder, 146
Beutler coachbuilder, 20
Bianchi, L., 162
Bianchi, M., 162
B.M.W. cars, 71
B.O.A.C. '500' race, *1967*, 133; *1968*, 146; *1969*, 169
Böhringer, E., 99
Boll, H., 58, 166
Bonnier, J., 39, 40, 41, 42, 48, 50, 51, 52, 57, 60
Borgward cars, 28, 32, 36
Brabham cars, 57
Bracco, G., 32
Brescia Corse, Scuderia, 140
Bridgehampton race, *1962*, 78
British Grand Prix, *1961*, 55; *1962*, 61
B.R.M. engines, 139, 140, 141
Brussels Grand Prix, *1960*, 48–9; *1961*, 52
Buenos Aires 1000 Km race, *1955*, 30; *1958*, 34; *1960*, 39
Bugatti, E., 16

## C

Camoradi Racing Team, 40, 42, 48
Canadian Grand Prix, *1962*, 78
Carrera Panamericana Mexico race, *1953*, 28; *1954*, 29
Chaparral cars, 100, 114–15, 122, 126–7, 128, 133, 134

Chevron cars, 134, 137
Chiti, Carlo, 132, 140
Cisitalia cars, 19, 21
Civil Governor's Cup, Lisbon, *1955*, 31
Claes, J., 29
Clark, J., 76–7
Cobra cars, 90, 92, 94
Colotti, V., 47
Cooper cars, 45, 46, 48, 49, 51
Coupe du Salon, Montlhéry, *1965*, 106
Coupe de Vitesse, Rheims, *1958*, 46; *1959*, 47

## D

Daimler company, 16
Daimler-Benz company, 16, 18
Davis, C., 113
Daytona Continental 3 Hours race, *1963*, 80; 2000 Km race, *1964*, 92; *1965*, 99; 24 Hours race, *1966*, 108; *1967*, 119; *1968*, 153; *1969*, 168
Drauz coachbuilders, 26
Dusio, P., 19
Dutch Grand Prix, *1961*, 53–4; *1962*, 59–60

## E

Elford, V., 70, 141, 150, 151, 152, 156, 157
E.M.W. cars, 31, 32
European Hill Climb Championship, *1964*, 98; *1965*, 106; *1966*, 118; *1967*, 137; *1968*, 142, 164–5
European Rally Championship, *1967*, 69–70; *1968*, 70–1
European Touring Car Championship, *1967*, 71

## F

Faroux, C., 22
Ferrari cars, 35, 36, 37, 39, 46, 49–50, 51, 52, 54–5, 57, 61, 84, 85, 86, 88, 90, 92, 102, 104, 105, 111, 112, 126, 128, 129, 131–2, 133–5, 144, 168, 169, 170
Filipinetti, Scuderia, 111, 122, 123, 131
Ford GT40 cars, 97, 99, 102, 103, 105, 108, 109, 110, 116, 120, 128–9, 135, 139, 140, 143–4, 145, 146–7, 152, 153–4, 155, 157, 160, 161, 168, 169, 170, 171
Forghieri, Mauro, 135
Formula Two Manufacturers' Championship, *1960*, 51
von Frankenberg, R., 28, 30, 31
French Grand Prix, *1954*, 46; *1961*, 54–5; *1962*, 60–1

## G

Gendebien, O., 49, 75
German Grand Prix, *1957*, 45; *1958*, 46; *1960*, 50; *1961*, 56–7; *1962*, 61–2
Ginther, R., 95
Glöckler, H., 28
Glöckler, W., 27
Glöckler-Porsche car, 22–3, 27
Goodwood Nine Hours race, *1955*, 31
Governor's Trophy race, Nassau, *1962*, 78
Grand Touring Championship, *1962*, 73, 78; *1963*, 89
Gregory, M., 144
Group 3 Championship, *1968*, 164
Guichet, J., 123, 125
Gurney, D., 49, 50, 52, 53, 57, 59, 60–1, 93–4

## H

von Hanstein, Baron H., 22, 27, 28, 31, 32, 37, 54, 60, 99–100, 114, 124, 125–6, 132, 133, 134, 141, 144, 157, 165–6
Hawkins, P., 124, 125, 145
Healey SR car, 161
Herrmann, H., 28, 29, 33, 37, 50, 136, 141, 171
Hetreed, B., 95

# INDEX

Hill, P., 86, 126
Holland, Racing Team, 101, 115, 136
Howmet cars, 141, 143

## I
Ikuzawa, T., 156–7
Ireland, I., 56
Italian Grand Prix, *1960*, 50; *1961*, 57; *1962*, 62
Irwin, C., 140, 152

## J
Jaguar cars, 86, 90, 95
Juhan, J., 30
JW Automotive Ltd, 139, 143

## K
Killy, J.-C., 148
Klass, G., 123, 124, 125, 131–2

## L
Le Mans 24 Hours race, *1951*, 22; *1952*, 22; *1953*, 28; *1954*, 29; *1955*, 30; *1956*, 33; *1957*, 34; *1958*, 35; *1959*, 38–9; *1960*, 41; *1961*, 43–4; *1962*, 78; *1963*, 88–9; *1964*, 96; *1965*, 105; *1966*, 115–16; *1967*, 128–30; *1968*, 158–63; *1969*, 170-171
Le Mans Practice Week-end, *1964*, 92; *1965*, 101; *1967*, 121
Liège-Rome-Liège Rally, *1951*, 22
Lindner, P., 86
Lola cars, 139
Lourenco Marques race, *1967*, 136
Lumsden, P., 87
Lyons-Charbonnières Rally, *1955*, 30; *1967*, 70

## M
Maglioli, U., 32, 33, 45, 93, 152
Mairesse, W., 60, 84–5, 122
Makinen, T., 99
Mann, A., 140
Marcos cars, 140, 155–6
Matra cars, 128, 138, 139

Maserati cars, 31, 43, 49
Mays, R., 16
McCluskey, R., 129
McLaren, B., 146
McLean, R., 109
Mercedes-Benz cars, 16, 17, 99
Midnight Sun Rally, *1950*, 21
Mille Miglia, 117; *1954*, 28–9; *1955*, 30; *1956*, 32; *1957*, 33
Mirage car, 122, 125, 126–7, 139, 143
Mitter, G., 101, 106, 113, 118, 144, 147, 151, 165, 166
Monaco Grand Prix, *1959*, 47; *1961*, 53; *1962*, 60
Mont Ventoux Hill Climb, *1965*, 106
Monte Carlo Rally, *1965*, 99; *1967*, 70; *1968*, 70–1; *1969*, 71
Monza 1000 Km Race, *1965*, 101; *1966*, 110; *1967*, 121–2; *1968*, 147–9; *1969*, 169
Moser, R., 95
Moss, S., 34, 41, 48, 49, 53
Mugello, Circuit of, *1966*, 117; *1967*, 130–3; *1968*, 157–8
Muir, B., 160
Müller, H., 98, 124

## N
Nation Preis race, Hockenheim, *1968*, 164
Neerpasch, J., 94, 143, 155, 166
Neubauer, A., 166
Nöcker, P., 114
North American Racing Team, 105
North-Western Grand Prix, *1962*, 78
Nürburgring 1500 cc Sports Car Race, *1954*, 29
Nürburgring 500 Km Race, *1955*, 31; *1966*, 117; *1967*, 135
Nürburgring 1000 Km Race, *1956*, 32; *1957*, 34; *1958*, 35; *1959*, 38; *1960*, 40–1; *1961*, 43; *1962*, 75–6; *1963*, 86–8; *1964*, 95; *1965*, 103–4; *1966*, 114–15; *1967*, 125–8; *1968*, 152–5; *1969*, 170

## O

Ollon-Villars Hill Climb, *1965*, 106
Oulton Park Circuit, 133

## P

Paris Salon, *1952*, 28
Paris 1000 Km Race, *1955*, 30; *1962*, 78; *1964*, 98; *1966*, 117; *1967*, 136; *1968*, 147–9
Parkes, M., 87, 111, 112
Patrick, S., 157
Pau Grand Prix, *1959*, 47–8; *1960*, 49; *1962*, 59
Pescara Four Hours Race, *1961*, 44
Pescarolo, H., 163
Peugeot cars, 101
Piccionaia Racing Team, 150
Piech, F., 18, 166
Pon, B., 78, 103
Porsche, Ferdinand, 15–22
Porsche, Ferry, 19
Porsche cars: 356: 21–4; 356A: 24; 356B: 25–6; 356C: 26; Carrera: 25; 550 'Spyder': 27–32; RS: 32–4; RSK: 34–6; RS60: 40; RS61: 42; Formula 2: 47–8; Formula 1: 52–4, 58–9; 904: 90–1; 904 8-cylinder: 92, 101; 904 6-cylinder: 101, 104; 906 Carrera 6: 107–8; 906 8-cylinder: 111; 907: 121, 128, 141–2; 907 'Langheck': 142; 907 'Berg': 142; 908: 142, 166; 908 'Lang': 166; 917: 170; 908 'Spyder': 167; 908 'Berg': 167; 910: 120, 123, 142; 911: 64–9; 911E: 67; 911T: 67; 911S: 67; 911R: 67, 131, 142; 912: 66; 917: 170
Porsche Cars Great Britain Ltd, 108
Prototype Championship, 78, 108; *1966*, 116; *1967*, 135

## R

Rabe, K., 16
Rand Nine Hours Race, *1967*, 136
Redman, B., 143, 145, 154, 155
Renault, L., 19
Renault cars, 19
Reutter, 21
Rheims 12 Hours Race, *1956*, 33; *1964*, 96–7; *1965*, 105–6; *1967*, 130
Rheinland-Pfalz Preis, *1964*, 97
Rindt, K.-J., 135, 146
van Rooyen, B., 136
Rouen Grand Prix, *1959*, 48
Rover-B.R.M. car, 88
Rossfeld Hill Climb, *1964*, 98; *1965*, 106; *1968*, 165

## S

Salon, Coupe du, *1965*, 106
San Remo Rally, *1968*, 70
Scarfiotti, L., 84, 102, 106, 109, 141, 165
Schlesser, J., 129, 155
Schütz, U., 151
Sebring 12 Hours Race, *1955*, 30; *1956*, 32; *1958*, 35; *1959*, 36–7; *1960*, 39–40; *1961*, 42; *1962*, 73–4; *1963*, 80; *1964*, 92; *1967*, 120–1; *1968*, 145–6; *1969*, 168–9
Seidel, W., 59
Serenissima car, 158
Serenissima, Scuderia, 59
Sharp, H., 125
Shelby, C., 92
Siffert, J., 122, 126–7, 141, 154, 157, 158, 161
Silverstone 1500 cc Sports Car Race, *1954*, 29
Solitude Grand Prix, *1960*, 49; *1962*, 61
Spa Grand Prix, *1959*, 37
Spa 500 Km Race, *1963*, 85–6; *1964*, 94–5; *1965*, 103
Spa 1000 Km Race, *1966*, 113–14; *1968*, 155–6; *1969*, 171
Spa 24 Hours Race, *1968*, 71
Spanish Rally, *1968*, 70
Spence, M., 95, 127
Spoerry, D., 144
Sports Car Championship, 152; *1956*, 33; *1958*, 34, 36; *1959*, 37; *1960*, 41; *1968*, 152, 163
Steinemann, R., 166, 168

Stewart, J., 133, 134
Stommelen, R., 137
Stoop, R., 86, 97
Strahle, P., 37
Stuttgart, Preis von, *1965*, 106
Surtees, J., 49, 50, 84, 87, 101
Swedish Grand Prix, *1955*, 31
Swedish Rally, *1968*, 70, 71
Syracuse Grand Prix, *1961*, 53

*T*

Targa Florio, *1956*, 32–3; *1958*, 35; *1959*, 37; *1960*, 25, 40; *1961*, 42; *1962*, 74–5; *1963*, 81–6; *1964*, 92–4; *1965*, 101–3; *1966*, 111–13; *1967*, 123–5; *1968*, 149–52; *1969*, 170–171
Tartaruga, Squadra, 159
Taruffi, P., 33
Taylor, S., 139
Thompson, R., 125
Tourist Trophy, *1955*, 31, 133; *1958*, 36; *1959*, 39; *1960*, 41; *1961*, 44; *1964*, 97
Trento-Bordone Hill Climb, *1964*, 98; *1965*, 106
von Trips, G. W., 32, 47
Tulip Rally, *1967*, 70

*U*

de Udy, M., 108

Ugolini, N., 59
United States Grand Prix, *1961*, 57; *1962*, 62

*V*

V.D.S. Racing Team, 150
Vaccarella, N., 32, 83, 86, 102, 103, 113, 122, 124
Venezia, Scuderia, 74
Volkswagen car, 17
Volpi, Count, 59

*W*

Waaldegaard, B., 70, 71
Walker, R. R. C., 48
Wanderer car, 16
Watkins Glen Six Hours Race, *1968*, 156–7
von Wendt, K. F., 166
Williams, J., 132
Woolfe, J., 139, 171
Wyer, J., 139, 166

*Y*

Yorke, D., 166

*Z*

Zandvoort, Circuit of, *1965*, 106
Zasada, S., 70
Zeltweg, Circuit of, *1958*, 36; *1960*, 51; *1966* 117; *1967* 135–6